THE PROFESSION OF E⌐⌐⌐⌐⌐⌐⌐⌐⌐ ⌐⌐⌐

Historians of the English legal profession have written comparatively little about the lawyers who served in the courts of the Church. This volume fills a gap; it investigates the law by which they were governed and discusses their careers in legal practice. Using sources drawn from the Roman and canon laws and also from manuscripts found in local archives, R. H. Helmholz brings together previously published work and new evidence about the professional careers of these men. His book covers the careers of many lesser-known ecclesiastical lawyers, dealing with their education in law, their reaction to the coming of the Reformation, and their relationship with English common lawyers on the eve of the Civil War. Making connections with the European *ius commune*, this volume will be of special interest to English and Continental legal historians, as well as to students of the relationship between law and religion.

R. H. Helmholz is Ruth Wyatt Rosenson Distinguished Service Professor of Law at The University of Chicago Law School. He is the author of *Marriage Litigation in Medieval England* (Cambridge University Press 1974), *Roman Canon Law in Reformation England* (Cambridge University Press 1990), and *Oxford History of the Laws of England: The Canon Law and Ecclesiastical Jurisdiction from 597 to the 1640s* (2014).

LAW AND CHRISTIANITY

Series Editor
John Witte, Jr., Emory University

Editorial Board
Nigel Biggar, University of Oxford
Marta Cartabia, Italian Constitutional Court / University of Milano-Bicocca
Sarah Coakley, University of Cambridge
Norman Doe, Cardiff University
Rafael Domingo, Emory University / University of Navarra
Brian Ferme, Marcianum, Venice
Richard W. Garnett, University of Notre Dame
Robert P. George, Princeton University
Mary Ann Glendon, Harvard University
Kent Greenawalt, Columbia University
Robin Griffith-Jones, Temple Church, London / King's College London
Gary S. Hauk, Emory University
R.H. Helmholz, University of Chicago
Mark Hill QC, Inner Temple, London / Cardiff University
Wolfgang Huber, Bishop Emeritus, United Protestant Church of
Germany / Universities of Heidelberg, Berlin, and Stellenbosch
Michael W. McConnell, Stanford University
John McGuckin, Union Theological Seminary
Mark A. Noll, University of Notre Dame
Jeremy Waldron, New York University / University of Oxford
Michael Welker, University of Heidelberg

The Law and Christianity series publishes cutting-edge work on Catholic, Protestant, and Orthodox Christian contributions to public, private, penal, and procedural law and legal theory. The series aims to promote deep Christian reflection by leading scholars on the fundamentals of law and politics, to build further ecumenical legal understanding across Christian denominations, and to link and amplify the diverse and sometimes isolated Christian legal voices and visions at work in the academy. Works collected by the series include groundbreaking monographs, historical and thematic anthologies, and translations by leading scholars around the globe.

Books in the Series

Law, Love, and Freedom: From the Sacred to the Secular Joshua Neoh

Great Christian Jurists in French History Olivier Descamps and Rafael Domingo

Church Law in Modernity: Toward a Theory of Canon Law Between Nature and Culture Judith Hahn

Common Law and Natural Law in America: From the Puritans to the Legal Realists Andrew Forsyth

Care for the World: Laudato Si' and Catholic Social Thought in an Era of Climate Crisis edited by Frank Pasquale

Church, State, and Family: Reconciling Traditional Teachings and Modern Liberties John Witte, Jr.

Great Christian Jurists in Spanish History Rafael Domingo and Javier Martinez-Torron

Under Caesar's Sword: How Christians Respond to Persecution edited by Daniel Philpott and Timothy Samuel Shah

God and the Illegal Alien Robert W. Heimburger

Christianity and Family Law John Witte, Jr. and Gary S. Hauk

Christianity and Natural Law Norman Doe

Great Christian Jurists in English History edited by Mark Hill, QC and R. H. Helmholz

Agape, Justice, and Law edited by Robert F. Cochran, Jr and Zachary R. Calo

Calvin's Political Theology and the Public Engagement of the Church Matthew J. Tuininga

God and the Secular Legal System Rafael Domingo

How Marriage Became One of the Sacraments Philip L. Reynolds

Christianity and Freedom (Volume I: Historical Perspectives, Volume II: Contemporary Perspectives) edited by Timothy Samuel Shah and Allen D. Hertzke

The Western Case for Monogamy Over Polygamy John Witte, Jr.

The Distinctiveness of Religion in American Law Kathleen A. Brady

Pope Benedict XVI's Legal Thought Marta Cartabia and Andrea Simoncini

The Profession of
Ecclesiastical Lawyers

AN HISTORICAL INTRODUCTION

R. H. HELMHOLZ
University of Chicago

CAMBRIDGE
UNIVERSITY PRESS

CAMBRIDGE
UNIVERSITY PRESS

University Printing House, Cambridge CB2 8BS, United Kingdom

One Liberty Plaza, 20th Floor, New York, NY 10006, USA

477 Williamstown Road, Port Melbourne, VIC 3207, Australia

314-321, 3rd Floor, Plot 3, Splendor Forum, Jasola District Centre, New Delhi - 110025, India

103 Penang Road, #05-06/07, Visioncrest Commercial, Singapore 238467

Cambridge University Press is part of the University of Cambridge.

It furthers the University's mission by disseminating knowledge in the pursuit of education, learning and research at the highest international levels of excellence.

www.cambridge.org
Information on this title: www.cambridge.org/9781108713092
DOI: 10.1017/9781108614887

First published 2019
First paperback edition 2022

A catalogue record for this publication is available from the British Library

Library of Congress Cataloging in Publication data
Names: Helmholz, R. H., author.
Title: The profession of ecclesiastical lawyers : an historical introduction / R. H. Helmholz.
Description: New York: Cambridge University Press, 2019. |
Series: Law and christianity | Includes bibliographical references and index.
Identifiers: LCCN 2019000692 | ISBN 9781108499064 (hardback) |
ISBN 9781108713092 (paperback)
Subjects: LCSH: Christian lawyers – England – Biography. |
Law – England – Christian influences – History. | Ecclesiastical courts – England – History. | BISAC: LAW / Legal History.
Classification: LCC KD620.H45 2019 | DDC 262.9092/242–dc23
LC record available at https://lccn.loc.gov/2019000692

ISBN 978-1-108-49906-4 Hardback
ISBN 978-1-108-71309-2 Paperback

Contents

Preface

For two particular reasons, I am grateful for the opportunity to publish this book. One is that it has enabled me to make good use of information uncovered in the course of my research in the archives of the English ecclesiastical courts – a task and a pleasure that has occupied virtually all of my academic career, now over fifty years in length. The other is that it has given me the opportunity to remedy one of the deficiencies of the survey of the history of the English ecclesiastical courts that appeared as a volume in the *Oxford History of the Laws of England* (2004). It left out the people. Here I have endeavored to put some of them back.

For the chance to do this, I owe a special thanks to John Witte, Jr., the Robert Woodruff, McDonald Distinguished Professor of the Law at Emory University. He suggested the possibility to me, and he encouraged me to persevere and to make use of the opportunity. The special combination of scholarly expertise and entrepreneurial ability, both of which he possesses in abundance, are matters of wonder to me. I am grateful for both of them. Two other scholars have also contributed in a special way to the appearance of this book. One is Robert Ombres, OP. He first suggested that I might undertake the collection of short biographies of English civilians that would appear in the *Ecclesiastical Law Journal*. When I demurred, he insisted. I had no alternative, he told me. I surrendered, and it turned out that he had been right. The results form Part Two of this book, and what at first seemed like a chore turned out to be a source of learning and even enjoyment. The other is Sir John Baker. Every living English legal historian owes a debt to him and to his scholarship, of course. I do myself, but his lead in producing the first collection of short biographies of the English civilians, published as *Monuments of Endlesse Labours* in 1998, paved the way for my own efforts along the same lines. In addition, I wish to thank the anonymous reviewer for the Press, who both read the book's text with care and saved me from mistakes and infelicities aplenty.

I am of course aware that some of the conclusions I reached in the course of research that are presented in these pages are out of line with those of many other writers on the same subject, historians whose work I admire. This book paints a rosier picture of the world of the English ecclesiastical lawyers than the one found in most of these accounts. They see decline; I see stability and even advance in the years before the outbreak of the English Civil War in the 1640s. Some part of this difference is attributable to my own reliance on the evidence found in the manuscript records of the ecclesiastical courts themselves, compared to their preference for governmental and societal sources drawn from outside that circle. But I think not all. In this context, I can only hope that, despite this disagreement, the book manages to add something to the history of the legal profession in England. That is its purpose – to show that the lives and careers of English ecclesiastical lawyers have played a legitimate part in the growth and development of the legal profession.

Abbreviations

For references used to refer to the works of commentators on the texts of the *ius commune*, treatises written by English civilians, and other legal works cited in the notes, see the Bibliography at the end of this volume.

Bracton, De Legibus	*Bracton on the Laws and Customs of England*, ed George Woodbine, trans Samuel Thorne (1968–77)
C & Y Soc.	Publications of the Canterbury & York Society
Coke on Littleton	Edward Coke, *First Part of the Institutes ... or Commentarie on Littleton* (1628)
Councils & Synods II	*Councils & Synods with other Documents Relating to the English Church II, A.D. 1205–1313*, ed F M Powicke and C R Cheney (1964)
CUL	Cambridge University Library
DD	*Doctores* or *Domini*
d.p.	*dictum post*
Ecc LJ	*Ecclesiastical Law Journal*
EHR	*English Historical Review*
LPL	Lambeth Palace Library, London
LQR	*Law Quarterly Review*
NILQ	*Northern Ireland Legal Quarterly*
ODNB	*Oxford Dictionary of National Biography* (2004 et seq.)
SS	Publications of the Selden Society
Wilkins, *Concilia*	D Wilkins, *Concilia Magnae Britanniae et Hiberniae* (London 1757)
ZRG	*Zeitschrift der Savigny-Stiftung für Rechtsgeschichte*

Records in Diocesan Archives

References to act books and other manuscript material in the records of the English ecclesiastical courts are given by diocese or archdeaconry, followed by the classification used in the office or archives where these records are kept. The latter are:

Canterbury	Canterbury Cathedral Archives, Canterbury
York	Borthwick Institute for Archives, University of York, Heslington, York
Bath & Wells	Somerset Archives and Local Studies, Taunton
Bristol	Bristol Archives, Bristol
Buckingham (archdry)	Centre for Buckinghamshire Studies, Aylesbury
Carlisle	Cumbria Archive Centre, Carlisle
Chester	Cheshire Archives and Local Studies, Chester
Chichester	West Sussex Record Office, Chichester
Cornwall (archdry)	Cornwall Record Office, Truro
Coventry & Lichfield	Lichfield Record Office, Lichfield
Durham	University of Durham Library, Palace Green, Durham
Ely	Cambridge University Library, Cambridge
Essex	Essex Record Office, Chelmsford
Exeter	Devon Archives & Local Studies, Exeter
Gloucester	Gloucestershire Archives, Gloucester
Hereford	Herefordshire Archives and Records, Hereford
Hertford (archdry)	Hertfordshire Archives and Local Studies, Hertford
Lincoln	Lincolnshire Archives, Lincoln
London	London Metropolitan Archives, London
Norwich	Norfolk and Norwich Record Office, Norwich
Oxford	Oxfordshire Archives, Oxford

Peterborough	Northamptonshire Record Office, Northampton
Rochester	Kent History and Library Centre, Maidstone
St. Albans (archdry)	Hertfordshire Archives and Local Studies, Hertford
Salisbury	Wiltshire County Record Office, Trowbridge
Sudbury (archdry)	Suffolk Record Office, Bury St Edmunds Branch
Winchester	Hampshire Archives and Local Studies, Winchester
Worcester	Worcestershire Archive and Archaeology Service, Worcester

Table of Citations to the Roman and Canon Laws

ROMAN LAW

CANON LAW

PART I

The Profession Described

Introduction

This book is meant to contribute to the history of one segment of the legal profession, that which was occupied by English ecclesiastical lawyers. It deals with their lives and professional careers from the time a system of ecclesiastical courts, in which most of them practised, came into existence in the thirteenth century up to the time of the curtailment of the scope of ecclesiastical jurisdiction that occurred towards the end of the nineteenth century. It pays particular attention to the years between 1500 and 1640, when the character and future of the courts in which they served was called seriously into question but nonetheless survived, only to be abolished during the Interregnum and then brought back to life in the 1660s.

The book has two parts. The first describes the law that regulated their professional conduct, the nature of their education in becoming lawyers, their reaction to the English Reformation, and the changes and developments during the years that led up to the English Civil War. The second part consists of eighteen descriptive portraits of noteworthy ecclesiastical lawyers. My hope has been that the book's two parts will complement each other, the second providing specific examples of lives and careers spent in the profession described in the first. There is some obvious overlap, repetition even, in the coverage of the two parts. This has proved inevitable. They are both built upon the same body of evidence that is today found in the archives of England's ecclesiastical courts.

Akin to the English common law's division of lawyers into two classes – barristers and attorneys – the profession of the men who administered the church's law was divided into two basic classes: advocates and proctors. The similarity between the divisions in these two English court systems was never exact, and some variety in the terms used within each category also existed.[1]

---

[1] Barristers were sometimes described as advocates, for example.

Common law barristers were sometimes described as advocates, for example. But even when different terms were used, in substance a similarity between these two parts of the legal profession remained. It has long been recognized as an apt parallel. John Cowell (d. 1611) made the connection in his *Interpreter*, for example,[2] and several other writers, both then and now, reached the same conclusion.[3] There were two different classes of lawyer within each jurisdictional system, and in both, the primary distinctions between the two were ones of function and learning. Advocates and barristers argued in favor of the legal positions of their clients; proctors and attorneys took their place in court, thus effectively standing in the client's stead.[4] Both advocates and barristers were also better educated and more fully versed in legal doctrine than were proctors and attorneys. The judges, who were usually called *Officiales* during the Middle Ages, and later more usually Chancellors in the ecclesiastical courts, were drawn from the first group, only rarely from the second, just as the judges of the courts of common law were chosen from among the barristers.

Recognition of this parallel between the lawyers of the common law and those of the ecclesiastical law also turned out to have at least one meaningful consequence. When the general jurisdiction of the ecclesiastical courts was drastically curtailed in the nineteenth century, the men who had served as advocates in them were invited to continue in practice as barristers without further training; the proctors were similarly permitted to act as solicitors.[5] At least in areas of law taken over by the common law, the similarity in their prior professional careers was close enough for them to be allowed to continue under a new name.

This book, however, is not directly concerned with this comparison, intriguing though it is and worthy as it also is to be kept in mind. It is about the professional life and work of English advocates and proctors, who were often called civilians from their education and continuing connection with the civil or Roman law. It attempts to describe their preparation for work in the courts of the church and the use they made of what they had learned in

---

[2] *The Interpreter (or Booke Containing the Signification of Words)* (Cambridge 1607), s.v. *Attorney.*

[3] G Jacob (d. 1744), *New Law Dictionary*, v *advocate* (London 1732); T Wood (d. 1722), *Institute of the Law of England*, Bk IV, c 1 (London 1772), pp 444–45; *Bl. Comm.* vol III *25–26; see also the examples in F Pollock and F W Maitland, *History of English Law*, vol I, (2d edn reissued, Cambridge 1968), p 215, and B Levack, 'The English Civilians, 1500–1750', in W Prest (ed), *Lawyers in Early Modern Europe and America* (London 1981), pp 110–11.

[4] P Tucker, *Law Courts and Lawyers in the City of London, 1300–1550* (Cambridge 2007), p 272: 'An advocate spoke for his client in the client or attorney's presence … whereas the attorney substituted for his client'.

[5] Court of Probate Act, 20 & 21 Vict. c. 77 §§ 40–41 (1857).

that preparation, either at university or as a clerk in an apprenticeship-like position.

Historical study of the legal profession is far from a new subject. In fact, the last quarter of the twentieth century witnessed something close to an explosion of scholarly interest in the history of the legal profession in England. Most of it has focused upon the common lawyers.[6] That is as it should be. However, even though much less attention has been devoted to the professional work of English civilians, the lawyers whose primary source of employment was in the courts of the church, several exceptions do exist. One need only cite books by Daniel Coquillette,[7] Brian Levack,[8] G D Squibb,[9] J H Baker[10] and also several chapters in academic journals and books of collected essays.[11] In addition, several books written to describe the history of the courts themselves have also devoted at least incidental attention to the lawyers who made the system run.[12] So the subject treated here is not written on a blank page. What it is meant to add to the existing studies is derived primarily from two sources not much used in the earlier English language scholarship. The first is the legal literature of the time – the treatment of the lawyers and the legal profession that is found within the *ius commune*. Both the Roman and the canon laws contained rules and principles devoted to the subject, and jurists in England and on the Continent paid attention to it. This mattered in practice. The second addition comes from information derived from an exploration of the

---

[6] See the review of the subject by A Musson, 'Men of Law and Professional Identity in Late Medieval England', in T Baker (ed), *Law and Society in Later Medieval England and Ireland: Essays in Honour of Paul Brand*, (London and New York 2018), pp 225–53, at p 225. Its footnotes draw particular attention to works by Brand himself, and also to works by E W Ives, J H Baker, C W Brooks, W R Prest. It also lists other articles devoted to the subject.

[7] *The Civilian Writers of Doctors' Commons, London* (Berlin 1988).

[8] *The Civil Lawyers in England 1603–1641* (Oxford 1973).

[9] *Doctors' Commons: A History of the College of Advocates and Doctors of Law* (Oxford 1977).

[10] *Monuments of Endlesse Labours: English Canonists and their Work 1300–1900* (London and Rio Grande, OH 1998).

[11] See, e.g., P A Brand, *The Origins of the English Legal Profession* (Oxford and Cambridge, MA 1992), pp 143–57; C T Allmand, 'The Civil Lawyers', in C Clough (ed), *Profession Vocation, and Culture in Later Medieval England* (Liverpool 1982), pp 155–82; M Beilby, 'The Profits of Expertise: The Rise of the Civil Lawyers and Chancery Equity', in M Hicks (ed), *Profit, Piety and the Professions in Later Medieval England* (Gloucester 1990), pp 72–90; R O'Day, 'Rise and Fall of the Civilians', in her *The Professions in Early Modern England, 1450–1800* (Harlow 2000), pp 151–61.

[12] See C Chapman, *Ecclesiastical Courts, their Officials and their Records* (Dursley 1992), pp 33–34; R Marchant, *The Church under the Law: Justice, Administration and Discipline in the Diocese of York* (Cambridge 1969), pp 41–60; R Houlbrooke, *Church Courts and the People during the English Reformation, 1520–1570* (Oxford 1979), pp 40–43, 51–52; Brian Woodcock, *Medieval Ecclesiastical Courts in the Diocese of Canterbury* (Oxford 1952), pp 40–45.

archives of England's ecclesiastical courts. These contents include the contemporary records and ancillary literature compiled by the English civilians
(formularies, case reports, and manuscript notes) for their own use in day-to-
day practice. There is a lot of it, and it sheds light on the subject's history that
is not available from any other source. The book's primary focus is also upon
the working lives of ordinary ecclesiastical lawyers rather than those of the
most prominent and successful among them.

One additional word of introduction. The book's concentration is upon
what happened in the courts of the English church. It is true that other courts
were open to the professional lawyers described in its pages. For instance,
courts of Admiralty, Chivalry, and the two English universities all adopted the
procedural system in which the civilians were at home. They acted profes-
sionally in them. Even the court of Chancery provided a workplace for some
of the lawyers trained in the canon and civil laws. In addition, it is true that
English civilians were often called upon for diplomatic service; their knowledge of Roman and canon laws was thought to qualify them for dealing with
European lawyers. They spoke a common language, one that most English
common lawyers were thought not to possess. Some of the best existing scholarship on these lawyers deals with those aspects of the careers of the same men
to be described here, as well as the contributions made by civilians to the field
of general jurisprudence. Indeed, some of the work of civilians in England has
seemed deserving of study because it can be said to have had an impact in the
development of aspects of today's legal systems.

Though a legitimate way of studying the subject, this book does not adopt
it. The English civilians were primarily ecclesiastical lawyers. The courts of
the church provided careers for most of them, and it is upon these courts that
this book focuses its attention. Their records have provided the primary basis
for descriptions herein. It is also true that much of what the English civilians
accomplished in the centuries covered by this book has been swept away by
later jurisprudence. Much of it is now obsolete. Some of it now strikes us as
unduly harsh or even as slightly foolish. But this book is a work of history, and
it appears as part of a series meant to explore different aspects of the relationship between Law and Christianity. From both these perspectives, devoting
attention to the routine work of the lawyers who appeared in what were then
often called the 'Courts Christian' seems appropriate.

1

The Law of the Legal Profession: Advocates and Proctors

A history of the profession of ecclesiastical law in England should begin with Roman law. Appropriate terminology is one reason. The terms used to designate the lawyers who served in the courts of the Church from the thirteenth century to the nineteenth were the contributions of the ancient Romans. So too was a considerable part of the law that determined the character of the work these men performed. Texts from the civil law used to define their duties and regulate their conduct were taken from the *Corpus iuris civilis*, the great collection of ancient law texts made at the instigation of the Emperor Justinian in the sixth century. The Digest (Dig. 1.19; 3.3.1–78), the Codex (Cod. 2.7–8), and even the Novels (Nov. 71.1) contained titles devoted specifically to advocates and proctors. So did the *Codex Theodosianus* (Cod. Th. 2.10.1–5; 2.12.1–7). These same two offices also appeared incidentally elsewhere in the texts found within these great collections of law.

The connection to Roman law was not simply a matter of names. It turned out to matter a great deal in the later development of a European legal profession, one that directly shaped the legal practice of ecclesiastical lawyers in England. That development effectively began at Bologna. When the texts from the Digest came to light and began to be taught in the Schools there in the late eleventh century, they were put to practical uses as well as to those of the Schools. Of course, this is well known.[1] The civil law dominated several different facets of the legal renaissance that began with the Digest's recovery, not simply the contents of lectures given in university law faculties. However,

---

[1] The modern literature on the subject is extensive; see, e.g., E Cortese, *Il Rinascimento giuridico medievale*, 2d edn (Rome 1996); F Wieacker, *History of Private Law in Europe*, T Weir (trans) (Oxford 1995), pp 28–41; A Gouron, 'Some Aspects of the Medieval Teaching of Roman Law', in J Van Engen (ed), *Learning Institutionalized: Teaching in the Medieval University* (Notre Dame, IN 2000), pp 161–76; J Fried, *Die Entstehung des Juristenstandes im 12. Jahrhundert* (Cologne and Vienna 1974), pp 61–67.

the dual role played by the civilian texts is worthy of particular note here. It had consequences for this book's subject, because those jurists who had an eye on the world of law as it was applied in courts themselves turned to the ancient texts in determining how lawsuits were to be conducted. Their move devoted to the conduct of litigation was thought to require more than the presence of the parties and a judge. Reliance on experts was needed. Men who were familiar with the relevant laws and who could speak on behalf of the litigants were needed. That is what the medieval jurists thought, and for this purpose, they took what they required from the ancient texts of the Roman law.

When this moment for action arrived in the twelfth century, the consequences of the recovery of these sophisticated sources of law must be seen as a real change of direction. The period from the fall of Rome to the years around 1100 has sometimes been described as a 'World without Lawyers'.[2] Perhaps that is an exaggeration. The notarial tradition never disappeared completely.[3] The church itself preserved relevant aspects of Roman traditions.[4] Collections of conciliar and papal decrees had long been made, and there were men who knew how to use them. Diocesan synods had also met in the centuries before 1100. In them disputes had been aired and decided, though we rarely know much about the details. References to *advocati* and *procuratores* also appear from time to time in early medieval sources, though it is not always certain what functions they performed.[5] Penetrating the realities of early medieval law as it was put into practice has proved to be no simple matter. It does seem right to say, however, that the centuries between the sixth and the eleventh produced nothing like a legal profession as we know it today. In that sense, it was indeed a world without lawyers. True, most European rulers did promulgate laws dealing with what one could call legal rights and wrongs. True also, there were men who had acquired a special familiarity with those laws. However, there was no group of professional lawyers if one takes the term to mean men trained in law who devoted their careers to it and made a living

---

[2] J A Brundage, *The Medieval Origins of the Legal Profession: Canonists, Civilians, and Courts* (Chicago, IL 2008), pp 46–74; see also M Bellomo, *The Common Legal Past of Europe 1000–1800*, L Cochrane (trans) (Washington, DC 1995), pp 34–44; P Brand, *Origins of the English Legal Profession*, pp 2–3; H Berman, *Law and Revolution: The Formation of the Western Legal Tradition* (Cambridge, MA 1983), pp 50–84.

[3] E.g., C M Radding, *Origins of Medieval Jurisprudence: Pavia and Bologna, 850–1150* (New Haven, CT 1988), pp 23–24.

[4] See M Schmoeckel, 'Procedure, proof, and evidence', in J Witte Jr. and F S. Alexander (eds), *Christianity and Law: An Introduction* (Cambridge 2008), pp 143–62.

[5] Several of them are collected in J Hogan, *Judicial Advocates and Procurators* (Washington, DC 1941), pp 25–31. The situation in England is described in J Hudson, *Oxford History of the Laws of England, Volume II 871–1216* (Oxford 2012), pp 63–64.

from its practice. No settled and enforceable rules for the place of lawyers in the procedural process used to settle disputes existed. Contestants in them must have been guided by long-established custom. They made their way without the professional help a lawyer provides.

THE RENAISSANCE IN LAW

By the years around 1200, that state of affairs came to an end. It appeared to thoughtful men that something more was required than adherence to customary norms and good sense. A set of formal rules for the conduct of litigation would become a matter of necessity for the church's bishops, just as it did for secular rulers.[6] Effective diocesan organization, it could accurately be said, 'demanded intensive and a quite legally technical administration'.[7] Rulers and jurists responded, and as a matter of course they turned for help to the Roman law's texts. This was the step taken in the temporal forum, and the church's procedural law followed the same path. Development in both halves of societal regulation virtually always began with Roman law,[8] though never in the church's jurisdiction without reference to spiritual principles and more strictly canonical sources. What the jurists – canonists and civilians alike – did was to make a sensible choice too. Although it would have been impossible to recreate the system of ancient Rome, what the civil law's texts contained on the subject of the practice of law provided a start for the creation of something that was new and useful. It provided procedural principles and building blocks for the development of a class of professional lawyers.[9]

---

[6] See W Trusen, 'Advocatus – zu den Anfängen der gelehrten Anwaltschaft in Deutschland und ihren rechtlichen Grundlangen' in H Kipp et al. (eds), *Um Recht und Freiheit: Festschrift für August Freiherr von der Heydte zur Vollendung des 70. Lebensjahres* (Berlin 1977), vol II, pp 1235–48; L Fowler-Magerl, *Ordines Iudiciarii and Libelli de Ordine Iudiciorum* (Turnhout 1994), pp 16–28; L Mayali, 'Procureurs et representation en droit canonique médiéval' (2002) 114 *Mélanges de l'Ecole française de Rome. Moyen-Age* 44–57; K Pennington, 'Representation in Medieval Canon Law' (2004) 64 *The Jurist* 361–83.

[7] A Hope, 'Bishops' Deputies and Episcopal Power in Medieval law, c.1150 to c.1350', in P Coss et al. (eds), *Episcopal Power and Local Society in Medieval Europe, 900–1400* (Turnhout 2017), pp 195–217, at pp 213–14; K Pennington, 'Due Process, Community and the Prince in the Evolution of the Ordo iudiciarius' (1998) 9 *Rivista internazionale di diritto comune* 9–47.

[8] See G Gottschalk, *Über den Einfluss des römischen Rechts auf das kanonische Recht* (Mannheim 1866, reprint 1997), pp 95–105; K W Nörr, *Romanisch-kanonisches Prozessrecht* (Heidelberg 2012), pp 28–36; K-H Ladeur, *Der Anfang des westlichen Rechts* (Tübingen 2018), pp 120–23.

[9] See C Donahue, Jr, 'Procedure in the Courts of the Ius commune', in W Hartmann and K Pennington (eds), *History of Courts and Procedure in Medieval Canon Law* (Washington, DC 2016), pp 74–124, esp. 80–83; S Reynolds, 'The Emergence of Professional Law in the Long Twelfth Century' (2003) 21 *Law & History Review* 347–66.

One sign of this usage was that regular reference to the texts involving Roman advocates and proctors appeared prominently in some of the earliest *ordines judiciarii*, the guides compiled to meet the need for direction in the details of court procedure. Bulgarus (*fl. c.*1130), the leader among the 'four doctors' who followed Irnerius, was one of the first to take this step.[10] He devoted a title in his brief treatment of procedure to describing 'advocates' as men who lent their aid to parties to litigation by arguing persuasively on their behalf.[11] Other examples followed, such as the Anglo-Norman *Ordo iudiciarius* from just a few years later. It contained short chapters on both proctors and advocates, using the categories from the law of Rome.[12] Later but of more lasting effect was the inclusion in the *Ordo iudiciarius* compiled by Tancred of Bologna (d. *c.*1236) of titles devoted expressly both to advocates and proctors.[13] His definition of advocates began with texts from the Roman law; their duty, he recorded, was to formulate a petition for themselves or for a friend, and to present it before a judge who held jurisdiction over the matter raised by the petition.

Under the civil law, the position of an advocate was an honorable one. According to then current norms, it followed that this office could not be held by children, women, slaves, or lunatics (Dig. 3.1.3).[14] To this list of obvious exclusions, Tancred added heretics and monks, taking as his authority for their exclusion texts from Gratian's Digest and a decretal of Pope Innocent III.[15] His formal definition of a proctor – a man who transacts the business of another in accordance with the terms of the latter's mandate – similarly began with a text taken from the Roman law (Dig. 3.3.1), adding an open-ended statement that

---

[10] A Gouron, 'Le rôle de l'avocat selon la doctrine romaniste du douzième siècle', in A Gouron, *Pionniers du droit occidental au Môyen Âge* (Aldershot 2006), n XV.

[11] *Summa de Iudiciis*, tit. 3, in A Wunderlich (ed), *Anecdota quae processum civilem spectant* (Göttingen 1841), p 3. Bulgarus is often credited with having compiled the first such *ordo* but what he composed is something less than that; see Fowler-Magerl, *Ordines Iudiciarii*, p 24; P Landau, 'The Origin of Civil Procedure', in Uta-Renate Blumenthal, A Winroth and P Landau (eds), *Canon Law, Religion and Politics: Liber Amicorum Robert Somerville* (Washington, DC, 2012), pp 136–43.

[12] See the edition in B Brasington, *Order in the Court: Medieval Procedural Treatises in Translation* (Leiden and Boston, MA 2016), pp 139–40, 148–50.

[13] 'Ordo iudiciarius', Pt. I, tits. 5–6, in F C Bergmann (ed), *Pillius, Tancredus, Gratia, Libri de iudiciorum ordine* (Göttingen 1842, reprint 1965), pp 111–23. See also 'Ordo judiciarius', C. 1 §§ 7–9, in L Rockinger (ed), *Briefsteller und Formelbücher des eilften bis vierzehnten Jahrhunderts* (Munich 1864, reprint 1961), vol II, pp 998–99.

[14] The second was a text from the vulgate version of the *Decretum* that had been taken from the Digest: C. 3 q. 7, c. 2, taken from Dig. 3.1.1.

[15] Dist. 7, De pen. c. 1; X 5.7.10 (Comp. III, 5.4.1).

the proctor should not be of a lesser status than the principal. However, he did not accord to proctors the same high status advocates held in the civilian texts.

Tancred also added a dictum, one again taken over from the Roman law, that was to have great importance in European legal history. It stated that except in special circumstances proctors could not be appointed to act in criminal trials.[16] Both the accuser and the accused must be present and speak for themselves.

The careful attention paid to advocates and proctors by the medieval proceduralists continued in the lengthiest, the most used, and still the best known of the relevant treatises, the *Speculum iudiciale* of William Durantis (d. 1296). His treatment of procedural law contained lengthy titles devoted to both offices, covering the basics of the subject and providing appropriate forms for possible use in a wide variety of circumstances.[17] It was meant for practice. He even included what he thought would be of practical use for advocates, telling them (for example) what they might do when speaking before the pope in consistory. It may well be, Durantis wrote for their use, that your face will pale, your tongue will stutter, and your limbs will tremble as you stand before the apostolic throne. For these lawyers he provided sixteen different ways of beginning – all florid set pieces sufficiently respectful of the occasion.[18] Presumably, the most suitable among them could be chosen and memorized beforehand, then honed for the occasion itself. That would give any advocate a start. Durantis even went a little further, providing textual authority drawn from the Roman and canon law texts for an advocate's assistance with the speeches he provided for the papal consistory. Who knows if they were actually used? We do know, however, that much of his text was put into practice; it was one of the most frequently cited sources of the *ius commune* throughout the Middle Ages and even into later times.

Despite the habitual reliance of medieval jurists such as Durantis on the texts of the *Corpus iuris civilis*, the advocates and proctors who emerged to serve in medieval courts were not equivalent in function to the men who appeared in the ancient texts. They did hold the same titles and they were governed by many of the same rules, but it is only a slight exaggeration to say that the medieval jurists took the material they found in the civilian texts and transformed it, using it for their own purposes and creating a new institution in the process. In other words, they made creative use of what they found.

---

[16]   Pt. I, tit. 6 § 5, citing a text from the *Decretum,* C. 5 q. 3 c. 2 and Dig. 48.1.13.

[17]   Willelmus Durantis, *Speculum iudiciale,* tit. *De procuratore,* Lib I, pt 3, (Basel 1574), pp 202–29; and tit. *De advocato,* Lib I, pt 4, pp 259–71.

[18]   Ibid., tit. *De exordiis et arengis advocatorum,* Lib I, pt 4, nn 34–5.

In doing this, however, they did not turn their back on the older meanings found in the civilian texts. In fact, they virtually always began their discussion by citing them as authoritative. Their contents were the bedrock guides. But a new institution emerged in the process nonetheless. This shift was formally recognized among commentators when they divided 'judicial' advocates and proctors from 'extra-judicial' advocates and proctors.[19] Making that distinction allowed them to avoid confusion – to select rules applicable to each and to concentrate the greater part of their attention on the judicial branch. It is also noteworthy that, despite the disagreements that sometimes existed between canonists and civilians on jurisdictional questions, with few exceptions they both treated advocates and proctors without regard to the division between temporal and spiritual courts in which they served. In function and conduct, the lawyers were not divided between the secular and ecclesiastical spheres. In England, of course, that division would be made and it would have consequences. But it was otherwise in the learned literature used on the Continent.

For both advocates and proctors, the changes from ancient times in what the terms meant after 1200 were particularly significant. The classical Roman advocate was an expert in persuasion, usually trained in rhetoric and skilled in argument in a public forum. He was not a jurisconsult or *jurisperitus*. By contrast, the term was later used to describe men whose expertise lay in the mastery of legal doctrine. Roman advocates had not necessarily been that, although it is true that some movement towards requiring legal learning among advocates gained ground under the late Roman Empire.[20] One such text called for their formal education (Cod. 2.7.11). It was not so earlier, how-ever, and this particular change was not reflected in the Digest's texts. Cicero (d. 43 BC), for example, was an advocate. His career clarifies what the term meant. He did take part in public litigation and he did come to know some-thing of the law, but his primary function was to apply oratorical skills to defend those who called upon him for aid.[21] The medieval advocate was something different. He did argue on behalf of his clients and they paid him for doing so, but his mastery of the law was what principally set him apart from both the parties and their proctors. Normally, men were admitted to the office of advo-cate only after formal education in a University's law faculty, and his assistance

[19] Caspar Manz, *Tractatus de advocatis, procuratoribus, defensoribus, syndicis et negotiorum gestoribus*, tit. *De procuratoribus* (Ingolstadt 1659), n 3.

[20] F Schulz, *History of Roman Legal Science* (Oxford 1946, reprint 1963), pp 267–77; J A Crook, *Legal Advocacy in the Roman World* (Ithaca, NY 1995), pp 6–17.

[21] See Jill Harries, 'Cicero and the Law', in J Powell and J Paterson (eds), *Cicero the Advocate* (Oxford 2004), pp 147–63; E P Parks, *The Roman Rhetorical Schools as a Preparation for the Courts under the Early Empire* (Baltimore, MD 1945), pp 21–60.

in providing counsel to those who called upon his legal expertise was as important a part of his career as was his ability in forensics. Only incidentally was he a qualified rhetorician.

The nature of the office of the Roman *procurator* was also different in its origins from that of the lawyer who emerged in medieval practice. Originally, proctors had been men appointed by the mandate of a Roman citizen to administer the latter's affairs during his absence from Rome. It appears that departure from the city of Rome *rei publicae causa* was the most common circumstance that led to the appointment of proctors and legal recognition of their wide powers.[22] The ability to delegate the management of one's property to a trustworthy person had been a strong inducement for service to the Roman republic, and that was the reason for its introduction. However, the institution also proved useful in a variety of circumstances, and its purpose was gradually broadened to include other causes of absence. A man could be legitimately absent for many legitimate reasons, and he would need someone to carry on his affairs, whatever those reasons happened to be. Eventually the law would drop any requirement of absence at all. The more specialized term *procurator litis* then came into use to designate the man appointed to take the principle's place in litigation.[23] What would matter then was the mandate delegating specific powers to the proctor. It could be drawn up to cover full or partial representation in a particular court and matter. It was this usage that later became a routine procedure in civil causes brought before the courts of spiritual and temporal jurisdiction during the Middle Ages.[24]

The term *procurator* did not, however, cease to carry a broader meaning. Proctors still served other functions than those of a courtroom lawyer. The representatives of the lower clergy to the English parliaments were also called proctors, for example.[25] A man or woman could even enter a valid marriage through the service of a proctor.[26] Similarly, the term *advocatus* was also used to describe the patron of an ecclesiastical living.[27] However, a court of law was

---

[22] G le Bras, *L'Evolution générale du procurateur en droit privé romain des origines au IIIe siècle* (Paris 1922), pp 30–56.

[23] See A H J Greenidge, *The Legal Procedure of Cicero's Time* (London 1901, reprint 1971), pp 237–43.

[24] E.g., Constitution of a proctor by Agnes Durant (Ely 1376), Act book EDR D/2/1, f 48 (18 different specific powers granted coupled with a grant of power 'omnia alia et singula faciendi et exercendi que in hac parte necessaria fuerint').

[25] See P Bradford and A McHardy (eds), *Proctors for Parliament: Clergy, Community and Politics, c.1248–1539* (C & Y Soc. 107, 2017).

[26] Abundant learning on this subject is found in Tomas Sanchez, *De Sancto matrimonii sacramento*, Lib. II, disp. 11, nn 1–32.

[27] Sext 1.6.13.

the natural venue in which these two institutions flourished. There, use of the two terms to refer to lawyers became a matter of routine in the Middle Ages. The men who served in specific diocesan courts became known as *procuratores generales* in ordinary usage. In the hands of the medieval jurists and under the influence of customary usage, that recognition of professionalization in the office followed as a matter of course, even though the original connection of both terms to the Roman institutions never dropped wholly out of use.

Starting with the Roman law's texts also led naturally to an expansion of legal learning about the work and powers of advocates and proctors at the hands of medieval jurists. Evidence of growth was found within the texts of the canon law itself. Gratian's *Decretum* (c.1140) and the glosses in its margins contain references to both offices, as in the statement that judges must listen and pay heed to the words of advocates before pronouncing a definitive sentence.[28] The *Liber Extra*, the *Liber Sextus*, and the Clementines all contained titles called *De procuratoribus*,[29] and advocates were mentioned by those terms in several of the decretals and conciliar decrees that dealt with court procedure and were placed in the church's lawbooks.[30] As in so much of the medieval church's procedural law, Roman law shaped its development, but the needs of contemporary court practice also made a difference in what these terms meant in fact.

MEDIEVAL JURISTIC LITERATURE

The developments in the law inevitably led to extensive discussion of the subject in the canonistic and the civilian literature of the later Middle Ages – much of it found in contemporary glosses and commentaries on the legal texts. Examples of the interest the medieval canonists took in this subject are found in many treatises. They are not hard to locate. Nor are they difficult to describe in outline. Hostiensis, an early and famous canonist of the thirteenth century, took up the office of an advocate in his *Summa aurea*, placing it under the heading *De postulando* in his treatment of Book One of the Gregorian Decretals. After setting out its formal requirements for entry and the exclusion of those who did not fit them, he went on to discuss the conduct that ought to mark an advocate's conduct. To this office, he wrote, belongs the

---

[28] Gl. ord. ad C. 35 q. 10 c. 7, s.v. *quia veritas*: 'Optima allegatio est contra iudices qui nolunt audire advocatos … Non enim potest ad veritatem pervenire nisi respiciatur'.

[29] X 1.38.1-15; Sext 1.19.1-9; Clem. 1.10.1-4.

[30] See, e.g., X 1.37.1 (prohibiting clerics from acting as advocates in temporal matters); X 1.32.1 (directing a judge to provide an advocate for a party in need of one); and X 1.37.3 (recognizing some of the duties of an advocate in not perverting the cause of justice).

requirement that the advocate should 'pursue no cause against conscience'. In addition, he held that 'as soon as he perceived that it was a hopeless cause he should withdraw from it'.[31] These directives turned out to be a more controversial position than his text itself indicated.[32] They also turned out to have a decided impact on court practice in England's consistory courts. The ecclesiastical lawyers sometimes acted upon them by withdrawing from causes they regarded as either hopeless or unjust.[33] As such, this was a significant addition to the civilian texts.

The process of elaboration of the characteristics attached to these offices was ongoing. One example of similar treatment, lengthier and more sophisticated legally than that of Hostiensis, is the commentary of the leading canonist of the fifteenth century, Nicolaus de Tudeschis, commonly known as Panormitanus. He devoted almost nine double folio pages in one edition to the discussion of a single decretal on the subject from Pope Innocent III. Its terms invited that treatment; it included many things. One was that which prohibited the introduction of proctors in criminal trials (X 5.1.15), always a matter of importance and interest to the canonists.[34] There were always exceptions to this rule and Panormitanus explored several of them. For instance, despite the prohibition against participation of a proctor, under ordinary circumstances a proctor could be admitted 'to excuse' a defendant's absence from court on the day he was summoned to answer a criminal charge.[35] The common legitimate excuse was that the accused man suffered from an illness that rendered travel impossible. If a proctor could do this, Panormitanus went on, could the same proctor not also be admitted 'to excuse him by virtue of his innocence'?[36] That might be characterized as only a short step. Suppose the proctor could show that the accused man had also been bed-ridden at the time the crime

---

[31] Hostiensis, *Summa aurea*, Lib. I, tit. *De postulando*, n 4.

[32] Some commentators, noting that such a withdrawal put the party in an impossible position, held that the lawyer could do so, but only with the permission of the judge. See, e.g., A Fritsch, *Advocatus peccans: sive, Tractatus de peccatis advocatorum et procuratorum*, Concl. IV (Frankfurt and Leipzig 1678).

[33] One probable immediate source of this prohibition was Council of Lyons II (1275), c. 19, in *Decrees of the Ecumenical Councils*, vol I, p 324. The practice is described more fully in my 'Ethical Standards for Advocates and Proctors in Theory and Practice', in S Kuttner (ed), *Proceedings of the Fourth International Congress of Medieval Canon Law* (Vatican City 1976), pp 283–99.

[34] Panormitanus, *Commentaria* ad X 5.1.15.

[35] D.p. C. 5 q. 3 c. 1. This usage is occasionally found in the court records; see *Ex officio c Robatham* (St Albans 1633), ASA 7/30, f 42v.

[36] *Commentaria* ad X 5.1.15, n 23 ('Item textus ibi dicit quod admittitur ad excusandum innocentiam, et sic loquitur quando excusat de crimine, ostendo eum innocentem et facit optime text. in arg. in [Dig. 40.1.6]'.

was alleged to have been committed. Should that be ignored? And suppose that no one had objected when he proffered this denial of guilt and the judge had absolved him. Would that absolution be a nullity? Perhaps this could be treated as one among the many cases in the canon law where an action that should not be done was still valid if it was done in fact without timely objection? Panormitanus discussed these questions (and others like them) with the caution that is one of the marks of a pure lawyer and also one of the stumbling blocks to modern historians in search of unambiguous answers to medieval questions. On this particular subject, investigation leads only to the conclusion that in the end he left some questions open.

Examination of the commentaries of many of the medieval civilians produces similar results. On this subject at least, no real division separated them from the canonists. The commentaries of Bartolus de Saxoferrato (d. 1357), to take only the most famous among them, discussed many of the same questions the canonists did, although it was the texts from the Digest not the *Liber extra* with which he normally began his discussion. The Digest's title *De procuratoribus* contains seventy-eight chapters (Dig. 3.3.1–78) and he commented on most of them. The contents of some that will surprise most modern readers often turn out to have been quite important in medieval practice. One such instance was the position Bartolus took towards a principal party who sent a proctor to appear in court with an insufficient mandate of procuration (i.e. one that did not grant all the powers needed to deal with the issues involved). In his view, that person was to be treated as contumacious.[37] He was to receive no further citation. The Digest's text itself did not go that far, but behind this jurist's seemingly harsh conclusion about what may have been an innocent mistake lay a problem that long troubled the medieval courts. If the mandate of procuration did not cover a specific action – say, the right to appeal – the proctor's action in entering an appeal would have been a nullity. It might thus happen that the right to appeal would be lost by such a result, since there were time limits on how soon after a sentence an appeal could be made.[38] It was important, therefore, that mandates were worded with care. If an appeal was likely, authority to enter an appeal must be included within the mandate. One way of assuring that it would be, Bartolus must have thought, was to visit penalties on those parties who failed to take due care in defining the powers of their proctors, even to the extent of anticipating what

---

[37] Bartolus de Saxoferrato, *Commentaria* ad Dig. 3.3.1.2 ('Iste [the principal party] non est amplius citandus, tanquam vere contumax').

[38] E.g., Braine c Gilane (Bristol 1564), Act book EP/J/1/6, p 29 (the proctor for one party 'allegavit tempus fatale fuisse et esse lapsum eo quod non constat de aliqua appellatione interposita').

they might be called upon to do in the event of an adverse sentence. We know too little about court practice to say what the results of his treatment meant in practice, but it is useful to have it as one example among many of the care medieval jurists customarily took in dealing with the subject of professional requirements.

DEVELOPMENTS IN THE SIXTEENTH AND SEVENTEENTH CENTURIES

In the sixteenth century and continuing even into the age of Enlightenment, the primary focus of scholarship on this subject, like most other parts in the *ius commune*, turned away from glosses and commentaries tied directly to the texts. It turned instead to a more varied and specialized legal literature. Some of it took the form of monographs on special subjects, and the law of advocates and proctors was one among them. A glance at the entries in Martin Lipenius, *Bibliotheca realis iuridica* (Leipzig 1757) produces an abundant harvest of the titles devoted to the legal profession written during those years. A simple count produces a total of 113 different authors on the subject listed under the heading *De advocatis*. The number found under the title *De procuratoribus* was lower – only fifty were listed. Even that is a substantial number, however, and many of the treatises cited did cover both branches of the legal profession within the same section. It is worth saying also that some of those I was able to locate and read proved to be slight things – very short doctoral dissertations, for instance. They could have been meant only to demonstrate that the candidate had gained enough familiarity with the texts of the Roman and canon laws on the subject to allow him to pass to the next stage of his career.[39] At the same time, some of the treatises listed in the Bibliography proved to be quite impressive in their coverage. Lengthy and detailed treatments on this subject are there to be discovered. A general similarity in content existed among those I was able to find and read through. That was only to be expected. But reading slight variants of the same theme turned out to be a worthwhile task nonetheless. Repetition provided a sufficient familiarity with the subject to provide a fair picture of the two institutions as they were then understood.

Moreover, such a study shows clearly one thing about medieval treatises. The discussion found in the treatises was not intended to be a search for originality or new ideas. Such a search would have been no virtue in a lawyer.

---

[39] E.g., Julius Pacius, *Theses de procuratoribus et defensoribus* (Geneva 1597) (four pages divided into twenty points with citations to Roman law and to the *Paratitla*, a much-used commentary on the civil law by Matthaeus Wesenbecius (d. 1586).

Most importantly for present purposes, the treatises covered much of the same ground in dealing with the law that governed the professional lives of the English civilians. They were meant for use. To be complete, to be useful, they had to be repetitive. They should not be despised on that account. The themes they raised and discussed at length proved relevant in the careers of English ecclesiastical lawyers. At least four of these themes raised matters of particular importance in common practice within the English courts. Each illustrates the utility of treatments that now appear to have been unoriginal and tedious.

Qualifications Necessary for Entry

The first – one commented upon by all writers on the subject – were the formal qualifications necessary for serving as advocates and proctors. It might be more accurate to say that the writers concentrated their attention upon the disqualifications. They normally began their treatment with a juristic commonplace of the canonists – all persons were qualified to act unless they were expressly disqualified. However, it turned out that there were quite a few persons who were in fact disqualified. Neither a woman, nor a soldier, nor anyone with a chronic disease could act (Dig. 3.3.54). The first of these followed from accepted medieval thought about feminine capacity. Law was classed as a 'masculine office'. The third existed because chronically ill persons were not likely to meet the requirement that they always be present in court. But why the second? It was said to be because the tasks of an advocate or proctor might distract a soldier from service to the public.[40] Thus, it did not apply to veterans.[41] According to Durantis, if a soldier did act as a lawyer, the proceedings he conducted remained valid, but in his view soldiers should not be admitted to ordinary practice before the courts.[42] Slaves were also disqualified, and so were monks. The consequences that followed from a lack of personal freedom must have been obvious as to the first; slaves might be called away at any time. But why the second? Because they had renounced the world and, like slaves, they lacked a distinct and recognized legal personality.[43] They were 'soldiers in the celestial army', as one jurist put it.[44] This was a medieval addition, to be sure, but it seemed that the same rationale applied that Roman lawyers had applied to slaves. Lack of sufficient age was also a disqualification. Eighteen

---

[40] Manz, *Tractatus*, tit. De procuratoribus, n 83.
[41] Ludovicus Cencius, *Tractatus de procuratoribus*, C. XXII, n 14 (Florence 1857).
[42] *Speculum iudiciale*, Lib. I, Pt. 3, tit. De procuratore, n 21.
[43] Manz, *Tractatus*, tit. De procuratoribus, n 77.
[44] Cencius, *Tractatus de procuratoribus*, C. XX, n 9.

was recognized by some as sufficient; parallel texts from the Institutes defining the age for making a valid last will and testament (Inst. 2.12) were said to support that cut-off point.[45] In practice, however, twenty-five years apparently became the canonical norm. A text from the canon law's *Liber sextus* so stated it (Sext 1.19.5) and this was widely taken over as a matter of customary practice even in the temporal forum.[46]

Among the most prominent additions to the list of those disqualified from legal practice during the Middle Ages was that excluding the clergy, at least those in major orders. This was not a matter of personal incapacity. Some clerics made good lawyers. It was rather a disqualification designed to protect spiritual men from the sordid details of wrangling in courts and so to secure the reputation of the clerical order. Hostiensis commented that their routine participation in litigation, particularly secular litigation, would both harm the reputation of the church and hinder the performance of the divine offices.[47] However, like many of the rules in this area of the canon law, this one admitted of exceptions. For a cleric to serve as an advocate or proctor on behalf of his own church was permitted. It furthered a legitimate goal of the canon law. Something like the same rationale applied to representing *miserabiles personae* in court. Both exceptions (and others like them) served a greater good than that of protecting the clerical order from public scandal.[48] And, as several jurists conceded, this was also an area of the law where custom did not always match the law's stated mandates.[49] Medieval England was one venue in which it did not.[50] In fact, a diocesan statute of 1287 enacted what appeared to be the opposite rule. The statute excluded laymen from practicing as advocates.[51] The proctors named in the earliest surviving act book from the diocese of Ely, for instance, seem all to have been clerics, although it is not clear that they

---

[45] Harpprecht, *Disputatio de procuratoribus*, n 7.

[46] Ibid. 'Sane iure canonico quo usu hac in parte observatur'.

[47] X 1.37.1; Hostiensis *Summa aurea*, tit. *De postulando*, n 7. See also J P Lancellotus, *Institutiones iuris canonici*, Lib. III, tit. 2 § 13, but also listing exceptions and several disputed questions among the jurists.

[48] See, e.g., P P Guazzini, 'Tractatus moralis' in *Opera omnia juridica et moralia*, vol III, nn 7–13 (stating the fact that exceptions to the rule were made 'in multis casibus'). On the scope of the concept of scandal in this context, see W Druwé, *Scandalum in the early Bolognese Decretistic and in Papal Decretals (c.1140–1234)* (Leuven 2018), p 93.

[49] It is worthy of note that the Roman Rota was one of the venues where the hold of custom contrary to the law's texts was described as particularly strong. See, e.g., Cencius, *De Procuratoribus*, C. 102, n 37. See also K Salonon, *Papal Justice in the Late Middle Ages* (Oxford and New York 2016), 39–41.

[50] See, e.g., William Lyndwood, *Provinciale* (Oxford 1679, reprint 1968), p 113, v. *competente*; see also Introduction, D M Owen (ed), *John Lydford's Book* (London 1974), pp 5–11.

[51] *Councils & Synods*, Pt II, p 1030 (Statutes of Exeter II, n 34 (1287)).

were in priest's orders.[52] It is matter of initial surprise to discover that the canon law's ideal excluding the clergy from the ranks of professional lawyers was only achieved after the Protestant Reformation.[53]

Distinctions between Kinds of Legal Representative

The second contribution of the later jurists to this subject was the clarification of the differences between the different types of agents and representatives recognized in the *ius commune*. Commentators took pains to distinguish advocates and proctors from other kinds of agents, listing and explaining the differences between them. One commentator named fifteen similar positions of representation found within the *ius commune*, all of them similar but not identical in name, function, or authority.[54] Guardians (of infants or the insane) were the most obvious example. They could act for a ward and were bound by a duty to act as a fiduciary on the ward's behalf, but they were not considered either as an advocate or a proctor. Their authorization to act came from the law itself, or at least from a person in lawful authority, rather than from the principal party in litigation. That distinguished them formally, and it carried with it a number of differences in practice. The availability of *restitutio in integrum* at the termination of the guardianship was probably the clearest example of the latter. It was appropriate to undo the improper actions of guardians, but not those of proctors.[55]

There were several other such distinctions commonly drawn by the jurists, some of them seemingly of no great importance but nonetheless likely to occur in practice. What about a husband acting for his wife? The law considered him to be a *coniuncta persona*, but it was an open question whether that status was sufficient to allow him to represent his wife's interests in court without a specific mandate from her. There were distinct opinions on the subject.[56] In appearance this does not appear to have mattered very much, but the question may have been relevant in England's ecclesiastical courts. Husbands did sometimes appear for their wives, and at least as far as I have been able to discover from the formal records, the practice was allowed to pass unchallenged.[57]

---

[52] See, e.g., Katherine Hunt's Action (1375), EDR D/2/1, f 43v (constitution by her of several proctors all of whom were described as *clerici*). Contrast Charles Eden's Action (17th century) EDR F 5/41, f. 60 (constitution of three proctors none of whom was stated to be a cleric).

[53] Marchant, *The Church under the Law*, p 49.

[54] Manz, *Tractatus*, tit. De procuratoribus, n 10: 'Quaeritur itaque quanto [et] quomodo differat procurator ab advocato, syndico, excusatore, etc'.

[55] Harpprecht, *Disputatio*, n 23.

[56] Cencius, *De Procuratoribus*, C. V, nn 1–21.

[57] E.g., Case of Joan Colfax (Chichester 1554), Ep I/10/20 (appearance by John Colfax 'nomine uxoris sue'); Alice Harewell c Elizabeth Keild (Worcester 1607), Act book 794.011, BA 2513,

The records actually produce at least one case in which the wife acted for her husband.[58] That too seems to have been allowed in the absence of objection.

The distinction discussed in treatises of greatest relevance to the subject of this study was that between advocates and proctors themselves. It turns out that in practice an overlap developed between the status and functions of these two classes. According to the learning inherited from antiquity this was not so, and later commentators on the subject sometimes so stated the difference. A wide gap was thought to have existed between them. Not only did proctors serve a different function in cases brought before the courts than did advocates, they also stood well below advocates in terms of prestige and levels of remuneration. The former was a common office of no particular prestige; the latter an honorable one charged with a public character.[59] Thus, it made some sense that according to one opinion a man tainted by *infamia* could lawfully serve as a *procurator iudicialis*, but not as an advocate.[60]

It appears, however, to have been an open question how fully this ancient learning still applied in later medieval centuries and into the sixteenth century. A few medieval glosses recognized the similarity of the functions advocates and proctors performed,[61] and by 1500 in practice the gap between the two halves of the legal profession had narrowed.[62] Caspar Manz took note that 'today at least in the greater courts [proctors] are no longer taken *pro vilibus*'.[63] The difference in function between them certainly existed, but the gap in status between proctors and advocates was less marked in practice than it had been in ancient times. In England this was true. Many of the men who served as proctors were university graduates in law – though almost invariably recipients only of the first degree (LLB). The records and the notebooks they kept also show that many of them had gained a working familiarity with the

---

p 310 (appearance by husband 'tanquam coniuncta persona' who 'constituit procuratorem pro uxore sua Archer seniorem').

[58] Ex officio c Crane (London 1589), Act book MS. DL/C/B/043/M50 9064/13 (Joan, the wife, alleging that her husband could not attend because of a sore leg).

[59] Manz, *Tractatus*, tit. *De procuratoribus*, n 14.

[60] Ibid., nn 110–11, citing as authority Inst. 4.13.11(10), which mentioned only proctors, not advocates.

[61] Many of the rules and requirements that applied to one also applied to the other.

[62] See, e.g., William of Drogheda, *Summa aurea*, C. 119, quaest. 9 ('Posset opponi quod non est differentia alia inter procuratorem et advocatum, quia advocatus postulat et procurator postulat in iure', but going on to discuss the matter and draw an operative distinction between them). This was apparently a widespread feature of European law; see R A Houston, 'The Composition and Distribution of the legal profession and the use of law in Britain and Ireland c.1500-c.1850' (2018) 86 *Tijdschrift voor Rechtsgeschiedenis* 123–56, at 128–29.

[63] Manz, *Tractatus*, tit. *De procuratoribus*, n 18 (speaking of the greater courts in Germany).

legal resources available in the European *ius commune*.[64] They knew enough, both from reading and from experience, to give advice and assistance on most legal questions to their clients. The distinction between the two halves of the profession was clearly maintained. In function and in learning, there continued to be a clear difference. But some of the old distance between them in expertise narrowed.

Exclusion of Proctors from Criminal Causes

A third topic treated regularly by later commentators on this aspect of the canon law, one already mentioned briefly in discussing the work of Panormitanus, was the exclusion of lawyers from criminal causes. In England's consistory courts, the crimes within the church's jurisdiction ranged from *ex officio* actions against persons who had misbehaved during church services to the offense of heresy, a crime for which conviction could lead to the horrors of being burned alive. From such cases proctors were excluded. And for the most part, the records of the English ecclesiastical courts show that the rule was followed in fact. With few exceptions, proctors were absent from *ex officio* causes, including those brought for 'heretical depravity'.[65] The normal procedure called for men and women charged with a crime to appear before the judge and hear the charge against them. If they denied it, they were assigned canonical purgation. Success in it required an oath by the defendant denying the commission of the crime of which they were suspected. It was supported by a number of compurgators who swore that they believed the oath to be worthy. If that failed or if they admitted the charge, they were assigned appropriate public penance. No lawyers (except the judges) were involved.

This procedure became a matter of controversy in the seventeenth century. In fact, it had long been controversial. The judges themselves seem sometimes to have violated its spirit by appointing proctors to act as 'promotors' in *ex officio* causes.[66] They may have been encouraged to do so because some areas of ecclesiastical jurisdiction could be invoked either as civil or as criminal matters – defamation or failure to make a payment of tithes, for example.

---

[64] See 'Notebook of William Colman', in R H Helmholz (ed), *Three Civilian Notebooks 1580–1640* (SS 127, 2010), pp 117–46.

[65] E.g., Ex officio c Busship (Bath & Wells 1510), Act book D/D/Ca 1a, p 73. The defendant was given a term to undergo compurgation three-handed. A proctor appeared for the defendants in Ex officio c Bradshaw (London 1588), Act book MS. DL/C/B/043/M50 9064/13, ff 15v-16, but he asserted only that a similar cause was pending before the Dean of the Court of Arches. A proctor also appeared in Ex officio c Palmer (Norwich 1577), Act book ANW/2/31, f 11; he objected to the overly general form of the presentment against his client.

[66] E.g., Ex officio c Sybley (Hertford 1632), AHH 5/11, f 56.

So too could disciplinary actions be brought *ex officio promoto*, with a proctor serving as the promoter.[67] Objections were sometimes raised to this practice,[68] and a few disputes also arose when defendants in these cases demanded to be represented by a lawyer but were denied the privilege. In 1635, in the court of the archdeaconry of Sudbury, a man named Humphrey was cited to appear to answer for violation of an offense within the court's jurisdiction. He came and demanded that a proctor be assigned to him. The judge refused, whereupon he is recorded as having 'said petulantly, Let the judge do his worst, I appeal'.[69] Unfortunately, no result survives.

This prohibition of legal representation in criminal matters, never without exception and always controversial in the hands of commentators, was of course one part of the inheritance of Roman law. It was the rule stated in the *Corpus iuris civilis*, and its prohibitions applied to both the accuser and the accused. The reason given for it in the texts was derived from the *poena talionis*. Under ancient Roman law a man condemned for a wrong must suffer the same harm (or greater) than the wrong he himself had caused.[70] This general idea was carried further. The man who brought a false accusation against another must also undergo the same fate he would have inflicted upon the person he had accused, a rule and result replicated in part by the English common law's ancient criminal appeal.[71]

A colorable reason therefore stood behind the prohibition against allowing lawyers to appear in criminal matters. It was found within the law itself. If a proctor were allowed to stand in the place of either accuser or accused in such a case, as he would be by becoming *dominus litis*, logically he would stand in the shoes of one of the parties.[72] As such he should be subject to the same penalties and punishments meted out to the men he represented. Since this result would be quite unjust – the proctor would have done nothing deserving of punishment – he should not be admitted at all.[73] If the practice were allowed, moreover, every person accused of a crime would send a proctor to appear

---

[67] E.g., Ex officio promoto c Hustler (York 1596), Chanc.AB.13, f 66v (the defendant appeared 'et statim dictus Hustler constitut magistrum White suum procuratorem in omnibus suis causis'); Ex officio promoto c Keggrell (Lincoln 1604), DIOC/Cj 15, f 71 (proctors for both).

[68] See Precedent book (Carlisle 17th century) DRC 3/62, f. 86v (raising the possibility of appeal).

[69] Archdeaconry of Sudbury, MS. 909/6, f. 14v. The nature of his alleged offense was not stated. In the same cause, however, one of the proctors was also appointed as 'coadiutor officii', suggesting that the judge was taking liberties with the established rule. Similar is an earlier case: Ex officio c Clerk (London 1513), MS. DL/C/B/043/M50 9064/11, f 112.

[70] See H F Jolowicz, 'The Assessment of Penalties in Primitive Law', in P Winfield and A McNair (eds), *Cambridge Legal Essays* (Cambridge 1926), pp 203–22.

[71] J H Baker, *Introduction to English Legal History*, 4th edn (London 2002), pp 502–05.

[72] Cencius, *De Procuratoribus*, C. 58 (in part criticizing the aptness of the concept).

[73] Cod. 7.45.1 and gl. ord. ad id, v. *non fuit*; the subject is more fully discussed in Durantis, *Speculum iudiciale*, tit. *De procuratore*, Lib. I, pt. 2, rubr, n 9, and Julius Clarus, *Practica criminalis* (Venice 1595), Quaest. 32, n 3.

in his place and thus avoid condign punishment, as by flight if the sentence went against him. The medieval canon law took seriously the principle that crimes should not be left unpunished.[74] Here was a conclusion drawn from that principle and a plausible reason for acceptance of the prohibition in the canon law.

By the sixteenth century, however, this line of reasoning had lost much of whatever cogency it once enjoyed, at least in the courts of the church.[75] The *poena talionis* was no longer exacted; in practice the punishments meted out to most of the guilty were also designed to heal a wound, right a wrong, or restore harmony among the populace. These sentences and goals had replaced those of the ancient law. Moreover, in consequence of a canon of the Fourth Lateran Council of 1215, the private accuser had been replaced in virtually all circumstances by allowing *ex officio* prosecution of persons suspected of having committed a crime or misdemeanor.[76] Public fame among responsible men and women in effect served the role of the ancient accuser. Despite these developments, the rule against allowing proctors in criminal cases remained.

This denial provides an example of a feature common to many legal regimes – the reason for a rule may change from one age to another, but the rule itself remains the same. In this situation, whatever justification existed for the rule's continuation was found in the same perceived dangers that English common lawyers used to justify denying a place for counsel to accused persons in criminal cases.[77] Too often, they concluded, lawyers stood in the way of discovering the truth. Lawyers took advantage of legal technicalities. They thus diverted the attention of finders of fact from their proper task. The presence of defense counsel too often stood in the way of the infliction of condign punishment of the guilty. Far better from that perspective that a defendant should appear in person. Once in court, the judge (or a jury) could hear him and observe the countenance and quality of his person. They assumed that the person accused knew the truth better than anyone else and concluded that finders of fact would be better informed by observation of his constancy (or trepidation) in sight and speech.[78] If a strictly legal question arose, the accused

---

[74] R Fraher, 'The Theoretical Justification for the New Criminal Law of the High Middle Ages: Rei publice interest, ne crimina remaneant impunita' (1984) *University of Illinois Law Rev.* 577–95.

[75] See Clarus, *Practica criminalis*, Quaest. 32, n 5: '[H]odie cessat haec ratio, cum sit sublata poena talionis'.

[76] Lat. IV c. 8 (X 5.1.17).

[77] See Ferdinand Pulton, *De pace regis et regni* (London 1609) tit. *Pleading not guiltie*, n 2, pp 192–93. Compare Durantis, *Speculum iudiciale*, tit. *De positionibus*, Lib II, Pt 2 § 3 nn 10–13.

[78] Manz, *Tractatus*, tit. *De procuratoribus*, nn 146–47.

person might have a learned advocate assigned to him, but short of that it seemed best that he should speak for himself. Modern sentiment has turned away from this way of thinking about the subject, and I think rightly so, but we should not suppose that nothing other than the blind reverence for Roman law and the dead hand of the past lay behind its acceptance.

The Contents and Wording of Mandates of Procuration

A fourth feature of the commentaries compiled about and useful to proctors and advocates was a scrupulous attention to the wording in the mandates under which proctors served. Although it was always possible to appoint a proctor *apud acta*, doing so required the presence of the principal and it did not solve the question of the kinds of future conduct by the proctor the appointment covered. This subject was mentioned briefly above in describing the contributions of Bartolus of Saxoferrato to the development of a workable law in this area. The varieties of possible forms to be used in the appointment of proctors was a regular theme found in the later treatises on the subject. It may seem that this was a holdover from the notarial culture present in Italian cities at the time the institution was being formed. Notaries were always present in the English consistory courts, and long treatises on the *Ars notariatus* were compiled in the sixteenth and seventeenth centuries to guide them. In fact, however, the variant forms given in the procedural literature of the time was more than following the path laid out in the old texts. If anything, the attention paid to the subject and thought about its reach grew over the centuries. Caspar Manz (d. 1677) devoted seventy-seven different paragraphs in his monograph to this matter.[79] Ludovicus Cencius (*fl.* 17th century) included a lengthy treatment called 'Of ambiguous mandates' to his treatise.[80] To them it was important. It was mentioned as of interest in the notebook of a seventeenth-century English law student.[81] Recognition of its significance also finds some support in the English church court records; the actions of a proctor were treated as invalid where he could not produce a sufficient proxy.[82] Manz himself began discussion of the subject realistically, noting that although for many purposes the constitution (in the sense of a letter of appointment)

---

[79] Ibid., nn 186–262.
[80] Cencius, *De Procuratoribus*, Cap. 28, nn 1–41.
[81] BL, MS. Harl. 3190, f 48 (dealing with Cod. 2.12(13).10.
[82] In re George Langmere, (Lichfield 1534), Act book B/C/10/1, f 51 (he was rejected as proctor of the wife of Thomas Screven). See also C Ritchie, *The Ecclesiastical Courts of York* (Arbroath 1956), pp 77–83.

of non-judicial *procuratores* required little attention to detail, with judicial proctors it was otherwise. With them, careful planning was required.

Why was that? Manz provided several examples to illustrate and justify his attention to the subject. One that points to his reason for laying stress on the wording of these mandates discussed the possibility of compromise in litigation. Of course, compromise of a dispute was a frequent occurrence then, just as it is today. The subject occupied a separate title of the Gregorian Decretals (X 1.36.1–11). But would a proctor be able to agree to a compromise and settlement? That was the relevant question. The ordinary mandate used in litigation gave him the power *ad agendum*. It did not confer the power *ad concordandum*, and settling a case seemed more like that than the power to dispute. It thus appeared to be outside the mandate's terms. There was an answer to this, however. As just noted, the ordinary rule was that the proctor became *dominus litis* after the *litis contestatio*, i.e. the joinder of issue, and if this meant a true *dominus* he ought to hold the same power the litigant himself had. The proctor should therefore be allowed to proceed as fully as the actual party, even to the end of the suit. There was an answer to this too, however. He may have been *dominus litis*, but this was only while the *lis* lasted. Once it had been abandoned, his authority ceased. Perhaps a fresh mandate, giving him specific powers to agree to the terms of a compromise, was therefore required under the circumstances. The pages of Manz's treatment did not produce a definitive answer to the question, but modern lawyers will recognize situations like this – cases where caution trumps an argument, even a good argument. The important point here, however, is that this was a lawyer's question, and it was a real question. In raising it and discussing it at length, Manz and other jurists who discussed matters like it were not simply demonstrating the extent of their erudition. They had a practical reason for their concern.

The records of the English courts show that the jurists' attention to this subject was not misplaced. Questions about the sufficiency of proxies arose with some frequency.[83] One example was the power of substitution. Did a general power to represent a person in litigation allow the proctor so appointed to substitute another proctor in his place? If he held plenary power, it seemed that he could. However, it was questionable to suppose that this had actually been the intent of the principal. The question arose surprisingly often in practice.[84] As a counsel of prudence, surely it made sense to include the power of

[83] See the example in L Poos L R (ed), *Lower Ecclesiastical Jurisdiction in Late-Medieval England* (Oxford 2001), pp 242–43.
[84] See, e.g., Prior of Bolton c Ellys (York 1521), Cons. AB.9, f 20v.

substitution expressly in appointments, and that is what the records show was often done.[85]

OPEN QUESTIONS AND OMISSIONS IN THE TEXTS

The thoroughness with which these four subjects were treated in the learned literature of the time should not close our eyes to another feature of that literature, one that ran in the opposite direction. A lot was left out. Quite a few subjects of immediate relevance to practicing lawyers, both then and now, were not discussed at all in it. If one picks up a modern handbook on the practice of law, it is striking how wide a variety of subjects are raised and discussed within it. Many of them would have been relevant even in past centuries. As a rule, however, many of them are not found in the learned treatises of that earlier time.[86] Rules of professional conduct – matters such as the avoidance of conflicts of interest or the duty to protect the confidences of one's clients – find scant place in the literature. Guidance about ongoing relations with clients, including the setting and collection of fees for services rendered, are also conspicuous by their absence. Questions about the proper relationships between proctors and advocates where both took part in determining the course of litigation are simply not present either. They must have arisen. Indeed we know that some of them did arise, because they appeared in contemporary court records.

A part of whatever blame exists for the absence of treatment of relevant topics like these from the treatises must be laid at the door of the sources available to their authors. The texts in the *Corpus iuris civilis* (and the *Corpus iuris canonici* too) either did not address them or mentioned them without adding anything to regulate them. Even after the expansion of scholarly interest from glossing to treatise writing had occurred, the attention of jurists who wrote about the church's law continued in many of the old ways, including this one. No clear fault could exist in following a well-worn path. However, there is also an alternative explanation, one that finds some support in the treatise literature. It is that the commentators themselves recognized that many such matters would be better regulated locally, either by local custom or diocesan legislation. The *Corpus iuris canonici* was far from being a code in the modern sense of a statement of law that was 'complete, coherent, and clear'.[87]

---

[85] Ibid., f 43 (Constitution of a proctor by R Beisley, noting that it was done 'iuxta formam registri').

[86] I used N Taylor (ed), *Guide to the Professional Conduct of Solicitors*, 7th edn (London 1996) as a guide in making this comparison.

[87] Taken from J H Merryman and R Pérez-Perdomo, *The Civil Law Tradition*, 3d edn (Stanford, CA 2007), p 33.

It contained contradictions, and it also left room for local customs. That may indeed have been by design. In England (as in other parts of Europe) some of the gaps were filled by provincial and diocesan legislation.[88] Three subjects recurred in that legislation.

Educational Requirements

Although the subject of education was not wholly absent from the formal sources, its details were largely left up to local decision. Statutes and customs, it seemed, could best determine what academic qualifications were necessary to render a man fit to practice in the consistory courts. The English bishops responded. They dealt with the problem only a few years after the institution of consistory courts that met regularly in their dioceses. A canon of the Council of Lambeth (1281), one strengthened by recitation of a text from the Book of Jacob (1:19) to the effect that wise men should always be quicker to listen than to speak, made a start. It imposed a requirement of three years' study of the canon and civil laws before exercising the profession of an advocate.[89] The canon itself described the need in dramatic terms. Men who had scarcely studied more than one law book and who were almost entirely ignorant of the law's nature had been arrogating this office to themselves. The inevitable result was obstruction of the truth and even the perpetration of frauds. Formal education was one answer to the problem, though it is not clear that it was ever an absolute requirement for entry into the profession, despite the existence of statutes like this one. A respectable opinion had long held that the only fair test was a candidate's actual knowledge of the law, no matter how it had been acquired.[90] Statements to that effect appeared in some of the letters of English bishops to their officials requiring them to admit suitable men to practice in their courts.[91] In others, nothing whatsoever was said of their education.

A second expedient in dealing with ignorance, one arranged locally, was the creation of corporation-like bodies of advocates in ecclesiastical centers. Apparently later in their creation in England than in France[92] and in the papal court in Rome,[93] a Doctors' Commons was organized in London as the

---

[88] For Italy, see M Ascheri, *Laws of Late Medieval Italy (1000–1500)* (Leiden and Boston, MA 2013), pp 323–24.

[89] *Councils & Synods*, Pt II, pp 917–18.

[90] See the opinion in Lyndwood, *Provinciale*, p 76, v *audiverit*.

[91] See York, MS. Box Proct. Adm.

[92] P Fournier, *Les officialités au moyen âge* (Paris 1880, reprint 1984), pp 32–33.

[93] See Salonen, *Papal Justice in the late Middle Ages*, pp 39–41.

center of learning in the *ius commune* towards the close of the fifteenth century. Just what educational functions it served, if any, has never been clear. The assumption – a reasonable one – has been that none existed. However, its extensive library was surely a source of learning in the civil law, and its members must have shared what they knew with each other. But this conclusion does not rise to the level of formal education.

Ecclesiastical court practice in England went further than endorsing these possible ways of learning. It was an almost universal custom to require a 'Year of Silence' between the acceptance and admission of an advocate in a bishop's court and the commencement of his gainful employment.[94] University lectures would not have conveyed much information about the actual jurisdiction exercised by the English courts. Nor would they have acquainted men with the forms used in practice. During that year the new advocate could at least have been given a start on that aspect of his profession. Little is actually known of exactly what young men did during this year, but its purpose is not in doubt. It was to absorb the rudiments of practice. Learning that at least two copies of a libel had to be prepared so that one could be given to the other party, for example, would not have been a lesson learned in school. It would, however, have become known to beginners during the Year of Silence.

Of course, this is not just an old problem. Law schools today may do slightly more. Clinical legal education in the United States has made some progress in bridging the gap between schoolroom and courtroom. However, it may also be true that the requirements for successful navigation in law practice are best learned under the guidance of an experienced man who is not a professor. Whatever the best path may be to deal with this controversial subject, what has just been described is the way most English proctors received their initiation into practice, a subject that will be explored more fully in Chapter 2.

Ethical Standards and Professional Conduct

The scarcity of texts defining and requiring ethical practice among lawyers is one of the more surprising features of the texts found in both the Roman and canon laws. This may have been a reflection of the free-for-all oratory characteristic of Roman advocates. It was, however, a strong concern of the church's leaders during the century in which consistory courts came into regular

---

[94] Statutes of the Court of Arches (1342), c 4, in F D Logan (ed), *The Medieval Court of Arches* (C & Y Soc. 95, 2005), pp 34–35; Squibb, *Doctors' Commons*, p 32. The same requirement is found in the archives of the northern diocese of Carlisle; see Carlisle, MS. DRC 3/62, but it appears to have been derived from the London statutes.

existence in Europe.[95] Indeed, reading the diocesan statutes on the subject suggests that in the thirteenth century it came as a bit of a shock to them to discover that the law's technicalities could be used to reach results of which they disapproved. Matrimonial causes were their initial and immediate focus. English diocesan statutes repeatedly forbade advocates from maliciously proposing exceptions in matrimonial causes. The inevitable result was that true marriages were not recognized or enforced.[96] If lawyers did this, they were declared excommunicate. To us, the statutes seem not to have recognized that under the then current matrimonial law, the situation was bound to arise. The enforceability of purely oral contracts, the possibility of adding conditions like a father's consent or the payment of a wedding gift, and the fallibility of human memory spurred by self-interest all invited contention. One party might remember a simple contract, the other a conditional one.[97] A lawyer for the second would only be doing his duty by entering an exception as a defense to the first's suit to enforce the contract. This might look like the product of malice or chicanery to an observer, particularly an observer who took sides with the party seeking to enforce the contract. The perception of wrong would almost inevitably ensue. The remedy of excommunicating the proctor or advocate who had entered the exception – a crude remedy without doubt – would not have solved the problem. Good faith was a defense – a matter that is often difficult to prove one way or the other. Perhaps unsurprisingly, no cases have yet been uncovered in the English procedural records where the penalty was actually imposed.

Other means of securing upright professional conduct on the part of advocates and proctors also existed. The canonists did part of the work,[98] and standards of conduct are found stated repeatedly in diocesan legislation. Supervision by the judges was one way of enforcing them. The oaths each ecclesiastical lawyer took upon admission to practice and (at least according

---

[95]   See C Morris, 'From Synod to Consistory: the Bishops' Courts in England, 1150–1250' (1991) 22 *Journal of Ecclesiastical History* 115–23.

[96]   See, e g. Council of Oxford (1222), c. 3–4, in *Councils & Synods* I, p 107; Statutes of Salisbury II (1238x1244), c 59, in *Councils & Synods*, p 387; Statutes of Wells (1258), c 72, in *Councils & Synods*, p 622; Statutes of York I, c 37, in *Councils & Synods*, p 493.

[97]   I have taken this example from a cause heard by the commissary court at Canterbury: Bertelot c Hornes (1377), Act book Y.1.1., f 28v (the defendant, a woman, answered the man's suit to enforce a marriage contract, contending that 'huiusmodi contractus fiebat sub tali conditione si amici dicte mulieris vellent consentire').

[98]   See, e.g., Durantis, *Speculum iudiciale*, tit. *De positionibus*, Lib II, Pt 2 § 9 n 6 (citing X 5.36.9, which dealt with causing damage to another, he argued that a proctor or advocate who advised his client to respond untruthfully to his opponent's *positiones* should himself be liable for the opponent's losses).

to stated rule) each year thereafter was another.[99] Proctors and advocates were obliged to swear not to introduce unwarranted delays in litigation, to avoid any taint of ambidexterity, to act in good faith in all things, and (as noted above) to withdraw from any cause they learned to be without merit. The canons of 1604 added a prohibition against excessive and vociferous clamor among the proctors, an ugly development that was said to have become common in the courts of the archbishop of Canterbury.[100] The canons threatened removal from practice for a second offense. Whether this happened in fact we do not know. The efficacy of all supervisory canons like these is not easy to test or describe. Still less can we trust the polemical literature of the 1640s, in which a proctor named 'Sponge' made an appearance in order to boast of having committed virtually every offense against justice forbidden under the statutes.[101] Who knows what to make of texts like this? There is a timelessness about such satirical screeds. Probably a grain of truth too. Chaucer's Summoner comes to mind.[102] So do the views of Francesco Petrarch.[103] Indeed the English ecclesiastical court records themselves contain prosecutions of men and women who had voiced similar negative sentiments about the honesty of the ecclesiastical lawyers.[104] It would go far beyond the available evidence to speak confidently of either success or failure in this perennially problematic area of the law.

Regulation of Fees and the Size of the Profession

How (and how much) professional lawyers should be paid for their services was another sore point with the many critics of the church's tribunals, never more so than in the seventeenth century. The size of the fees he secured was

---

[99] E.g., Admission of Nicholas Fyssh (Bath & Wells 1459), Act book D/D/Ca 1, f 9 (said to be 'iuxta exigenciam statutorum eiusdem consistorii'). See also the examples and discussion in Brand, *Origins*, pp 146–47.

[100] Canon 113, in G Bray (ed), *The Anglican Canons 1529–1947* (London 1998), pp 434–35. The medieval background to this subject is found in J A Brundage, 'My Learned Friend: Professional Etiquette in Medieval Courtrooms', in M Brett and K Cushing (eds), *Readers, Texts and Compilers in the Earlier Middle Ages* (Farnham and Burlington, VT 2009), pp 183–96.

[101] Anon., *The Proctor and Parator their Mourning* (n p 1641).

[102] See, e.g., the summoner's depiction in 'The Friar's Tale'. See also Anon, 'Satyre on the Consistory Courts (*c.*1298)', in T Wright (ed), *The Political Songs of England* (Camden Society 6, 1839), pp 155–60, and the commentary in L A Haselmayer, 'The Apparitor and Chaucer's Summoner' (1937) 12 *Speculum* 43–57.

[103] See E Peters, 'The Sacred Muses and the Twelve Tables: Legal Education and Practice', in K Pennington and M Eichbauer (eds), *Law as Profession and Practice in Medieval Europe: Essays in Honor of James A Brundage* (Farnham 2011), pp 137–51.

[104] E.g., Ex officio c Agnes wife of William (London 1483), MS. DL/C/B/043/M50 9064/02, f. 27v (prosecution for saying that a proctor 'will be foresworn for a grote and so will all those that are of his occupation').

one of the 'abuses and exorbitancies' of which Sponge the proctor had been most boastful. The pamphlet portrayed him as finding it hard to face the future without them. He could not, however, have lawfully claimed to have charged his clients whatever he liked. The size of professional fees in the church's tribunals was not left to the market. Instead, the fees to be paid to lawyers were set according to the perceived value of each specific task performed, and both advocates and proctors were required both by statute and by the canon law itself to offer their serves for nothing *in causis pauperum*.[105]

The scale of fees was not a matter that could have been fixed realistically in the formal canonical texts. It called for local choice and at least occasional amendment.[106] That was the system adopted in England – so much for each court appearance by a proctor, so much for the examination of witnesses by an examiner appointed for the task, and so forth. These fees were made a matter of public display. A table stating them was to be displayed both in the courts where ecclesiastical causes were heard and also in the offices of the registrar of each court.[107] And litigants did have a choice. No rule obliged them to appear by proctors, and in point of fact, more than a handful chose not to. They appeared in person even in instance causes. Some of the causes heard by the church's tribunals involved no difficult points of law or fact – litigation involving defamation for instance – and it would not have been a foolish choice for a man or woman involved in one of them to decide against appointing a proctor or employing an advocate. A concrete example is found in the thirty-two instance causes recorded in the act book inserted into the epis-copal register of Hamo of Hethe, a fourteenth-century bishop of Rochester. In only seven of them were both parties represented by a proctor. In twelve, both parties appeared and acted in person. In thirteen causes one of the parties only appeared by proctor; the other party appeared in person.[108]

---

[105] See, e.g., M Ingram, *Church Courts, Sex and Marriage in England, 1570–1640* (Cambridge 1987), pp 55–57.

[106] In England, this required consideration of the common law itself, as in offering advice on how to avoid a writ of prohibition in a suit to recover a proctor's fees. See the example in the Ely diocesan records, EDR F/5/41, f 304 (1609) (advising the proctor not to plead 'any promise or assumpsit'). The advice was apparently heeded, as in Clarke c Parsons (Bath & Wells 1611), Act book D/D/Ca 173, s.d. 1 October (suit by proctor against a client styled as 'subtractio salarii').

[107] An example titled 'Table of ancient fees' preserved from the seventeenth century is found in Worcester Record Office, MS. 777.713, BA 2090, pp 97–99, and from Bristol from the same period, Bristol Record Office, MS. EP/J/10.

[108] See *Acta iudicialia*, April 1347–October 1348, in C Johnson (ed), *Registrum Hamonis Hethe*, (C & Y Soc. 49, 1948), pp 911–1043. See also M Bowker (ed), *An Episcopal Court Book for the dio-cese of Lincoln, 1514–1520* (Lincoln Record Society 61, 1967); the numbers for the commissary

Similar but not identical to the regulation of court fees was the control on the number of advocates and proctors allowed to practice at any one time. There were always limits set. As with the question of fees, a free market for entry was not desired. No one has yet compiled a list that would show the extent of the control that was exercised on their admission to practice, although several useful lists of the names and degrees of successful candidates do appear in the records.[109] The only courts for which we have anything like a complete picture are those in London held in the name of the archbishop of Canterbury. In 1295, Archbishop Winchelsey established the numbers – ten proctors and sixteen advocates were to be permitted in the Court of Arches.[110] No more; and no expansion in this statutory limitation was made for centuries. However, the number of proctors was allowed to expand well beyond ten, and by the reign of Henry VIII, the number of proctors permitted to practice in the London courts had grown to twenty-one. In 1528 Archbishop Warham issued a statute that no more proctors were to be admitted until the statutory number of ten was reached, but this too failed. In the 1560s the number stood at twenty-two. Archbishop Whitgift later responded by increasing the allowable number to twenty-eight.[111] Where these numbers stood in the nineteenth century when the jurisdiction of the ecclesiastical courts came under frontal attack has not yet been fully worked out. A nineteenth-century manuscript now in the Lambeth Palace Library put the number of proctors admitted to general practice in the Court of Arches at thirty-four,[112] and the annual Law Lists show that the number admitted was actually greater than that.

EFFECTS ON LAWYERS IN COURT PRACTICE

The actual effect of the canon law on practice within the English ecclesiastical courts is the final topic that requires exploration on the basis of what is shown by the records found in diocesan archives. Did English ecclesiastical lawyers actually follow the texts of the Roman and canon laws which defined the tasks and powers of advocates and proctors, at least as those texts had been interpreted by the Continental jurists? It is a legitimate question. European

---

court at Canterbury during the late fifteenth and early sixteenth centuries were also roughly equivalent; see Woodcock, *Medieval Ecclesiastical Courts in the Diocese of Canterbury*, p 44.

[109] E.g., Logan, *Medieval Court of Arches*, pp 209–23; Marchant, *The Church under the Law*, pp 247–54 (advocates and proctors in York and Nottingham); B Woodcock, *Medieval Ecclesiastical Courts*, pp 121–23 (proctors active in commissary court).

[110] Wilkins, *Concilia*, vol II, p 205.

[111] I Churchill, *Canterbury Administration* (London 1933), vol I, p 451.

[112] LPL, MS. Arches K/21; there were also 'supernumerary proctors', but their number is not given.

commentators on this subject left room for the force of local custom in interpreting the texts and determining the scope of lawful jurisdiction. In addition, the dominance of the common law in England might appear to have threatened or at least complicated application of the civil law to advocates and proctors. The question is whether the temporal laws would have been an impediment to the use of Continental laws and treatises, particularly after the Protestant Reformation in the sixteenth century. What actually happened?

There are two ways of seeking an answer to that question. The first is by examining the literature compiled by English civilians – the men who practiced as lawyers in the courts of the church and wrote about it. The second is by looking at the court records that were compiled and have been preserved. Both now exist in considerable quantities in English record offices and in national repositories. They are the best guides we have to what happened in practice before the English courts.

For the medieval period, these sources show that English ecclesiastical lawyers regularly relied on the Continental literature for authority and for help in their professional lives. In one fourteenth-century civilian's notebook, for example, one finds authority for situations where a formal libel was unnecessary that were drawn from William Durantis' treatise of judicial procedure.[113] This was advice any lawyer could use. Similarly, a treatise on the procedure used in the Court of Arches from the second quarter of the fifteenth century, one designed to inform the advocates and proctors serving there, is filled with citations to the juristic literature discussed above.[114] Its compiler used both Roman and canon law texts to support his instruction in the details of correct procedural practice.[115] William Lyndwood, the greatest of the medieval English canonists, also did so in commenting upon the provincial constitutions of the province of Canterbury. He devoted two titles to advocates and proctors, and his marginal glosses are filled with references to the relevant texts that have been described above.[116] A second particularly interesting example is that of John Lydford, who served as judge of the consistory court at Winchester from 1377 to 1394. In his memorandum book, not only did he regularly cite texts from the learned laws to give direction to lawyers, he entered into detail about

---

[113] BL, Arundel MS. 437, f. 315v; the reference (to which others were added) was to Durantis, *Speculum iudiciale*, Lib. IV, Pt. 1 § 9. Similar is the fourteenth-century civilian's notebook now in Hereford Cathedral Library, MS. O.4.15, f 17v (dealing with the evaluation of evidence and citing as authorities texts from both Roman and canon laws).

[114] See Logan, *Medieval Court of Arches*, pp 97–114.

[115] Another example is found in the manuscript text of William of Pagula, *Summa summarum*, Huntington Library, San Marino, CA, MS. 9/H/3, f 296 (citing the gl. ord. ad C. 15 q. 3 c. 1 to enlarge the standing of women to initiate criminal causes in the ecclesiastical forum).

[116] See *Provinciale*, Lib I, pp 75–79 (titles 17–18).

their use in practice. For instance, he added two entries designed to deal with the necessity of providing mandates with sufficient language to allow proctors to agree to compromises in disputed causes.[117] It is evident that he was familiar with this difficult problem, one that was dealt with at length in the learned commentaries of his time.

Of course, this is what one should expect. Although it is true that many aspects of medieval legal practice were determined by the *stylus curiae* of individual places and tribunals, it is also true that the medieval English church was part of Catholic Christendom. Its bishops looked to the papacy and papal decretals for direction. The papal courts were the final courts of appeal. It was natural, therefore, that they should have defined and discussed the character of their own profession with the tools those laws provided. William Lyndwood's great effort, a theme which runs throughout the *Provinciale*, was to harmonize the effects of English provincial statutes with the formal law of the church.[118] His was an attitude also current among the English civilians.

What may be surprising is to discover that these same characteristics persisted after the English church had cut its ties with the papacy. Many historians have assumed that this breach signaled, indeed required, a rejection of the canon law itself. But this is too hasty a conclusion, one not based on the surviving court records. In fact, the canon law did not disappear. For one thing, the legal argument in favor of its retention was impeccable.[119] A Henrician statute provided that the existing laws of the church should 'be used and executed as they were before the making of this Act', unless they were either 'repugnant to the laws, statutes and customs of this realm' or contrary to 'the king's prerogative royal'.[120] Much the largest part of the existing canon law violated neither exception, apart from the fact that some of it had been stated in a papal decretal or a decree of a council under the presidency of the Roman pontiffs. In the main, the contents of the decretals and decrees dealt with private and procedural law. Think of the law of marriage and divorce or of defamation, or even the church's law of testamentary succession. Mainstays of ecclesiastical jurisdiction in England, they had nothing to do with papal power. Procedural law was even clearer. It was different than that of the common

---

[117] See Owen, *John Lydford's Book*, n 157 (p 81) (citing twice the *Liber sextus*) and nn 22, 24 (pp 34–35) (on the proxies).

[118] B E Ferme, *Canon Law in Medieval England: a Study of William Lyndwood's* Provinciale *with particular reference to Testamentary Law* (Rome 1996), p 142 (stressing 'his desire to hold English practice consistent with the *ius commune*').

[119] R E Rodes, *Lay Authority and Reformation in the English Church* (Notre Dame, IN 1982), pp 163–64.

[120] 25 Hen. VIII, c. 19 (1533); the act was repealed under Mary but renewed by 1 Eliz. I, c. 1 (1559).

law, but with one or two arguable exceptions it was not considered 'repugnant' to the common law.[121] Only in the eyes of some extremists were statements of rules and principles found within the texts of the Roman or canon laws on these subjects sufficiently different to constitute repugnancy with English laws and customs.[122] Few of them had anything in substance to do with papal power. Of course, the canonical texts that did actually clash with English law were treated as invalid under the statute's provision. An example is provided by texts vesting control of English benefices in the papacy. They did fit the statutory test of repugnancy. Otherwise, as the statute declared, the canon law remained in force in England. This was the view held by the English civilians, and it gave them the opportunity, indeed it required them, to make regular use of the canonical texts and the huge body of Continental writings that dealt with the organization and duties of their profession. They embraced that opportunity.

Particularly in the area of law dealt with in this book – the character and duties of the legal profession – the evidence from the post-Reformation procedural literature compiled by proctors is unambiguous on this point. Richard Cosin's *Apologie*, written in defense of ecclesiastical jurisdiction and first published in 1593, supported its treatment of *ex officio* procedure with copious citations to the Roman and canon laws, including treatises written by Continental jurists.[123] The elements that a proctor should include in a libel for the recovery of tithes, discussed in the Notebook of Dr Thomas Eden (d. 1615), were taken from and supported by texts of the canon law and by citations to commentaries by Panormitanus, William Durantis, Bartolus, and Robertus Maranta (d. 1540).[124] Thomas Ridley (d. 1629) buttressed his defense of the contributions made to English society by advocates with a text from the Roman law (Cod. 2.7.14).[125] Similarly, the entries for advocates and proctors found in John Ayliffe's guide to the law of the Church of England were both drawn from the texts of the Roman and canon laws.[126]

---

[121] The point was made clearly in BL, Harl. MS. 4117, f. 80 (c.1600): 'notandum est licere iudici ecclesiastico procedere in quacumque causa de iure canonico vel ecclesiastico' except where doing so was contrary to 'iura municipalia vel statuta huius regni').

[122] Compare, for example, William Stoughton (*fl.* 1584), *An Assertion for true and Christian church-policie* (Middelburg 1604), p 39 (asserting that 'the Papall and foreign canon law is already taken away and ought not to be used in England') with R Cosin, 'Preface', *An Abstract of Certain Acts of Parliament, of Certain Canons, Constitutions and Synodells Provincial* (London 1584) (emphasizing the harmony between the two).

[123] *Apologie for Sundrie Proceedings by Iurisdiction Ecclesiasticall*, Pt II, c 4 (London 1593).

[124] See Helmholz, *Three Civilian Notebooks*, pp 54–55.

[125] *View of the Civile and Ecclesisticall Law*, 3d edn, Pt. II, c. 2 § 6 (Oxford 1662), pp 135–36,

[126] *Parergon Juris canonici Anglicani*, v. *Advocates* and v. *Proctors*. See also the evidence and conclusions in Levack, *The Civil Lawyers in England*, pp 183–84.

The second possible source of information about the hold of the Roman and canon laws on the organization and conduct of English advocates and proctors comes from the court records themselves – investigation shows that the evidence there is much thinner. Unfortunately, the act books and cause papers rarely contain citations to legal texts, even in those of the medieval years. There were only a few exceptions to this rule, particularly on procedural matters, in which it may have seemed particularly important that a full record be kept in case of an appeal. Those exceptional references discovered so far have all been to the learned laws. One from the diocese of Ely during the fourteenth century involved a question of the payment of the expenses of the costs of litigation.[127] Another is a matrimonial cause from the diocese of York, in which the evidentiary value of a writing was assessed by its consistency with the requirements of a decree from the Fourth Lateran Council found in the *Liber extra*.[128] A third is a testamentary cause from 1531 on a point of admissibility and probatory value of a manorial court roll.[129] The same only occasional citation of notations to formal law continued in the post-Reformation court records.[130]

The evidence drawn from the court records also demonstrates that the distinction between advocates and proctors was preserved in practice. Advocates seem not to have been present in most of the lesser ecclesiastical courts, at least not regularly present. In the court records, sometimes one finds the same man described as both proctor and advocate.[131] Occasionally, a cause would be postponed so that an advocate could be summoned or at least consulted. However, the distinction between the two halves of the profession was never lost from sight, and not simply in Doctors' Commons; they were thus distinguished from the proctors in practice throughout the years. The judge in a fourteenth-century cause heard in the diocesan court at Canterbury, for example, recessed a testamentary dispute to allow the proctor to come with an advocate.[132] Apparently, he was dissatisfied with the proctor's

---

[127] Warde c Rector of Knappewell (Ely 1375), EDR D/2/1, f. 43 (citation to Sext 2.6.1, dealing with the payment by a party who had abandoned a cause).

[128] Hobbesdoghter c. Beverage (York 1392–94), CP.E.202. The applicable text was at X 2.19.11.

[129] Wethursbe c Kent (Worcester 1531), Act book MS. 794.011, BA 2513/1, pp 37, 40, 41 (citation to X 2.20.49). See also the invocation of the two laws as authority for permitting summary treatment of a fifteenth-century tithe cause in BL, Harl. MS. 862, f 3 and cited Clem. 2.1.2 and 5.11.2.

[130] See Helmholz, *Three Civilian Notebooks*.

[131] E.g., Bartholomew Lovell, described as 'procurator et advocatus curie predicte' in his admission to practice, recorded in the Act book (Rochester 1445), DRb Pa 2, f 27.

[132] Hamdenum c Executors of Speldeshall (Canterbury 1374), Act book Y.1.1, f. 62 (order to the proctor 'ad veniendum cum advocato sub pena preclusionis a patrocinio'). Similar is Tailor c Devon (Durham 1498), Act book CB.Pr.Off, f 128 (deferring a cause to the diocesan court 'eo quod [the defendant] non habet consilium nec potest adquirere consilium').

talents. Sometimes the separate presence and the names of both proctors and advocates were noted in the act book for a particular court.[133] Whether their work in specific cases heard before the courts was kept wholly separate or not, the distinction between these two halves of the legal profession, derived from the Roman law, continued to be respected.

CONCLUSION

Chance inclusions in the formal records such as those just described only confirm what is evident from the totality of the available evidence. The canon law of lawyering, including that part of it which was originally taken from the *Corpus iuris civilis* and then 'canonized' by the church, was regularly called upon as authoritative in the English ecclesiastical tribunals. It was always subject to the constraints of human weaknesses and the restraints of contrary custom, but its existence in the learned laws mattered in fact. It was added to, but it was only rarely overturned by the work of later jurists, the adoption of provincial statutes, and the observance of local customs. It was this that allowed the creation of a true profession of ecclesiastical lawyers.

The court records of the English church, surveyed in this chapter, show the results of this process. When one discovers causes in the act books in which proctors renounced further prosecution of one of those in which they had appeared after they had discovered it to be without merit, this must count as one instance of complying with the ethical obligations that had become one part of the obligations of a good ecclesiastical lawyer. Such obligations, important for the creation of a true profession, were the results of efforts of many jurists and administrators acting to expand the categories of ancient law. They were legitimate additions to offices that had owed their names, their reception, and even their continuing relevance to their inclusion centuries before within the laws of ancient Rome that were recovered at Bologna from the end of the eleventh century.

[133] E.g., list of lawyers present in Ex officio c Seaward (Exeter 1630), Chanter MS. 764. Similar is a fifteenth-century entry: Gregorie c Marshton (Bath & Wells 1458), D/D/Ca 1, p 247.

2

The Education of Ecclesiastical Lawyers

The first chapter dealt only briefly with the attempts that were made to require formal education in law for the advocates and judges who served in the English ecclesiastical courts. More, indeed much more, could be said about this subject on the basis of modern scholarship. The briefest of considerations will demonstrate the reasons for this developed state of our understanding. It is connected directly with the history of European universities, where future advocates prepared for their professional careers. Some of the scholarly works on the history of European universities have dealt in detail with legal education.[1] Articles and even books have also been devoted to the place of law within the universities in England.[2] Several lists of advocates that include a notation and a description of the education of the men listed exist.[3] Treatments of the scholarly literature produced by the English advocates also demonstrate the extent and the ambition of the learning some of these men possessed.[4] And a few serious studies of the general outlines of the education of advocates and judges – the top part of the legal profession – are well presented in one of James Brundage's contributions to the series on the history of medieval canon

[1] E.g., H Rashdall, *The Universities of Europe in the Middle Ages* (Oxford 1936), vol III, pp 156–57.
[2] A Cobban, *The King's Hall within the University of Cambridge in the Later Middle Ages* (Cambridge 1969), pp 54–55, and A Cobban, 'Theology and Law in the Medieval Colleges of Oxford and Cambridge' (1982) 65 *Bulletin of the John Rylands Library* 57–77; see also W Courtenay, *Schools & Scholars in fourteenth-century England* (Princeton, NJ, 1987).
[3] C Coote, *Sketches of the Lives and Characters of Eminent English Civilians* (London 1804); Marchant, *The Church under the Law*, pp 247–53; Levack, *The Civil Lawyers in England*, pp 204–82; Squibb, *Doctors' Commons*, pp 118–209.
[4] Coquillette, *The Civilian Writers*; W Holdsworth, *Sources and Literature of English Law* (Oxford 1925, reprint 1952), pp 203–38; H Coing, 'Das Schrifttum der englischen Civilians und die kontinentale Rechtsliteratur in der Zeit zwischen 1550 und 1800' (1975) 5 *Ius Commune* 1–55.

law being published by the Catholic University of America Press.[5] There has long been scholarly disagreement about the quality of legal education offered at Cambridge and Oxford,[6] but its requirement in the lives of English civilians who became judges and advocates has not been put in doubt.

Things stand quite differently with the history of the education of English proctors. Little has been done. Many of the books and articles written in the past fifty years about England's ecclesiastical courts do pay some attention to the learning of these men, but mostly only in connection with the litigation in which they took part.[7] It was never necessary for proctors to have been university graduates, although some of them were. It has therefore been difficult to estimate how much law they knew and still more difficult to be sure where they could have learned the tools of their trade. Their fees, their ubiquity, and their behavior in litigation have been usefully explored, but about their training much less has been discovered. What this chapter seeks to add to the subject is information about the nature of their education as lawyers that is derived from the archives of the courts where they served. It begins, however, with the advocates, adding information drawn from the same record sources.

THE EDUCATION OF ADVOCATES

Two additions to existing scholarship describing the education of advocates and judges are suggested by the records that inform this volume. The archives where court records are kept, contemporary descriptions found in manuscript formularies and precedent books, and manuscript collections in several of the colleges at Cambridge and Oxford are all useful in the pursuit of a fuller understanding of the subject.

Law Lectures and Associated Sources of Learning

The education of advocates in England, like that offered on the Continent, began with texts – the texts of Roman and canon laws.[8] A number of the

---

[5] 'The Teaching and Study of Canon Law in the Law Schools', in W Hartmann and K Pennington (eds), *History of Medieval Canon Law in the Classical Period, 1140–1234* (Washington, DC 2008), pp 98–120.

[6] For a negative view, see J L Barton, 'The Faculty of Law', in J McConica (ed), *History of the University of Oxford III: the Collegiate University* (Oxford 1986), pp 257–93. For a more positive view, see L Sutherland, *The University of Oxford in the Eighteenth Century: A Reconsideration* (Oxford 1973). My own understanding of the subject appears in 'University Education and English Ecclesiastical Lawyers 1400–1650' (2011) 13 *Ecclesiastical L J* 132–45.

[7] E.g., Woodcock, *Medieval Ecclesiastical Courts*, pp 40–45.

[8] See M H Hoeflich and J M Grabher, 'The Establishment of Normative Legal Texts: The Beginnings of the Ius Commune', in *History of Medieval Canon Law in the Classical Period,*

lectures based upon them have survived from the Middle Ages; much the larger part of them have remained in manuscript. Taken together they show how carefully lecturers dealt with the wording and the meaning of these texts. They proceeded methodically through them.[9] The texts were first read aloud and word for word. The Latin term *Lectura* applied to some of the treatises written by later civilians and canonists was no accident. Some of this concentration may have been a product of simple need. Students would not necessarily have owned the books where the laws were found. Books were expensive.[10] In this recitation, the lecturer's first object was to fix the text in the minds of his students. Just how medieval students were able to remember the contents of the texts from this system is difficult to understand today, but they seem to have been capable of doing so. Contemporary commentary treated the necessary memorization as within the capacities of law students.[11] One helpful clue as to how they managed is to stress that students would have heard the texts read more than once. The ordinary course of education called for students to have repeated the basic courses. They would have heard the sources read again in the course of their university education.[12] Of course these texts and commentaries on them would also have been available in college libraries. Moreover, *repetitiones* were also held for particularly important or difficult texts. Even so, it must have been a task. Students themselves appear to have themselves recognized both the need and the difficulties.[13] Their commonplace books, containing definitions of legal terms and (usually) some textual support for each of them, were one source of assistance.[14]

Lecturers commonly began with the texts and then moved outwards. Sometimes a considerable distance, but more often not very far. Reference to other texts in the *Codex* or *Digest*, texts that required harmonization with

pp 1–21 (stressing the similarity of the treatment of texts among contemporary theologians); F De Zulueta and P Stein, *The Teaching of Roman Law in England around 1200* (SS, Supplementary Series 8, 1990), p xiv ('almost biblical authority').

9   See, e.g., the sixteenth-century lectures on the title *De re iudicata* (Dig. 42.1.1–64) now found in Lincolnshire Archives, MS. For. 20.

10 'Letters of the Oxford Dictatores', in H G Richardson (ed), *Formularies which Bear on the History of Oxford c.1204–1420*, vol II (Oxford Historical Society n.s. 5, 1942), n X:11.

11 E.g., Ulric Huber (d. 1694), *De Ratione juris docendi et discendi diatribe*, M Hewett (ed) (Nijmegen, 2010), p 55 (describing the first step as reading 'assiduously and carefully the texts' and then considering their relation to other texts).

12 See Rashdall, *Universities of Europe*, vol III, p 157.

13 See F D Logan, 'The Cambridge Canon Law Faculty: Sermons and Addresses', in M J Franklin and C Harper-Bill (eds), *Medieval Ecclesiastical Studies in Honour of Dorothy M. Owen* (Woodbridge 1995), pp 151–64, at 157–58.

14 E.g., 'Legal Commonplace Book, c.1457', Princeton University Library, MS. 122 (Alphabetical treatment of terms, each with a citation to the basic texts of Roman and canon laws). See

the one under discussion, was a regular source of comment. Sometimes a further text provided additional support, or at least additional comment. Baldus de Ubaldis (d. 1400), for example, found it appropriate in commenting on a text from the Decretals (X 3.2.8) to prove that men commonly feign poverty, hiding their treasures from public view, with a citation from a text from the year 382 A.D. that had been incorporated into the Roman law's Codex.[15] He gave no apparent thought to providing evidence from his own time or even a contemporary legal citation. A civilian text from more than one thousand years in the past seemed a more appropriate way of making this point. A recent account rightly speaks of 'the glamour of the authorities'.[16] The longevity of the central place they occupied in the academy was not the result of blind habit or unthinking conservatism.[17] It was a choice.

Moreover, this preference for internal authorities did not always prevent lecturers from discussing matters of immediate relevance. For instance, a manuscript preserved in the Lincolnshire archives on the Digest's titles began with the plain statement that a party might send a representative to court where he himself was sick or injured. So much was found in the texts. However, the lecturer went on to clarify the question, contending that this was only a permissive power. The sick or injured man was not obliged to send a proctor to represent him simply because he had the power to do so. He was legally entitled to a delay, at least a temporary delay, under existing law. This was not a case, the lecturer thought, where a text was to be read *a contrario sensu* to exclude a possibility it replaced.[18]

It is easy to criticize the formalism characteristic of the lectures, and they have been criticized more than once. The mildest of criticisms is that this method of reading and relying on the texts caused them to be taken out of context, so that the lectures lacked a 'sense of history'.[19] A slightly more extreme form of criticism is that the jurists 'seemed to revel in the repetition of every conceivable text and

---

also M Carruthers, *The Book of Memory: A Study of Memory in Medieval Culture*, 2d edn (Cambridge 2008), pp 12–13, 127.

[15] *Commentaria in Decretalium Volumen* ad X 3.2.8, n 13. The text cited from Roman law is Cod. 11.26.1.

[16] O Weijers, *A Scholar's Paradise: Teaching and Debating in Medieval Paris* (Turnhout 2015), p 61.

[17] B Wauters and M de Benito, *History of Law in Europe: An Introduction* (Cheltenham and Northampton, MA 2017) 56, describing their attitude to the texts as 'works of universal value that bore truth and reason'.

[18] Lincolnshire Archives, For. 20, at Dig. 42.1.60 ('qui morbo vel alio impedimento est impeditus mittere procuratorem non tenetur' citing a further text).

[19] M Gilmore, *Argument from Roman Life in Political Thought 1200–1600* (Cambridge, MA 1941, reprint 1967), p 37.

argument, regardless of increasing confusion that resulted'.[20] This negative reaction to the civilians' reliance upon centuries-old texts, however sensible it seems in the twenty-first century, risks misunderstanding the actual use the texts then had for lawyers, which is what the students were learning to be. In a sense the medieval *ius commune* was a closed system. Many legal systems are. They treat a limited number of authorities as persuasive. Such a focus on a specific body of authority was particularly true of the *ius commune*.[21] Although subject in practice to the inroads of custom and desuetude and also to modification through invocation of the principle that all laws should be read in a spirit of equity, it was apparent that new texts could not be added to the *Corpus iuris civilis*. The medieval canon law was itself subject to limited amendment.

The resulting 'internal focus' of the *ius commune* is apparent in the arguments commonly made in litigation. What level of violent behavior by a husband was sufficient to permit a divorce *a mensa et thoro*? That depended on a text from the Gregorian Decretals and a commentary by the canonist commonly called Praepositus (d. 1507).[22] What standard of proof applied in a disputed case where summary rather than plenary procedure was used? That depended on a text from the Digest and commentaries on it by Bartolus and Jacobus Menochius (d. 1607).[23] What words spoken during a man's final illness amounted to an expression of testamentary intent that would be enforced by a judicial decree? That depended on a text in the Institutes and a commentary on it by Joachim Mynsinger (d. 1588).[24]

At the same time, it was not a static system. Many of the existing texts were regarded as containing more than one possibility within them, more than one understanding and more than one potential use. They possessed a 'mind' (Cod. 1.14.5). It might extend their meaning beyond the specific context or title in which they appeared.[25] The most famous example is the concept embodied in

---

[20] A Black, *Monarchy and Community: Political Ideas in the later Conciliar Controversy 1430–1450* (Cambridge 1970), p 56. See also J A C Smith, *Medieval Law Teachers and Writers: Civilian and Canonist* (Ottawa 1975), p 49.

[21] See P Weimar, 'Die legistische Literatur und die Methode des Rechtsunterrichts der Glossatorenzeit', in P Weimar, *Zur Renaissance der Rechtswissenschaft im Mittelalter* (Goldbach 1997), pp 3–43.

[22] Gurling c Gurling (Arches 1597), in Bodl. Tanner MS. 427, f 42 (citing X 2.13.13 and J A Antonio de Sancto Gregorio, *Commentaria super quarto decretalium* at X 4.19.1).

[23] Archbishop of York c Dean and Chapter of Durham (c 1580), BL, Lansd. MS. 135, f 74v (citing Cod. 6.33.3 and Philipus Decius, *Commentaria* ad id).

[24] Earl and Countess of Rutland c Alsop (c 1670), All Souls Coll. Library, Oxford, MS. 230 (no foliation, citing Dig. 32.1.39(37) and Bartolus, *Commentaria* ad id and adding more recent commentaries on the civil law).

[25] For a modern example of this potential, see R Zimmermann, *Contemporary Law, European Law: the Civilian Traditions Today* (Oxford 2001), p 123 ('venturing beyond Roman law by means of Roman law').

the maxim *Quod omnes tangit* (Cod. 5.59.5.2). It was widely used to support the creation of representative institutions or parliaments. What concerns a community should be consented to. In the Codex itself, however, the phrase itself did no such thing. It was taken from the Roman law of *tutela*, where it stated only that the joint administration of a minor's estate could not be terminated without the consent of all the *tutores*.[26] This text was given a wider use by the jurists who applied the reason that lay behind (or within) it to serve wider purposes. To us, this may appear to be a fanciful use, certainly an aggressive one, but it was a legitimate one according to the assumptions medieval jurists held. Learning how to draw such assumptions from the existing texts in this freewheeling fashion was something the students at Bologna (or Cambridge and Oxford) learned to do. A lecture on the positive benefits to mankind of representative institutions would have been of little use to them in practice. But a demonstration of the expansive use to which a text in the Digest could be put would.

It may be pointed out (with good reason) that European jurists in the sixteenth and seventeenth centuries went well beyond this text-bound system. Hugo Grotius (d. 1645) is the great and clearest example. His treatment of legal questions, organized by subject matter, not by titles from the Digest or Institutes, embraced evidence from historical, theological, and literary sources. The same could probably be said of the Second Scholastics in Salamanca. This enlargement in scope did not mean, however, that the texts themselves were forgotten. Even the legal humanists sought to uncover the true meaning of the texts, not to overturn them. The Renaissance efforts were additions to the texts, not substitutes for them. Grotius and the others took the contents found in the laws as the proper starting point for his analysis. The laws retained their status as the basic sources of authority, as they had for their medieval predecessors. What the learned additions of Hugh Grotius and others did was not to reject the texts of Roman and canon law as applicable sources of law. The additions supplemented them.[27]

The Cambridge law lectures of Francis Dickins (d. 1755), a law fellow at Trinity Hall, provide a relevant English example of the possibilities found in this approach, although his lectures were less learned and wide ranging

---

[26] See G Post, *Studies in Medieval Legal Thought: Public Law and the State, 1100–1322* (Princeton, NJ 1964), pp 163–238.

[27] J Muldoon, 'Hugo Grotius, Medieval Canon Law and the Creation of Modern International Law', in P Landau and J Mueller (eds), *Proceedings of the Ninth International Congress of Medieval Canon Law* (Vatican City 1997), pp 1155–65; R Feenstra, 'Grotius' Doctrine of Liability for Negligence: its Origin and its Influence in Civil Law Countries until Modern Codifications', in E J H Schrage (ed), *Negligence: the Comparative Legal History of the Law of Torts* (Berlin 2001), pp 129–71.

than those of Grotius.[28] Dickins had given up the medieval method of instruction that went methodically through the Digest and Codex, but he had not abandoned reliance upon the traditional authorities of the *ius commune*.[29] He always made reference to them, no matter the topic. They were the sources of law that counted. He was not a slavish admirer of every feature of Roman law, but he did admire the best of them, and he regarded the majority as belonging to that category. His students were not all destined for a legal career and he wished to educate them in principles of honesty and good government, principles he found stated clearly within the civil law.[30]

None of this is meant to suggest that during medieval times and afterwards future advocates spent their years in Oxford or Cambridge simply memorizing the texts of the Roman and canon laws. Still less is it to suppose that the system was without fault. What kind of legal education ever has been? Still, students in the law faculties did more than listen to lectures. They also had opportunities (as we might say) to put the texts to work. They entered into disputations on points of law,[31] and if they went ahead with a doctorate in law,[32] they produced and defended a thesis. They made use of the opportunities for private study,[33] and they had access to the immense body of learned literature that provided commentary on the laws, including summaries and compendia of their contents.[34] Letters from law students show that they were learning to use these resources to deal with specific questions.[35] In addition, it has been suggested that aspiring advocates attended sessions of the university courts as a first-hand way of learning about relevant procedural and substantive

[28] See Chapter 20 in Part II of this book.

[29] Ibid.

[30] See also W Ellis (ed), *Summary of the Roman Law, taken from Dr. Taylor's Elements of the Civil Law* (London 1772, reprint 2005).

[31] B Levack, 'Law', in N Tyacke (ed), *History of the University of Oxford*, vol IV (Oxford 1997), pp 559–68, at p 566 (noting that some of them concerned matters of ecclesiastical jurisdiction in England); O Pedersen, *The First Universities*, R North (trans) (Cambridge 1997), pp 259–62.

[32] L. Boyle, 'The Curriculum of the Faculty of Canon Law at Oxford in the First Half of the Fourteenth Century', in *Oxford Studies Presented to Daniel Callus* (Oxford Historical Society, n.s. 16, 1964), p 152; A Wijffels, 'A Seventeenth Century English Commentary "De regulis iuris" (D.50.17)', in O Condorelli (ed), *Panta rei. Studi dedicati a Manlio Bellomo*, vol V (Rome 2004), pp 473–96.

[33] Barton, 'Faculty of Law', vol III, pp 270–71, 278–79.

[34] E.g., Joannes Schneidewein (Ointomus), *In Institutionum imperialium commentarii* (Venice 1701) (a double folio work of over 600 pages in double columns summarizing and commenting on the learning found in the civilian sources).

[35] For an example from a law student in thirteenth-century Oxford, see N R Ker and W Pantin, 'Letters of a Scottish Student at Paris and Oxford c.1250', in *Formularies which bear on the History of Oxford c.1204–1420*, vol II (Oxford Historical Society n.s. 5, 1942), XI1:1.

law.[36] These visits would have provided an appropriate avenue to becoming an advocate or a judge in one of England's consistory courts. The Year of Silence spent before entering into active practice may well have been an important addition to what legal learning any advocate needed. However, it would not have rendered useless what he had learned in the law faculty of a university. When one looks, for example, at the section of a thirteenth-century *Summa* on the office of advocates that provided suggested forms for the libels to be used in the courts, what one finds are not only the forms, among the most practical of documents, but also abundant citations to the texts of Roman and canon laws to explain and justify them.[37] Law students, or former law students, would have recognized their source at once.

The Two Laws

Most medieval universities where the law was taught had separate faculties: one for Roman law, one for canon law. That division suggests that the two laws must have been rivals, competing for students and for prestige. There may well have been some personal rivalry between the men in them, but whatever enmity did exist should not be transferred to their subjects. Roman law was not treated as a competitor to the study of canon law, still less as an enemy. Indeed, its study provided the normal starting point for lawyers, even those whose careers would be spent in the courts of the church. Its intellectual relevance for canonists is illustrated by the prior chapter's treatment of the origins and development of the medieval legal profession. This was a repeated pattern in many parts of the canon law. The existence of a useful introduction to the law, found in the Institutes and leading into the Digest's more sophisticated coverage of so many areas of law taken over by the canon law made its study a natural way to begin.

And so it happened. At Oxford the normal course of education for a canonist began with study of civil law. Five years' study of the civil law was the recommended norm – not mandatory, it seems – but what was expected in the normal course of an advocate's education.[38] For those who moved to the study in

---

[36] This is the suggestion made by A Shepard, 'Trinity Hall Civil Lawyers and the Cambridge University Courts, c.1560–1640', *Trinity Hall 2000: Legal Education and Learning* (n.d.), pp 5–13. See also M Underwood, 'The Structure and Operation of the Oxford Chancellor's Court, from the Sixteenth to the Early Eighteenth Century' (1978) 6 *Journal of the Society of Archivists* 18–27.

[37] Bonaguida Aretinus, 'Summa introductoria super officio advocationis in foro ecclesiae', Pt. II, tits. 5–25, in A Wunderlich (ed), *Anecdota quae processum civilem spectant* (Göttingen 1841), pp 183–218.

[38] Rashdall, *Universities of Europe*, vol III, p 157.

the canon law faculty the starting point was Gratian's *Decretum*, followed by the second half of the *Corpus iuris canonici*, beginning with the *Liber extra* and the *Liber sextus* from the thirteenth century. It is unlikely, however, that this would have been a student's first encounter with the canon law. Even at an early date, some references to canon law were made, as is shown by the early *Brocardia* used in the schools.[39] It would have made little sense to treat the Roman law of marriage, for example, in complete isolation from the medieval canon law on the subject then in force throughout Europe, and of course many aspects of court procedure found in the civilian texts had been augmented, or at least affected, by laws found in the Decretals. Adoption of summary procedure is the most significant example. If nothing else, the civil laws invited comparison. In thinking about this subject it is well to recall the common maxim of the day: 'A civil lawyer without the canon law is little worth; the canon lawyer without the Roman law nothing'.[40]

The realism of this maxim becomes particularly important when one seeks to understand the continuation of learning in the canon law after the Reformation. The separate canon law faculties at Oxford and Cambridge were closed, but the advocates whose education occurred in the civil law faculty remained conversant with the traditional sources of the church's law. They used it in their own work. Take virtually any treatise on the law that was applied in the English ecclesiastical courts – one finds within it the regular citation to texts from the Gregorian Decretals and usually also a learned commentary on them.[41] Manuscript copies of university lectures on Roman law confirm this conclusion.[42] Canon law was kept 'in commendam' with the Roman law.[43] Historians who have concluded that the canon law ceased to be studied and applied after the Reformation have not looked at the details. The details make it evident that rejection of papal government did not require the rejection of the contents of papal decretals. Indeed, most of them were not rejected.

---

[39] E.g., H van de Wouw, 'Brocardia Dunelmensia' (1991) 108 ZRG *(Rom. Abt.)* 241–42.

[40] F Merzbacher, 'Die Parömie "Legista sine canoniibus parum valet, canonista sine legibus nihil"' (1967) 13 *Studia Gratiana* 273–82; I Baumgärtner, 'Was muss ein Legist vom Kirchenrecht wissen? Roffredus Beneventanus und seine *Libelli de iure canonico*', in P Linehan (ed), *Proceedings of the Seventh International Congress of Medieval Canon Law* (Vatican City 1988), pp 223–45.

[41] E.g., J Godolphin, *Orphan's Legacy: or a Testamentary Abridgement* (London 1701), Pt I, c 9 (references to persons deemed incapable of making a valid last will and testament, citing both Baldus and Panormitanus in support).

[42] E.g., see late-fourteenth-century English *Lectura* on Canon Law, BL, MS. Reg. 9.E.viii, f 27 ('Notandum iura civilia possunt in causis ecclesiasticis allegari et secundum ea iudicari' unless revoked by the canons).

[43] T Fuller, *History of the University of Cambridge*, M Prickett and T Wright (eds), (Cambridge 1840), p 225.

THE EDUCATION OF PROCTORS

Learning how proctors were trained presents more difficult problems than that of advocates. No autobiographical accounts have come down to us. A kind of apprenticeship or pupillage in the office of an established proctor seems to have been the normal point of entry. Some elementary guides to court practice have survived, however. They are enough to show what proctors were expected to know and to say in appearances before the courts. The notebooks kept by proctors also suggest possible answers. There are three principal subjects to be discussed. The first is an estimation of how many proctors had some university training in law. The second is a description of how proctors learned to represent their clients before a judge – that is, how they were taught what to say in court. The third is an examination of the ways in which proctors learned to prepare the documents needed at each stage of litigation.

University Education

The surviving act books and cause papers of England's consistory courts regularly record the names of the lawyers that represented parties to civil litigation, and it was not uncommon for the scribe to add a specific notation of their possession of a degree in law. Even where such a notation is not found, their names can be checked with the names of these men in the biographical registers of Oxford and Cambridge. The overall conclusion that emerges is that what might be termed a substantial minority of working proctors held the first degree in law, although never (so far as yet discovered) the doctorate. University training was by no means required for proctors, but neither was it a rarity among them. Perhaps one out of three would be an average figure for the proctors in most English courts.[44] University education probably did give aspiring proctors an advantage, at least initially. The diocesan statutes of Carlisle, for example, stated that possession of a degree in law entitled its holder to a preferred claim to a place in consistory court,[45] and education was singled out for mention in some of the testimonials of competence presented

---

[44] This is consistent with findings for the consistory court in Paris at the end of the fourteenth century; there six of the seventeen proctors can be shown to have studied law at the University of Paris. See J A Brundage, 'From Classroom to Courtroom: Parisian Canonists and their Careers' (1997) 83 ZRG (Kan. Abt.) 352–53.

[45] Carlisle, MS. DRC 3/62 (c.1600). See also Brand, *Origins of the English Legal Profession*, p 149 (same preference in the Court of Arches).

by ecclesiastical lawyers upon their admission to practice.[46] A degree must have given a man an advantage.

Although there were courts in which none of the proctors held an academic degree, in most places a few of them did during the Middle Ages. For instance, of the twelve proctors who appeared regularly in the commissary court at Canterbury between 1475 and 1500, four certainly and one probably were bachelors in law.[47] Of the eleven men who served as proctors general in the consistory court of the diocese of Bath and Wells between 1458 and 1498, four held university degrees in law.[48] Roughly the same held true during the first half of the next century. Elsewhere too; of the ten proctors entered in the first subscription book of Doctors' Commons in 1511, three held the first degree in law.[49] In the consistory court at Winchester, two of the five proctors who appeared in the first surviving instance act book (1526–30) held the first degree in law; the others did not.[50] The consistory court in the diocese of Lichfield appears, by contrast, to have more often done without university-trained proctors. None of the five men active as proctors in 1464–65 seems to have held a degree in law,[51] and of three proctors practicing regularly in 1525, only one held an LLB.[52]

The situation during the second half of the sixteenth century and into the seventeenth was not markedly different, despite a rising level of education among the English clergy. There were nonetheless a few apparent advances. At Hereford between 1567 and 1572, for instance, of the four proctors serving

---

[46] Admission of Giles Burton (York 1632), loose in MS. Box Proct. Adm.

[47] Woodcock, *Medieval Ecclesiastical Courts*, pp 121–22. See also J A Brundage, *Medieval Canon Law* (London 1995), p 137, noting that of the eight or nine men practicing before the consistory court of Ely during the 1370s and early 1380s, only 'two or three seem to have had university degrees'.

[48] R W Dunning, 'The Wells Consistory Court in the Fifteenth Century' (1962) 106 *Proceedings of the Somersetshire Archaeological and Natural History Society* 53.

[49] Squibb, *Doctors' Commons*, p 18.

[50] Taken from Winchester Act book, 21M65/C2/2. The two with degrees were John Lawrence and John Southwood; those without were Nicholas Hocker, John Lichfeld, and a man named Tadens, who quickly disappeared from the number of proctors. Lawrence was BCnL (Oxon.); he served as judge on occasion in this court, and later became archdeacon of Wiltshire.

[51] Taken from Lichfield Act book, B/C/1/1, beginning in April 1464. The proctors were William Calton, Thomas Colt, John Croftes, William Hudson, and John Paynell. At f 80v, Paynell is described as an advocate, but no degree is listed for him, and no entry for him appears in the biographical registers of Oxford or Cambridge.

[52] Lichfield Act book, B/C/2/1. The exception was Gregory Stonyng, LLB. The other two active proctors were Thomas Palmer and Thomas Lee. In the diocese of Gloucester in 1553, there appear to have been three proctors active: Hugh Evans, George Useleye, and Roger Lewis; only the last of these held the LLB degree. (See Gloucester Act book GDR 7B).

actively in the consistory court, three held a bachelor's degree in law.[53] More common, however, was the situation in the 1630s in the archdeaconry of Nottingham, where of the three proctors active in the official's court, apparently only one of them, George Saunders, a scholar of Trinity Hall, Cambridge, held the LLB.[54] In the consistory court of Worcester in 1607, four proctors appeared regularly in the act book. Two of them possessed the first degree in law.[55]

It must be said that these examples, although worth having, cannot give a full picture of proctors' education. For one thing, they are not the product of a complete survey. For another, some of the proctors were probably arts graduates, even though this reasonable supposition has turned out to be difficult to pin down. Most significantly, however, the figures almost certainly underestimate the extent of university training among proctors. Nothing prevented, and the expense involved encouraged, aspiring proctors to attend Oxford or Cambridge but to leave without having taken a degree.[56] The order supporting the admission of one York proctor mentions that he had spent two years at Sidney Sussex College, Cambridge, but it makes no mention of his having received a degree in law or arts.[57] The figures given above must therefore be regarded as stating a minimum of proctors' university education.

Preparation for Practice: Learning Court Procedure

Even if they held no university degree, English proctors prepared for their practice before being admitted to it, although their preparation was not formal education in the modern academic sense. Quite a few of them came from families of ecclesiastical lawyers – son following father – and they must

---

[53] Taken from Hereford Act books, HD4/1/9 and 1/10. The three were John Darnell, John Hodges, and Richard Maddocks (or Mathocks); William Darnell, son of John, seems not to have had a university degree in law.

[54] Marchant, *The Church under the Law*, p 254. The others were John Tiberd and David Royce: there is also some sign of practice by a proctor named Hatfield Reckles. The situation in the archdeaconry of Cornwall was similar, at least in 1610 (Cornwall, Act book ARD/3). There were four active proctors, Ralph Keate, William Friggens, Henry John, and Hugh Wills. Only Keate held a law degree.

[55] Taken from Worcester Act book, 794.011 BA 2513/6.

[56] The expenses of taking a degree were not inconsiderable; see, e.g., H E Malden, *Trinity Hall* (London 1902), pp 238–39.

[57] Admission of Peirs Lee (York 1632), in MS. Box Proct. Adm. (letter from the Archbishop stating that Lee 'hath been trained up as a clerke in and about my consistorie and exchequer courts at York' and adding that he had been two years at Cambridge).

have learned something of their profession growing up.[58] However, there was training of some sort for all. Letters of recommendation to the courts often stated that the applicants had been 'trained up as a clerk' before seeking formal admission,[59] and something resembling what eventually became a formal system of apprenticeship probably prevailed much earlier.[60]

It is worth noting that the initial admission of proctors sometimes occurred well before they actually represented clients in litigation. It was called the Year of Silence in the London courts, and a similar delay seems also to have occurred elsewhere.[61] Newly admitted proctors must have spent this time learning what to do and what to say when they came to represent a party in court. There is some evidence to suggest that in London they heard lectures about the law as part of this preparation.[62] Elsewhere, no such evidence has been unearthed, in part because the number of proctors in most consistory courts was too small to have supported a formal system of instruction. A period of apprenticeship or clerkship was the only realistic alternative.

It is impossible to penetrate very far into the practicalities of those clerkships, but one can point out the existence of many elementary procedural manuals designed to help these aspiring proctors. They exist today in almost every repository of consistory court records. These works must have been perused, perhaps even committed to memory. The most common was the textbook of civilian procedure. Most are quite elementary. Typically one begins: 'A trial consists of three elements: the beginning, the intermediate stages, and the end. The beginning of a trial is the *litis contestatio*, the intermediate steps

---

[58] Ritchie, *The Ecclesiastical Courts of York*, p 56; M Steig, *Laud's Laboratory: The Diocese of Bath and Wells in the Early Seventeenth Century* (London 1982), pp 172–73.

[59] George Dealtary (York 1681) in MS. Box Proct. Adm. (eight years). See also Houlbrooke, *Church Courts and the People*, p 17; A Tarver, *Church Court Records* (Chichester 1995), p 3, to the effect that seven years' apprenticeship with a notary public was required.

[60] See G I O Duncan, *The High Court of Delegates* (Cambridge 1971), p 197.

[61] At Lincoln, a statute promulgated in 1330 required a year's probation after four years' study of the law. See D M Owen, *The Medieval Canon Law* (Cambridge 1990), p 23. At Carlisle, the statutes regulating the consistory court read: 'Nullus in curia predicta procurator generalis admittitur nisi per annum et amplius in ipsa curia steterit pro practica cursu causarum et statutis et consuetudinibus addiscens'. See Cumbria Record Office, MS. DRC 3/62, *c.*1600. However, a post-Restoration handbook states that advocates, i.e. men with degrees in law, could be admitted to serve as proctors without waiting for this year; see BL, Add. MS. 72544(A), p 9 (Trumbell MSS).

[62] College of Arms, London, MS. Vincent 419 (c. 1420), seems to have been designed for such purposes; for example, at f 127 et seq. the law relating to marriage and the impediment of crime, one of the diriment impediments, is laid out briefly, and the account continues with the practical advice: 'Unde sic concipe libellum. Coram etc.' (going on to give the proper form to use in litigation).

consist of the proofs, and the end is the sentence'.[63] Then it goes on to give further detail. For example, it explains that the first of the three 'elements' was itself divided into several steps: the citation, the constitution of the proctor, the giving of the libel, the answer of the party, and the giving of the terms of proof in the second stage.

A few of these procedural treatises were more ambitious, sometimes adding authority from the Roman and canon laws or raising more detailed points of law, describing, for example, what a citation must include and the ways it could be delivered.[64] Francis Clerke's *Praxis in curiis ecclesiasticis*, printed after the Restoration but widely circulated in manuscript from the 1590s, is the best example of the elaboration that was possible in such manuals. Copies exist today in many English repositories.[65] Many of them were extensively glossed with references to treatise literature, a means of bringing proctors up to speed with the system they would encounter once they entered into active practice.

Similar manuals were available to men intending to become proctors. Most of them have remained in manuscript and largely left unexamined, but if used carefully they can be informative. For instance, an early seventeenth-century treatise of some 120 folios now in the Wiltshire Record Office seems almost to have been designed for men who were learning the law.[66] It is thin in its citation of learned works, and it eschews all questions of theory and academic debate. However, it does provide useful information about making inventories of decedents' estates, drawing up interrogatories, distinguishing

---

[63] This is taken from BL, MS. Add. 6254 (16th century), f 1, called 'Summarium processus iudicii in curiis ecclesiasticis huius regni'. The Latin, at f 2, is: 'Iudicium ex tribus constat, principio, intermediis, et fine. Principium iudicii est litis contestatio, intermedia sunt probationes, finis est sententia. Principiis iudicii praecedunt nonnulla praepatoria: citatio, certificatorium procuratoris constitutio, libelli oblatio; sequuntur nonnulla scilicet responsio partis principalis, termini probatorii datio …' This MS. also contains many references to the writing of jurists, including Baldus de Ubaldis, Panormitanus, Lyndwood, and Andreas Gaill.

[64] E.g., Norfolk Record Office, Norwich, PCD/2/5, p 3, called 'Regulae materiam citationis concernentes', one of which is that if it can be shown that a citation, otherwise defective, actually came to the notice of the party cited, it could serve to alert him to the nature of the cause; see also Martin Ingram, 'Reformation of Manners in Early Modern England', in Paul Grittiths et al. (eds), *The Experience of Authority in Early Modern England* (New York 1996), 47–88. It cited in support: 'Vant. de null. quibus modis null. repar. pot. n. 122. 123', which is Sebastianus Vantius, *Tractatus de nullitatibus processuum ac sententiarum* (Venice 1567), tit. *Quibus modis sententiae nullae defendi possint*, nn 122–23.

[65] See J D M Derrett, 'The Works of Francis Clerke, Proctor (A Chapter in English Romano-Canonical Law)' (1974) 40 *Studia et documenta historiae et iuris* 52–66, at 65–66, and R H Helmholz, *Roman Canon Law in Reformation England* (Cambridge 1990), pp 196–97.

[66] Wiltshire Record Office, Trowbridge, MS, D5/24/18.

between requirements for proper treatment of summary and plenary causes. In this the manuscript treatise is like the great bulk of this procedural literature in its coverage of, and indeed its insistence upon, the schematic nature of a canonical trial. 'You must learn the following procedural steps', it seems to tell its readers.

Manuals of varying length and degrees of sophistication exist in virtually every diocese from which court records have survived. The copy in the archives in Trinity Hall's Library is itself called *'Praeparatoria ad practicam'.*[67] A similar example, found in the county record office in Chichester, is more locally styled *'Practica curie Cicestriensis'.*[68] Books like these had little to say about the substantive law. Where they went beyond, what they did say about it was incidental to their description of the procedure proctors were expected to learn. One discovered necessary information about, say, the law of testaments or marriage by learning the procedures and the language used in practicing it.

The second kind of procedural training book directed proctors in the language they were to use in courts. It is fair comment that a canonical trial depended upon written documents submitted to the court, but this did not mean that there was no oral part. Much of what occurred was spoken.[69] The documents were introduced with words, and objections to them appear also to have been made orally. The process was apparently conducted primarily in Latin, and in theory it followed a dignified and relatively fixed pattern. Satires directed against the courts sometimes contended that there was often more noise than formality in what actually happened within the courts,[70] but even if their accounts contained some measure of truth, proctors had to know what to say when they appeared before a judge. The book they seem to have used most often to learn this aspect of their practice was a short – often very short – dialogue called *De forma procurandi,* or sometimes *Actor et reus.*[71] It contained a set and formal courtroom dialogue, rather like what is found in a play's script. A brief excerpt from one copy now in the University of Chicago's Library[72] gives a fair impression of the character of these entries:

[67] Trinity Hall, Cambridge, MS. 42/1, f 169v.

[68] Ep I/51/4, p 1.

[69] E.g., Cotyngworth c Buttre (York, 1507), Act book, D/C.AB.2, f 55v (the plaintiff's proctor 'excepit oretenus contra testes et eorum dicta').

[70] This characterization was admitted by a civilian serving as registrar; see J Addy (ed), *The Diary of Henry Prescott, LL.B., Deputy Registrar of Chester Diocese, Volume I, 28 March 1704–24 March 1711* (Record Society of Lancashire and Cheshire, 127, 1987), p 102.

[71] See the copy in the Cumbria Record Office, Carlisle, DRC 3/63, ff 268–73, or BL, MS Reg. 2.D.IX, f 135 et seq.

[72] Joseph Regenstein Library, University of Chicago, Special Collections, MS. 1660, f 19.

Procurator actoris	*Peto terminum mihi assignari ad proponendum in debita iuris forma sive ad libellandum.*
Iudex	*Assignamus tibi ad libellandum in proximo et parti adversae ad recipiendum.*
Procurator actoris	*Domine, peto quatenus admoneas R. ad interessendum omnibus et singulis actis usque ad finem litis.*
Iudex	*Admoneo te R. quatenus hic intersis omnibus et singulis actis usque ad finem litis.*

In this fashion, the dialogue continued. It included coverage of the various stages of litigation in Latin with equal formality, and was probably meant to be memorized.

Occasionally, proctors who used these dialogues annotated them with references to difficult practice points or sometimes to a treatise or legal text that supported the form's utility. For instance, beside the dialogue dealing with publication of the depositions, the compiler of the Chicago copy added a note that the depositions were always to be published in the presence of the parties and a copy given to each of them; he supported this note by a citation to Lanfrancus de Oriano's *Praxis iudiciaria aurea*, an early modern Continental manual of procedural law.[73] Such notes were, of course, additions to the basic information, and they are not found in all remaining manuscripts. However, the dialogues figure so frequently in the archives of the courts where papers of the registrars have survived that it requires no stretch of the imagination to assume that novice proctors found them useful in learning the mechanics of their profession.[74]

Preparations for Practice: Drafting Documents

The third aspect of the education of proctors involved the preparation of documents. A considerable part of their work (and their income as well) came from the preparation of the papers used in litigation – what are now

---

[73] Ibid., f 22v; the reference is written: 'Lanfran. test. depos. nu. 32 circa finem'. It is a reference to material in Lanfrancus de Oriano (d. 1488), *Praxis iudiciaria aurea* (Hildesheim 1757, reprint 1970–71), tit. *De testium depositione*, n 32.

[74] Other copies: CUL, MS. EDR F/ 5/32; Canterbury, MS. C.18, ff 242–50; East Sussex Record Office, Chichester, Ep I/51/4, pp 1–9; Dean and Chapter Library, Durham, MS. Hunter 18 (at start of volume); University of Durham, Department of Palaeography and Diplomatic, DDR XVIII/3, ff 123–24; LAO, FOR 21, nine folios; BL, MS. Add. 6254, ff 46–61; Norfolk Record Office, Norwich, Dn/PCD 2/6, p 5 et seq; Nottingham University Library, Manuscript Dept., MS. P. 282, ff 57v-63v.

called cause papers.[75] This class included articles, appeals, caveats, citations, commissions, exceptions, interrogatories, libels, replications, provocations, schedules of penance, schedules of expenses, sequestrations, sentences, and the like. Nor was this all. Proctors drafted administrative documents for many matters ancillary to litigation. A list includes admonitions, commissions, collations, confirmations, dispensations, licenses, presentments, resignations, tuition bonds, and the like. It was not simple prestige that led so many proctors to qualify as notaries public.

The primary resource proctors had for instruction in drafting was the formulary or precedent book, a volume of forms used in litigation. At least one is found in virtually every archive that contains ecclesiastical court records. These books had antecedents quite far back in the history of the *ius commune*;[76] and by the sixteenth century they were all but invariable features of ecclesiastical court archives in England. Their utility in training proctors seems evident. They contained the forms every proctor would need to use in practice. Of course formularies were not employed for educational purposes alone. Experienced practitioners also used them. But signs of educational use are also imprinted clearly on many of their pages.[77] One of them is the presence of instructional notes, either in the document's margins or included within the forms themselves. So in a note in a formulary from the diocese of Chichester were instructions that two different kinds of suit could lawfully be brought by executors against those who impeded collection of a decedent's assets.[78] It provided variant forms of both, allowing a proctor to select the one that would best fit his needs. Similarly, in a fifteenth-century formulary from the Court of Arches now in the British Library, variant forms for use in citing a person for spoliation of a church were given, but alongside them was an instruction

---

[75] An indication of the importance of this aspect of practice is the size of the fees involved. At Worcester (late 1600s), a proctor's fee for appearing in a cause was 12d. (after 2s. for the first appearance). The fee for drafting a libel was 3s. 4d. (Worcester MS. 777.713, BA 2090, p 96).

[76] See, e.g., the examples in L Wahrmund, *Quellen zur Geschichte des Römisch-kanonischen Prozesses im Mittelalter*, 5 vols (Innsbruck, 1905, reprint 1962). See also J E Sayers, 'An Evesham Manuscript Containing the Treatise Known as *Actor et Reus* (British Library, Harley MS. 3763)', in her *Law and Records in Medieval England* (London 1988), n VII; and L Fowler-Magerl, *Ordo iudiciorum vel ordo iudiciarius. Begriff und Literaturgattung* (Frankfurt 1984), in *Ius commune*, Sonderheft 19, pp 201–14.

[77] E.g., Library of the Dean and Chapter, Durham, MS. Hunter 70; f 4: 'Tene menti practicam quando in lite producitur tibi aliquod instrumentum …' See also Owen, *Medieval Canon Law*, p 42; J H Baker, *A Catalogue of English Legal Manuscripts in Cambridge University Library* (Woodbridge 1996), p 93 (a formulary is described as 'seemingly collected for instructional purposes').

[78] See MS. Ep 1/51/3, p 12: 'Duae sunt actiones quae competunt executori et sunt animadversione dignae, viz …'

that in England the custom was that an archbishop's citation should be drawn up in a particular way.[79] In yet another British Library formulary from the fifteenth century, in the margin beside a monition which could be issued against laymen claiming the right to sit in a chancel stood an additional note that the form was legal, based upon the first chapter in one of the books of the Gregorian Decretals.[80] Books like these were designed to teach the law by providing both the necessary forms, and sometimes the legal authority for them or else a brief commentary on their utility. Occasionally, as in a late-sixteenth-century manuscript now in the Buckinghamshire Record Office[81] or a late-fifteenth-century example now in the British Library, the commentator interrupted the forms to give some workaday advice about law practice.[82] This was one way to learn the law, and it is not very different from the 'chamber learning' or the 'private reading and study' that characterized training in the English common law. It was an important part of the education for aspiring English common lawyers, and so it appears to have been for new proctors in the courts of the church. Indeed the 'system' is not wholly different from what happens in law offices today. One learns by picking up a form book and making use of its contents. To understand the elements of, say, the English ecclesiastical law of defamation, one can do worse than beginning with a libel used in a defamation cause. It laid out the elements that had to be proved. Its intelligent use provided a 'way into' the relevant law. This is what most, or at least many, of the English proctors seem to have done.

Preparation for Practice: the Learned Laws

A feature of some English formularies is the inclusion of citation to texts from the Roman and canon laws alongside the forms of libels and other documents. Sometimes these notations also contain a reference to a learned commentary on those texts. They raise a fourth subject. How much did the proctors learn about the substance of the Roman and canon laws? The argument for a negative response is strong, at least for those proctors who had not taken a

---

[79] BL, MS. Harley 3378, ff 9–9v: ('Licet ad certos diem et locum et sub certo iudice debeat quis citari, hoc tamen consuetudo pertinet in Anglia quod archiepiscopus Cantuariensis ita citet' with another appropriate form).

[80] BL, MS. Harley 3300, f 38v: 'Monitio contra laicos calumpniantes locum in cancello'; the text from the Decretals was X 3.1.1 (noted in the MS. according to the medieval custom: 'fundatur per c. primum de vi et ho. cle. in antiquis iniunctum').

[81] Buckingham MS. D/A/X/4, ff 70–70v (information entitled 'Observanda in examinatione testium').

[82] BL, MS. Add. 41503, ff 148–5lv (entitled 'Informatio procuratorum' and providing advice on what to say under a variety of circumstances).

law degree at university. By our standards, they were given a poor legal education. And there was contemporary evidence to support a negative assessment of their expertise. Such criticism existed.[83] The canons of 1603/04 sought a remedy for the 'oversights and negligence' said to have been common among proctors by requiring that they consult with an advocate before accepting an offer to represent a client.[84] True, some of the negative evidence about their competence may have amounted to complaints about the common failings of humanity rather than to specific deficiencies in their legal training, but some of it did come from informed men who had no axe to grind.[85] There must have been something to it.

Nonetheless there is a positive side, and it is important to take note of it. The regular inclusion of texts and commentaries from the *ius commune* in the literature related to English ecclesiastical court practice shows that English proctors had the ability to make some intelligent use of the tools found within the learned laws. There can be little doubt about the availability in England of texts and treatises on the *ius commune*, even outside the great university and ecclesiastical centers.[86] Proctors employed this literature in practice. It cannot be said, one must conclude, that the typical English proctor was learned in the law in the way the advocates were. Henry Swinburne (d. 1624), *was* a truly learned man; and although he began his career as a proctor, he did not remain one.[87] Ordinary proctors, by contrast, appear to have had only a basic familiarity with the resources of the *ius commune*. Where they were out of their depth, they had the alternative of procuring a counsel's opinion. The archives contain some of them, kept by the proctors who had requested them and then preserved them in places where they have remained to this day. But the same archives show that not every case required a *consilium*. Practice, plus reading in the available literature, brought them into contact with the learned laws.

An easy way to appreciate the extent of what they knew is to take a look at Henry Conset's manual, *Practice of the Spiritual or Ecclesiastical Courts* (1685). He was a proctor, and his approach to legal questions was very like

---

[83] E.g., Ex officio c Richard Herford (Canterbury 1473), Act book Y.1.11, f 305, a prosecution accusing the court lawyers of being *latrones et bribours*. Much of such criticism is collected (and recounted in an entertaining fashion) in C Hill, *Society and Puritanism in Pre-Revolutionary England* (New York 1964), pp 298–343.

[84] Canon 130, in Bray, *The Anglican Canons*, pp 432–33.

[85] See, e.g., R A Houlbrooke (ed), *The Letter Book of John Parkhurst, Bishop of Norwich, Compiled during the years 1571–5* (Norfolk Record Society 43, 1974–75), p 263 (an effort to curb the issuance of citations that lacked adequate grounding in law).

[86] See, e.g., N P Tanner, *The Church in Late Medieval Norwich, 1370–1532* (Toronto 1984), pp 35–42.

[87] See J D M Derrett, *Henry Swinburne (?1551–1624) Civil Lawyer of York* (York, 1973).

that of his numerous fellow proctors of prior and succeeding centuries. For understanding the nature of an appeal *a gravamine*, for example, Conset cited one *consilium* of Panormitanus.[88] To show the existence of a right to appeal from an allegedly excessive taxation of costs, he cited a single entry from Lanfrancus de Oriano's treatise on procedure. There is, it is true, little or nothing of the elaborate accumulating and weighing of opinions one finds in most Continental treatises on procedure or published collections of *consilia*. Conset seems to have paid little attention to the complexities sophisticated jurists found lurking behind each rule. He gave a brief citation, and one that went to the point, presumably the point that would have mattered in practice. Perhaps it would be right to call his *Practice* unimpressive or unscholarly on this account. It seems so when compared with some of the huge and sophisticated works that were coming off Continental printing presses at the time he wrote. The manuscript copies of the literature produced by the English judges and advocates are also more complete in their coverage of contemporary authorities in procedural law. Even with this qualification, however, Conset's example demonstrates that English proctors did acquire a basic familiarity with the learned laws. Graduates or not, they succeeded in learning more of the *ius commune* than would come from simple observation of what was happening in the English courts Christian. His was a practitioner's approach to the subject, but it was one supported by a familiarity with the European *ius commune*.

---

[88] Part 5, § 5:2. This is consistent with the relatively small libraries that appear to have been held by most civilians; see, e.g., Allmand, 'The Civil Lawyers', pp 165–70.

3

Ecclesiastical Lawyers and the Protestant Reformation

How did the ecclesiastical lawyers react to the coming of the Protestant Reformation? A fair question. The primary sources of authority in the courts of the English church during the Middle Ages were found in the *Corpus iuris canonici*, and if one assumes, as many historians have, that the primary goal of that great collection of the church's law was to establish and enhance the power of the Roman pontiffs, the answer seems obvious. The civilians who had relied upon and enforced that law must have disliked and resisted the arrival of Protantism. J J Scarisbrick, one of the leaders of the 'revisionist' school of Reformation history, concluded that English reformers 'took a shoulder to [the filthy canon law] and heaved it over'.[1] If that were an accurate description of what happened, the Reformation would have appeared as a most unwelcome arrival to the lawyers who are the subject of this book. They had been trained in the canon law. They were accustomed to it, not excluding its source in papal legislation. They would therefore have regarded Protestantism as a threat to themselves and to their profession.

ECCLESIASTICAL LAWYERS IN YEARS OF RELIGIOUS CHANGE

There is some evidence supporting this exercise in deductive reasoning. Some radical Protestants did wish to rid the land of the canon law, and during these years several signs of popular discontent with the existing law of the church did make themselves felt among the English people.[2] The common lawyers expanded the scope of writs of prohibition in ways that curtailed enforcement of the canon law. Admission of students to the civil law faculties at Cambridge and Oxford also declined markedly in the middle years of the sixteenth century.

[1] *The Reformation and the English People* (Oxford 1984), p 162.
[2] See, e.g., R B Manning, *Religion and Society in Elizabethan Sussex* (Leicester 1969), pp 19–32.

Efforts to re-write the church's law in the *Reformatio legum ecclesiasticarum*, begun under Henry VIII and extended under Edward VI, similarly raised the possibility of real change, even of radical upset in the careers of the men who worked in the spiritual courts.

Of course, it is also true that the *Reformatio* never became law.[3] Admissions to the study of law at the Universities also recovered in numbers during the reign of Elizabeth and her immediate successors. It is also easy to exaggerate the effects of the threats to the church's courts posed by the common lawyers, as will be shown in Chapter 4. The question of reaction of English civilians to changed circumstances therefore requires a more detailed examination. This chapter adds to the relevant evidence by looking at what happened within the circle of lawyers serving in the ecclesiastical courts themselves during the sixteenth century. Did the lawyers who served there react negatively to the Reformation in their professional lives? It is impossible to look within their minds, but it is possible to have a closer look at what they did. It is also possible for historians to attempt to make sense of what they find.

The Reign of Henry VIII

From the perspective of the surviving court records, the initial break with the papacy appears to have made little difference to the careers of the great majority of English civilians. Perhaps lawyers make unlikely martyrs. These years did produce a few famous examples of heroic dissent among the episcopate, John Fisher of Rochester being the most important among them. But he was a theologian rather than a lawyer, and men like him were famous in part because they were exceptional. His example seems not to have reached down to the consistory courts. There, except for death or promotion, the same men continued to act as judges, advocates, and proctors throughout Henry's reign. The first attempt at producing a workable version of the *Reformatio legum ecclesiasticarum* itself came from the circle of lawyers within Doctors' Commons.[4] That connection suggests a willingness to experiment with amendments to the existing laws, but it was much less than an overthrow of their substance.

---

[3]   Its failure could be attributed to 'an act of malicious sabotage' by the Duke of Northumberland; see D MacCulloch, *The Boy King: Edward VI and the Protestant Reformation* (Berkeley and Los Angeles, CA, 1999), pp 154–55.

[4]   See G Bray (ed), *Tudor Church Reform: The Henrician Canons of 1535 and the* Reformatio legum ecclesiasticarum (London 2000), pp xxvi–xxvii.

In the diocesan courts, most practicing civilians also kept their places. For instance, Roland Lee served as judge of the consistory court at Lichfield during Henry's reign, continuing to do so until he became bishop of the see of Coventry and Lichfield in 1533. He died in office in 1543.[5] Nicholas Harpsfield acted as chancellor in the consistory court at Winchester in the late 1520s and served there throughout Henry's reign. He continued in office until he was made archdeacon of Canterbury during the reign of Queen Mary.[6] John Stilman, registrar of the diocesan court at Chichester, likewise served there from 1518 until his death in 1543.[7] Among the lesser civilians, the same pattern is discernable. They remained in place. At Winchester, for example, Nicholas Hocker and John Lichfield, the two proctors who lived throughout Henry's reign, both continued to exercise their office from the 1520s into the 1540s.[8] Stability seems to have prevailed.

Of course, these were troubled times. Who knew where things would end? The court records do produce occasional signs of unease, as for example the 1528 prosecution for heresy of a Lincolnshire sailor who had been stranded at Bremen in Germany and seen something of the changes effected by the followers of Martin Luther. Despite his protestations that he held no heretical views and the apparent lack of positive evidence that he did, he was subjected to a public penance and made to promise publicly never to 'teach nor show to any folks such erroneous opinions and damnable abuses' that he had heard during his sojourn in Germany.[9] Panicky reactions like this are not found among the ordinary records of earlier times. Orders against the importation of Lutheran books which appear in court records as they do in royal proclamations add to this impression of heightened worry about the future.[10]

---

[5] See Lichfield, Act book B/C/2/1, and B Jones (ed), *Le Neve, Fasti Ecclesiae Anglicanae 1300–1541: Coventry & Lichfield Diocese*, compiler (London 1964).

[6] See Winchester, Act books 21M65/C 2/2 (1526–30) and 21M65/C 2/3/1 (1541–49), and J Horn (ed), *Le Neve, Fasti Ecclesiae Anglicanae 1541–1857 III, Canterbury, Rochester and Winchester Dioceses* (London 1974), p 15.

[7] S Lander, 'Church Courts and the Reformation in the Diocese of Chichester, 1500–58', in R O'Day and F Heal (eds), *Continuity & Change: Personnel and Administration of the Church in England 1500–1642* (Leicester 1976), p 220.

[8] Ibid. The other proctor serving this court during Henry's reign, John Southwood, appears to have dropped out during the course of the 1520s.

[9] Ex officio c Barnett (Lincoln 1528), Act book DIOC/Cj/4, ff 16–16v.

[10] E.g., the injunction under penalties of heresy for importation of such books; it was also recorded in London, Act book (1526) MS. DL/C/303, f 123; see also the proclamation of 1529, in P L Hughes and J F Larkin (eds), *Tudor Royal Proclamations, Volume I: the Early Tudors (1485–1553)* (New Haven, CT 1964), n 122.

There were also public attacks on ecclesiastical jurisdiction during these years. One need only note the Commons Supplication against the Ordinaries or the aftermath of Hunne's Case.[11] They must be counted as indications of popular disquiet with ecclesiastical jurisdiction.[12] No period in English history, however, has been without such evidence. Courts of any sort are unlikely candidates for public enthusiasm. More significant is that for the most part, the church's legal institutions in England remained intact during these years.[13] The Reformation statutes, such as the one that amended the prohibited degrees of consanguinity and affinity in matrimonial law (25 Hen. VIII, c 19), were not dramatic in their effects. The Council of Trent would enact similar changes. Only statutory prohibitions against appeals to the Roman court (25 Hen. VIII c 21; 28 Hen. VIII c 10) should certainly be counted as apparently meaningful exceptions to the rule of overall stability in the diocesan courts. Ominous for the future they may have been, but they did not affect the substance of what ecclesiastical lawyers in England did in practice. These statutes simply changed the venue being assigned for hearing appeals, and that would not have required large changes in practice for the proctors and advocates who made the appeals. The *Reformatio* also failed to become law; its failure may have suggested that things would remain the same in the court system.

The Reigns of Edward VI and Mary

This pattern of relative stability in the profession continued through the reigns of Henry's two immediate successors, ironic though that result may appear. Edward and Mary embodied almost directly opposite ends of religious opinion. Even so, readers of the act books will discern little sign of dramatic change and none of principled disruption within the courts. Of course, two special factors may help explain this unexpected result. Fewer of the court records from Mary's reign have been preserved than from those of the other Tudor monarchs, and prosecutions for heresy were usually conducted by special commission, not in the consistory courts. Record searches may therefore be an incomplete way to approach the question.

---

[11] The former is found in *Letters and Papers, Foreign and Domestic, of the Reign of Henry VIII* (London 1880, reprint 1965), vol V, p 468. The classic account of the latter is A Ogle, *The Tragedy of Lollards' Tower* (Oxford 1949).

[12] See C H Williams (ed), *English Historical Documents, 1485–1558* (London 1967), nn 24, 80.

[13] E.g., C Kitching, 'The Prerogative Court of Canterbury from Warham to Whitgift', in R O'Day and F Heal (eds), *Continuity and Change: Personnel and Administration of the Church in England 1500–1642* (Leicester 1976), pp 191–214.

Even so, it is telling that the existing evidence of continuity in service among the ecclesiastical lawyers themselves is more prominent than the opposite. At the archiepiscopal court at York, for example, the two men serving as judges who had taken office under Henry VIII and lived through this period were still in harness there when Mary died in late 1588.[14] At Canterbury, Robert Colyns, the commissary general who had first appeared in the act books of the 1520s, was also still in his judicial place in 1559.[15] Of course, some of the judges had died or been promoted. An example is Hugh Curen, official principal at Hereford during the 1530s, who became Archbishop of Dublin in 1555. Men like these must be counted as survivors. In fact, Curen is a particularly good example. He survived the ups and downs of these years to become bishop of Oxford in 1567.

This pattern also holds true overall for the lawyers who acted in the consistory courts. The three advocates at York whose names are found in the Henrician act book and who had not died by the close of Mary's reign were still in place after Elizabeth's accession.[16] That stability was matched by that of the proctors at York. Five of them served throughout the reigns of Henry, Edward, and Mary.[17] In the diocese of Hereford, the two proctors acting there in the 1530s who also survived into the 1550s remained in place during Queen Mary's reign.[18] At Winchester, of the six proctors practicing in the consistory court during the last part of Henry's reign, three had died before that monarch and three remained in place into Mary's reign.[19] In other words, the comings and goings of ecclesiastical lawyers that we are able to trace did not coincide with the dramatic variations in religious policy that occurred under the Tudor monarchs. Doctrinal and liturgical swings appear to have had much less impact on the careers of ordinary ecclesiastical lawyers than one might suppose from looking at the question from the outside. Stability is the impression that emerges from looking at the court records themselves.

---

[14] They were John Rokeby and George Palmer. This is shown by the headings of consistories in the relevant York Act books: Cons.AB.14, Cons.AB.18, Cons.AB.21, and Cons.AB.22.

[15] He had first been official in the court of the archdeacon of Canterbury. See Woodcock, *Medieval Ecclesiastical Courts*, p 120. His subsequent service in the commissary courts is shown in Canterbury Act books Y.2.16, f 72 (1547) and Y.2.19, f 105 (1559).

[16] They were Richard Farley, Reginald Beysley, and William Turnbull.

[17] They were Thomas Standevin, John Todde, Christopher Beisley, John Wright, and John Shellito.

[18] They were John Dornell and Roger Lewes; this is taken from Hereford Act books, HD/4/1/6 and I/7; there is a lacuna for the years 1538 to 1552.

[19] Taken from Winchester Act books, 21M65/C 2/3/1, C 2/4, and C 2/5.

The Reign of Elizabeth

At the accession of Elizabeth, a change occurred that is discernible in the contemporary court records. It suggests that a division should be made between ordinary ecclesiastical lawyers and those who occupied or had moved to higher positions in the church. The latter were the men who had become bishops, archdeacons, or cathedral deans and were no longer active in the day-to-day running of the consistory courts. Something like half of this group refused to take the Oath of Supremacy and were deprived. The other half did take the oath and continued in possession of the dignities they had attained.[20]

Hugh Curen, already mentioned as official at Hereford and later successively archbishop of Dublin and bishop of Oxford is one of the best examples of a survivor – a successful one. There were others. At York, William Rokeby and John Rokeby, both judges in the consistory court there in the 1540s, achieved dignities, the first as precentor of the cathedral church, the second as archdeacon of the East Riding. They both died in office, the first in 1568 the second in 1573. By contrast, George Palmes, also a judge at York in the 1540s became archdeacon of York in 1544 and might have continued as such, but he was deprived when he refused to subscribe to the Act of Supremacy during the royal visitation in 1559. The most dramatic example of change so far discovered comes from the diocese of Winchester. Three of the four men who had acted as judges in the consistory court there and had also achieved higher office were deprived. They were Nicholas Harpsfield, who had become archdeacon of Canterbury,[21] Edmund Steward, who had become dean of Winchester,[22] and John Lawrence, who had become archdeacon of Wiltshire.[23] Only Robert Reynolds, who was given a canonry at Winchester in 1558, remained active in the work of the church. He died in office in 1595.[24]

The experience of the ordinary lawyers who staffed the consistory courts appears to have been different in character from that of many of the dignitaries. Although a few exceptions exist, by and large the advocates and proctors who had been active during the two prior reigns, including most diocesan registrars, remained in place under Elizabeth. The example of the diocese

---

[20] Besides the examples given below, see Houlbrooke, *Church Courts and People*, p 26, with reference to 'long serving chancellors at York, Chester, Chichester, and Gloucester' to which list he adds (p 25) Miles Spencer, sometimes archdeacon of Sudbury, who served as chancellor at Norwich from 1531 to 1570.

[21] J Horn (ed), *Le Neve, Fasti 1541–1857: Canterbury, Rochester and Winchester Dioceses*, p 15.

[22] Ibid., p 84.

[23] J Horn (ed), *Le Neve, Fasti 1541–1837: Salisbury Diocese* (London 1986), p 18.

[24] Horn, *Le Neve, Fasti 1541–1857: Canterbury, Rochester and Winchester Dioceses*, p 104.

of Winchester is again instructive. One finds six proctors in the act books who were active in Henry VIII's reign. Of these, three had died by 1547, two continued throughout the religious changes and were still active in the 1560s, and the sixth, the already mentioned Nicholas Harpsfield, was deprived on the accession of Elizabeth.[25] In the consistory court of the diocese of Exeter, the two proctors active in the 1530s who survived into the 1560s were still there and in practice.[26] At Lichfield, the history of the proctors was one of virtually complete continuity. Five men were serving as proctors there during the 1540s. Three of them continued under Elizabeth; one of them (Edmund Stretchey) died in 1547; and one (Richard Martyn) cannot be traced except to say that his disappearance from the act books did not coincide with the accession of Elizabeth.[27] In other words, most ordinary proctors continued in the careers they had begun despite the changes the English Reformation had brought in its wake.

INTERPRETING THE EVIDENCE

The evidence thus shows that the majority of English ecclesiastical lawyers in practice in the church's courts stuck to their posts and to their profession despite the changes in religion that occurred during the sixteenth century. It is not so clear, however, that there is a fully satisfactory explanation for this stability. None of the civilians who made that choice (at least knowable from evidence in the literature in the record offices) has left an account of the reasons that justified their conformity. Of course, it is both true and worth stating that under ordinary assumptions of the time the opinions of ordinary English men and women did not count for much in the choice of the realm's religion. That public opinion should have determined whether or not the Reformation would succeed, a premise that seems to underlie the recent 'revisionist' history of the subject, was certainly not one that would have been widely shared at the time, and certainly not by the English civilians. No principle was more firmly established in the ecclesiastical law than that which declared that 'the people are to be led, not to be followed'. It was stated clearly in several places

---

[25] The two continuing were John Pottinger and Gilbert Mather; the three who had died were Nicholas Hooker (or Hocker), Robert Raynold, and John Lichfield. Taken from the act books cited above in note 15.

[26] They were Michael Brown and Simon Beare; found in Exeter Act books, Chanter MSS. 778 and 779. Disappearance of the act books from the twenty-five years prior to 1560 prevents description of what happened to the other men.

[27] Taken from Lichfield Act books, B/C/2/4 and B/C/2/5.

in Gratian's *Decretum*,[28] as it was in the work of the later canonists.[29] True, most medieval canonists would have assumed that the leading of which they wrote would be done by senior clergy, most notably the pope. Still, one should hesitate before fastening modern respect for public opinion on the men and women of the sixteenth century. In this attitude towards authority the English ecclesiastical lawyers were no different than the great majority of English people. They conformed.

Even admitting the difference between attitudes then and now, the question remains. We know that some English men and women did react negatively to the changes in religion that occurred under the Tudor monarchs. The choice to reject them in favor of adherence to the forms of religion in which they had been raised was made by some of the men who were directly connected with the church's governance, as English ecclesiastical lawyers certainly were. Were these lawyers whose continuing conformity has been described therefore simple timeservers? Did they meekly comply with the wishes of those in power in their own self-interest but against their own better judgment? They would have forfeited their careers by refusing to conform and that cannot have been an easy choice to make. In support, they might have cited the words of a fellow civilian who had become a bishop, Stephen Gardiner. He wrote in a letter to Erasmus that 'only a fool questions what cannot be altered'.[30] It may be that this was a sentiment most of the civilians shared.

A different and more charitable understanding of the evidence is also possible. It is suggested by a noteworthy study of the English episcopate undertaken more than sixty years ago by Lacy Baldwin Smith.[31] He investigated the nature of the academic study and the later careers of the bishops who occupied the episcopal bench between 1536 and 1558. In examining their careers, he discovered that those men who had studied theology during their time at university were much more likely to have sided with the Protestant reformers than were those who had studied law. He did not find a perfect correlation, but it was close enough to provide a likely and interesting explanation of their behavior. Lawyers, he concluded, appear to have been conservative by training and habit, much more so than were theologians. As he saw it, the pattern of thought among the lawyers was dominated by 'the shrinking from innovation, the demand for order and for submission to existing conditions'.[32]

---

[28] E.g., Dist. 63 c. 12; Dist. 62 c. 2.
[29] E.g., Panormitanus, *Commentaria* ad X 1.6.2 (*Osius*), n 4, dealing with episcopal elections and stressing the canonical rules that minimized the laity's participation in them.
[30] J A Muller (ed), *The Letters of Stephen Gardiner* (Westport, CT, 1933, reprint 1970), p 3.
[31] *Tudor Prelates and Politics 1536–1558* (Princeton, NJ 1953).
[32] Ibid., p 45.

Becoming a bishop did not change that pattern for the English civilians. These lawyer bishops carried their conservatism into their careers after they had been promoted, and it was this that separated the lawyers from the theologians in their reaction to religious change.

If that was so of the lawyers who became bishops, it is likely also to have been so of the lawyers who remained in the ecclesiastical courts, the judges, advocates, and proctors who are the subject of this book. There is a difference, however, a significant one. The public world occupied by bishops was not the same as the arena of practicing ecclesiastical lawyers. 'Conservatism' did not mean the same thing for both groups. For bishops, conservatism meant continuing adherence to traditional religion and traditional forms of government. For proctors and advocates, it meant continuing adherence to established legal practice. Their attention would have been focused on the forum in which they served rather than on larger questions of church government or matters of salvation. For them, continued adherence to the work of their courts throughout the years of the Reformation would have been the more conservative path. As long as court practice remained largely untouched by the Reformation, they would have been content.

They must have thought – quite naturally – that the work they did in these courts was worth doing, even important. Why abandon it? If we remember, as we should, how little substantive change occurred in the jurisdiction exercised by the ecclesiastical courts in England over the course of the sixteenth century, it cannot be a surprise that ordinary civilians, sharing the basic attitude to change that was held by lawyers who became bishops, should have remained in place within the courts. The next chapter will examine the subject of ecclesiastical jurisdiction in more detail, including an assessment of some of the changes that did occur, but if we attempt to put ourselves into the shoes of ordinary English ecclesiastical lawyers, it is not difficult to understand their continuing adherence to the system in which they had been trained. The alternative would have been worse. Much worse. And not just for them. In their opinions, it would have been worse for both the church and the nation. They could not foresee what would happen in fact in the years after 1640.

4

English Ecclesiastical Lawyers before the Civil War

The years from 1600 to the 1640s were testing times for the English civilians. Some aspects of their professional lives must have appeared promising. The Reformation settlement was in place, and the advocates and proctors who served in the courts of the English church had not deserted their posts. They would not have regarded that settlement as a setback. It was not even a threat. Whatever their religious opinions were (and who can tell what they believed in their hearts?), most of the areas of practice the civilians had held in earlier centuries emerged unscathed from the changes in religion that began under Henry VIII and continued under his immediate successors.

What loss existed in the extent of ecclesiastical jurisdiction had already occurred during the years before the Reformation began. The disappearance of jurisdiction over contracts and debts accompanied by an oath, one that was held by the ecclesiastical tribunals under the rubric of breach of faith (*laesio fidei*) during the Middle Ages, had come under sustained and successful attack beginning in the last third of the fifteenth century. The force of royal writs of prohibition and prosecutions brought under the medieval Statutes of *Praemunire* caused them to disappear from the pages of the courts' act books prior to the arrival of the Reformation in England.[1] The loss of defamation causes involving the imputation of purely temporal crimes followed the same pattern.[2] In fact, these losses were part of a European-wide shift in thinking about jurisdictional boundaries. The same developments occurred on the other side of the English Channel.

This assessment is not meant to deny either the reality or the importance of religious change. Queen Elizabeth had assumed the title of 'Supreme

[1] See R H Helmholz, 'Assumpsit and *fidei laesio*' (1975) 91 *LQR* 406–32, at 426–27.
[2] See R H Helmholz, 'Introduction' in *Select Cases on Defamation to 1600* (SS 101, 1985), pp xliii–xlv.

Governor' in both the temporal and the spiritual spheres (1 Eliz. I, c 1 § 9). Appeals from the courts of the English church went to the new Court of Delegates, which sat in London, in place of the papal court in Rome. The English language ousted Latin from parish churches. The Book of Common Prayer replaced the medieval Mass books. But these alterations in government and religious life, however dramatic in appearance and in implication they were, made little difference in the day-to-day running of the English ecclesiastical courts and in the professional lives of the lawyers who served in them. Legislation restricting the reach of papal claims to exercise effective jurisdiction in England had long been part of English law.[3] Its effect in practice would have been old hat to English civilians, and for the most part, they were left free to continue along familiar paths.

This stability turned out to mean that the courts of the church maintained their jurisdiction over clergy and laity in a much wider sphere of human life than anyone would think appropriate today, indeed wider than some men thought at the time. Marriage and divorce, last wills and testaments, payment of tithes, defamation, several facets of economic life, control of ecclesiastical property, and a host of criminal offenses against morality all remained within the legitimate reach of the church's tribunals.[4] They preserved their jurisdiction over the laity to a greater extent than did the courts of the church across the Channel in France.[5] In England, the courts also retained use of a medieval sanction, one that had long been unavailable in the French *officialités*. This was the right to invoke the 'secular arm' to aid the church's jurisdictional rights. It could be used and was used to secure the imprisonment of any person who had remained excommunicate for more than forty days, and it was granted upon application to the Crown. This privilege, allowed as a matter of course in the royal chancery, was important in sustaining the effectiveness of ecclesiastical sanctions, and it was not lost.[6]

---

[3] E.g., Statute of Praemunire (16 Ric. II, c. 5, 1392). See also the discussion in R N Swanson, *Church and Society in Late Medieval England* (Oxford 1989), pp 182–86.

[4] R B Outhwaite, *The Rise and Fall of the English Ecclesiastical Courts, 1500–1860* (Cambridge 2006), pp 1–14.

[5] See A Lefebvre-Teillard, *Les officialités à la veille du Concile de Trente* (Paris 1973), pp 127–43; T Lange, *Excommunication for Debt in Late Medieval France: The Business of Salvation* (Cambridge 2016), pp 22–24.

[6] See F D Logan, *Excommunication and the Secular Arm in Medieval England* (Toronto 1968), pp 156–57; the noticeable decline in numbers mentioned in the chancery files was caused by a change in the procedures of record keeping rather than a change in substance or an actual decline in numbers.

AGGRESSION FROM WITHOUT

Continuation of the major parts of the medieval ecclesiastical jurisdiction within the courts is not the whole story. Far from it. Any description of the professional careers of English civilians during this era must include threats from without as well as insistence on continuity from within. There were real attacks on the Elizabethan settlement – most coming from what might be called the Puritan direction – that is, from those who regarded the courts presided over by the deputies of the episcopate as relics of popery, which to some extent they were. The more immediate threats to the English civilians, however, were those that came from the English common lawyers. An accomplished student of the history of the civil law in England described the final years of Elizabeth's reign as 'The Crisis of the Profession',[7] and there is evidence to support this characterization. Most serious in the long run was an expanded use of writs of prohibition to restrict the jurisdictional rights of the courts of the church.[8] Particularly threatening was the development of a test which excluded from ecclesiastical jurisdiction any subject over which the common law courts themselves exercised substantive or supervisory jurisdiction. The medieval standard for granting writs of prohibition had depended upon respect for long-accepted custom. It had been the reference point determining the proper jurisdictional boundaries between the two court systems. The new test left greater freedom for the common lawyers to decide where the boundary lines would be drawn. They did not do so greedily, but they did so with determination. Their change in attitude meant that whenever the common law's jurisdictional scope rose, that of the ecclesiastical law sank.

The subject of this chapter is the reaction of the English civilians to this development – something they regarded (correctly) as a threat to their independence and their livelihood. Examination of the evidence from the records of the ecclesiastical courts themselves shows, however, that the English civilians were not passive victims of aggression from without. Still less were they victims of a widespread contempt for their profession. A dismissive nickname – the bawdy courts – was fastened upon those tribunals, as in an amateurish rhyme from the 1640s: 'I care not a straw for thy bawdy law'. Ridicule is a powerful weapon, but it should not be applied anachronistically or one-sidedly. The act books from medieval times contain prosecutions for similar

---

[7] Levack, *The Civil Lawyers in England*, pp 50–85.
[8] The most complete study is C M Gray, *The Writ of Prohibition: Jurisdiction in Early Modern English Law* (New York 1994), reprinted and corrected form at www.lib.uchicago.edu/e/law/gray (2004); see also C W Brooks, *Law, Politics and Society in Early Modern England* (Cambridge 2008), pp 109–23.

instances of abuse and contempt. And much of the evidence from the records of the courts of the church after the Reformation suggests the opposite of a weak and vaguely comical ecclesiastical court system. So does some of the other evidence, even that which came from its critics. Consider for instance the Root and Branch Petition and the Grand Remonstrance of 1640 and 1641 that contained the grievances of the Parliamentary Party and were the prelude to the English Civil War.[9] A perceptive critic concluded that some of the grievances in them were aimed at the courts of the church. 'A system is here hinted at', he noted, 'especially a judicial system', adding that the document itself showed that in the eyes of the drafters of the two documents the courts of the church had 'proved prejudicial and very dangerous'.[10] This quoted language is not a normal way of speaking among men who regard the church's courts and the lawyers who served in them with mild amusement or contempt. It is the language of alarm. For that reaction, the judges and lawyers who served in them were not wholly responsible, but they did contribute to it, as the evidence drawn from the contemporary records of the courts of the church demonstrates. The records of the ecclesiastical courts hold the key to understanding the extent of the hostility of the Parliamentary party towards episcopal government and the courts that formed part of that system. They demonstrate that there was in fact some cause for apparent alarm.

INITIATIVES AND INNOVATIONS OF THE ECCLESIASTICAL LAWYERS

The first piece of evidence and the most obvious from the records of the ecclesiastical courts, however, appears to point in the opposite direction. The records repeatedly demonstrate that the judges in the ecclesiastical courts obeyed royal writs of prohibition when they received them. They were not scofflaws. Acceptance of these writs, normally suspending further proceedings in a cause before the court after the writ had been introduced, had been their practice throughout the Middle Ages,[11] and it continued in regular use afterwards. This

---

⁹ See S R Gardiner (ed), *Constitutional Documents of the Puritan Revolution, 1625–1660*, 3d edn revised (Oxford 1906, reprint 1962), pp 137–44, 202–32.

¹⁰ R Strier, 'From Diagnosis to Operation', in D L Smith, R Strier, and D Bevington (eds), *The Theatrical City: Culture, Theatre and Politics in London, 1576–1649*, (Cambridge 1995), pp 224–59, at 225. See also J Morrill, 'The Attack on the Church of England in the Long Parliament, 1640–1642', in D Beales and G Best (eds), *History, Society and the Churches: Essays in Honour of Owen Chadwick*, (Cambridge 1985), pp 105–24; C Haigh, *The Plain Man's Pathways to Heaven: Kinds of Christianity in Post-Reformation England, 1570–1640* (Oxford 2007), pp 213–14.

¹¹ This large subject is reviewed by W R Jones, 'Relations of the Two Jurisdictions: Conflict and Cooperation in England during the Thirteenth and Fourteenth Centuries', in W Bowsky

had never meant, however, that the English civilians regarded prohibitions as determinative of the proper extent of their own jurisdiction. Prohibitions were acts of power. As such they were construed narrowly, covering no more than the exact subject stated in their terms.[12] So, for instance, one judge allowed an appeal in a prohibited cause under the theory that the writ had only ordered its recipient to hear the cause no further. He had obeyed that order to desist (he said) by passing the cause to an appellate court.[13]

The civilians also wrote tracts to defend their jurisdiction, attempting to confine the too frequent issuance of writs of prohibition by emphasizing the value and tradition in England of the church's law.[14] They stressed the ill results that issuance of these writs had caused. So, for example, a man had been ordered to take out a bond to avoid keeping adulterous company with a Rose Symonds and 'signified' to the Chancery to be imprisoned when he refused. Instead of complying, he obtained a writ of prohibition by citing the provision of Magna Carta that no free man should be taken or imprisoned without the lawful judgment of his peers or the law of the land. The end result: he returned to live in adultery with Rose.[15] Surely the king's justices would not have wished that result, the commentator assumed, but that was one of the evil ways prohibitions were being used in the world as it was. Once informed of the consequences, the judges in the royal courts might change their ways. The civilians were hopeful.

The civilians also adopted devices – most of them variations in the wording in libels and articles – in order to avoid writs of prohibition by emphasizing the spiritual nature of the causes begun in the consistory courts.[16] The words

(ed), *Studies in Medieval and Renaissance History*, vol VII (Lincoln, NE, 1970), pp 79–210. Specific to writs of prohibition is G Flahiff, 'The Writ of Prohibition to Court Christian in the Thirteenth Century (parts 1 and 2)' (1944 and 1945) 6 and 7 *Medieval Studies* 261–313 and 229–90.

[12] See, e.g., Ford c Doffyn (Exeter 1599), Chanter MS. 784C, s.d. 5 June (supersedeas granted 'quoad contenta in prohibitione tantum'); Lillingstore c Verey (Buckingham 1639), Act book D/A/C/12, f 69 (construing writ to apply to only one of two causes brought to recover tithes). This subject is treated at greater length in my *Roman Canon Law*, pp 172–88.

[13] Swifte c Johnson (Durham 17th century) DDR XVIII/3, f 125.

[14] E.g., the tract in Lincoln's Inn Library, Maynard MS. 59, fols 473-76v (Jurisdiction over tithe causes, invoking the medieval writ *Circumspecte agatis* (13 Edw. I, st. 4) that had been given the effect of a statute); see also Cosin, *Apologie for Sundrie Proceedings by Iurisdiction Ecclesiasticall*, Pt. I, cc 8–9.

[15] Ex officio v Giles (1610), BL, Stowe MS. 424, ff 158–158v.

[16] See, e.g, form (Canterbury early 17th century), MS. Z.3.27, f 74v: 'Protestationes ad evitandum prohibitionem regiam ubi agitur pro decimis silve ceduae'; Formulary (Durham 17th century), DDR XVIII/3, f 245v ('Processus cum adfertur regia prohibitio' with advice on preserving testamentary jurisdiction against these writs); Smyth c Over (1520), in E M Elvey (ed), *Courts of the Archdeaconry of Buckingham 1483–1523*, (Buckinghamshire Record Society 19, 1975), p 270.

used could be tailored to stress that the claim was not one that involved a conflict with the common law.[17] Failure to pay church rates, for instance, could be stated in terms of neglect of an ancient custom rather than a matter of collecting a sum of money. The courts also assessed expenses (what we would call court costs) against those who introduced writs of prohibition that had accrued prior to the time the writ had been introduced.[18] Failure to pay those legitimate expenses was treated as a separate matter from the underlying cause that had been prohibited, at least in the eyes of the English civilians. Anyone who refused to pay the expenses was subject to suit in their courts and even excommunication for failure to comply with such an order to pay accrued expenses. The judges even made provision for charging a fee 'for the opening of any writ of prohibition'.[19] Their effort sought to ensure that those who considered purchasing a writ of prohibition would first count the cost.

During this period English civilians also entertained prosecutions brought 'for the violation of ecclesiastical liberty' when a suit brought before a secular court encompassed a matter that properly belonged only within the church's jurisdiction.[20] Actions like these were means of resisting encroachments on what the civilians regarded as their rightful place in the government of the realm. How successful they were in the end we rarely know. What we do know is that the English civilians had not surrendered control in many of the matters of contemporary dispute. In assessing the actual force of individual prohibitions, it is also important to stress that the common law judges did not all agree on exactly what matters should be prohibited. Their reports contain many instances of disagreement. A notebook of the prominent civilian, Sir Julius Caesar (d. 1636), contains a case in which one of the parties first obtained a writ of prohibition, only to have the other party obtain a writ of consultation from the same court.[21] Such instances must have encouraged the civilians to stand fast. They must also have deterred some potential litigants from choosing a course that would lead them into a morass of conflicting

---

[17] E.g., Lowthe c Saintandrewe (Nottingham Archdeaconry/York 1583), Trans. CP 1584/3 (dealing with tithe of underwood of less than twenty years growth).

[18] See Formulary, (Salisbury 17th century), MS. D 5/24/18, f 71 ('De expensis retardati processus'). See also Grindall c Thomson (Carlisle 1607), MS. DRC/3/62, s.d. 20 October (judicial order after introduction of a prohibition 'ad solvendum xx li. pro expensis taxatis'); Potts c Davy (Buckingham 1601), Act book D/A/C/25, f 29 (53s 4d assessed as expenses in a cause that had been decided ultimately in favor of the ecclesiastical court's jurisdiction).

[19] Formulary (Lincoln 17th century), MS. For.22 at end.

[20] E.g., Ex officio c Dicson et ux. (Durham 1593), DDR IV/3, f 96 (apparently defamation).

[21] Case of Margary Hunt (c.1599), BL, Lansd. MS. 160, f 226 (seemingly brought 'for reviling and laying violent hands upon a minister'). On some of the ambiguities in this area, see S F C Milsom, *Historical Foundations of the Common Law* (London 1969), pp 13–15.

opinions as well as the difficulties they faced in the ecclesiastical courts themselves.

In the end, of course, efforts like these went for nothing. At some point after the restoration of ecclesiastical jurisdiction in the 1660s, the English civilians came to accept the common lawyers' position that writs of prohibition marked the legitimate boundaries of their own jurisdiction. But that moment had not yet come by 1640. It had been the operative opinion among the common lawyers long before that date, but the point was not good law from the perspective of ecclesiastical lawyers. Into the 1630s this subject was still open to question among them. Generally, the king was on their side, and they thought that the history of the scope of jurisdiction in their courts was too. Like many of the constitutional disputes of those years, it was a matter of contention, one not solved at the time.

Besides these partial acts of resistance against the incursions of the common law, the advocates and proctors in the ecclesiastical courts had other reasons for optimism about their future. The evidence to show this falls into three categories: the overall amount of litigation in the ecclesiastical courts; the expanding nature of instance causes (i.e. private disputes between parties); and the growth of the reach of *ex officio* jurisdiction (i.e. prosecutions brought to punish infractions of the criminal law of the church). Not all the evidence in each of these categories points unambiguously towards growth in vigor within the church's legal system, but on balance, each of the three areas demonstrates more signs of strength than they do of weakness from the 1590s to the late 1630s. These signs of strength alarmed contemporary critics of the Church of England and its judicial system. And indeed they had some reasons for alarm.

LEVELS OF COURT ACTIVITY

The first – levels of court activity – is probably the most impressive. At least it is the easiest to appreciate. An influential survey of sixteenth-century ecclesiastical jurisdiction concluded with the words, 'The ecclesiastical courts emerged from the Reformation gravely weakened'.[22] This was true in a sense. They had accepted the obligation to enforce statutes enacted in Parliament. They had lost contact with and respect from the courts in Catholic lands across the English Channel. However, no decline occurred in terms of the amount of litigation being brought before the courts. In fact, levels rose right up to the years immediately prior to the 1640s, and that is what would have

---

[22] Houlbrooke, *Church Courts and the People*, p 266.

been most immediately meaningful to advocates and proctors. It is essential to recognize the existence of greater secular interference in spiritual jurisdiction by common lawyers than had existed in, say, 1450. At the same time, however, it is not correct to conclude that this interference caused the amount of litigation brought before the courts of the church to shrink or shrivel. It did not.

What decline existed in levels of litigation in the courts of the church actually occurred in the late fifteenth and early sixteenth centuries. It came to a halt and was indeed reversed under Elizabeth and her immediate successors. For example, 133 instance causes were brought before the consistory court in the diocese of Chichester in 1544. Fifty years later, the number had more than doubled; 278 causes were introduced.[23] In the consistory court at York, a detailed study has shown that 213 causes were introduced in 1561–62. By the 1620s and 30s, the numbers had grown by not quite 50 percent.[24] In the chancery court for the same diocese, the increase was even greater – up from 27 causes in 1571–72 to 203 for 1634–35.[25] In the diocese of Norwich, the number of causes listed as before the consistory court in the 1580s came to fewer than 200 per session, but by the late 1620s the total had risen to over 300.[26] These are examples only; virtually every serious study of the levels of litigation has found similar evidence of expansion in numbers. At least from that viewpoint, ecclesiastical jurisdiction was not a system in decline. It was growing. In some areas of the law, plaintiffs had a choice of forum; they could, for example, have sued over tithes in a common law court and they could have brought many aspects of the law of last wills and testaments before the Court of Chancery. The numbers show that enough among them continued to prefer ecclesiastical jurisdiction in situations where they had a choice.[27]

Did this matter? Is it an accurate measure of the attitudes of contemporary ecclesiastical lawyers? Certainly it would strain credulity to suggest that any civilian routinely sat in one of England's consistory courts toting up the number of causes introduced there and then comparing the totals with figures drawn from previous decades. The numbers may prove to be as ambiguous as

---

[23] C A Haigh, 'Slander and the Church Courts in the Sixteenth Century' (1975) 78 *Transactions of the Lancashire and Cheshire Antiquarian Society* 1–13, at 2; see also J Vage, 'Records of the Bishop of Exeter's Consistory Court c.1500–c.1660' (1982) 114 *Reports and Transactions of the Devonshire Association* 79–98, at 80 (the opening decades of the seventeenth century saw the bishop's court 'at the height of its activity').

[24] Marchant, *The Church under the Law*, p 62.

[25] Ibid., p 68.

[26] Figures taken from act books containing litigation: DN/ACT 15 with DN/ACT 59.

[27] See Houlbrooke, *Church Courts*, pp 276–77; W J Sheils, 'The Right of the Church: the Clergy, Tithe and the Courts at York, 1540–1640', in W J Sheils and D Wood (eds), *The Church and Wealth* (1987), pp 231–55.

they are tedious to compile. Increases in litigation are not often treated as signs of health and prosperity in any society. One should also factor in the increase both in population,[28] and in general levels of litigation that were a feature of English life during this period.[29] In other words, many things may lie behind the increase in activity in the consistory courts. Admitting the ambiguities, however, it is hard to deny that litigation is the lifeblood of any system of public courts. Although administrative tasks are sources of revenue and the lives of English civilians were occupied with many of them, litigation undeniably brought income and grudging prestige to the practitioners within the system. It provides a crude but acceptable means by which to measure the system's perceived significance among the people subject to it. For purposes of assessing of the state of health of the ecclesiastical courts under the early Stuarts, at least one must conclude that the figures support a positive conclusion (or a negative conclusion if one takes the perspective of critics of the English church's legal system). Whichever perspective one chooses, the courts and the lawyers who practiced in them were kept busy with professional work. They had some reasons to worry, but they also had some reasons to be optimistic.

Much the same thing can be said of the level of activity on the *ex officio* side – the criminal jurisdiction of the courts, although the evidence is a little harder to evaluate because for a variety of reasons the records are not as full or reliable as they are on the instance side. Nonetheless, what indications there are also suggest an expansion in numbers. A reliable study of the incidence of presentments by churchwardens for offenses committed in three deaneries, one in York, one in Cheshire, and one in Suffolk, found increases between the 1590s and the 1630s of an average of 33 percent.[30] In the archdeaconry of St. Albans, 135 *ex officio* prosecutions were entertained in 1583; by the year 1625 the number had risen to 294.[31] Other indications point in the same general direction. These numbers may be crude, but they are not impressionistic. In particular, they do not give a reliable picture of the number of criminal defendants who actually appeared before the courts, were found guilty, and then duly performed their penance. They do not tell us whether or not

---

[28] E A Wrigley and R S Schofield, *Population History of England, 1541–1871* (Cambridge, MA 1981), pp 69–71.

[29] C Brooks, *Lawyers, Litigation and English Society since 1450* (London and Rio Grande, OH 1998), p 66 and passim.

[30] Marchant, *Church under the Law*, p 219. See also O'Day, *The Professions in Early Modern England*, pp 151–58.

[31] R Peters, *Oculus Episcopi: Administration in the Archdeaconry of St. Albans 1580–1625* (Manchester 1963), pp 65–67.

sentences of excommunication were actually feared by most people. These might be truer tests of the status of ecclesiastical jurisdiction. Regrettably, the records were not preserved with a view to helping the curious historian answer the question. All we can say for sure is that the incidence of ecclesiastical litigation, instance and *ex officio* both, was rising in most places between 1560 and 1640. The point worth insisting upon is that the figures we do have, crude as they may be, give evidence of the existence of a vigorous court system and the likelihood of prosperity for the lawyers who served within it.

This advance was also matched by the creation of an expanded body of published works on English ecclesiastical law. Men like Henry Swinburne (d. 1624), Thomas Ridley (d. 1629), Richard Cosin (d. 1597), and Francis Clerke (*fl.* 1594) rose up to fill what may have looked like a void.[32] They were needed. Except for William Lyndwood, medieval England had produced few learned writers on the canon law. The works of these new authors, based on traditional law, described the law applied in the English ecclesiastical courts in the years that followed the Reformation. They were also joined by civilian authors whose ambitions stretched further. William Fulbecke (d. 1603), Arthur Duck (d. 1648), John Cowell (d. 1611), and Richard Zouche (d. 1662) contributed to the field of general jurisprudence. Starting with the traditions of the *ius commune*,[33] Zouche's works even attracted the interest of Continental jurists. His *Elementa jurisprudentiae* and his *Quaestiones juris* were printed in Leiden, Mainz, and Berlin. In other words, an expansion in the production of legal commentaries occurred at the same time as an expansion in numbers of causes brought before the courts. For proctors, none of this would have been a source of enrichment, though it might have helped them in practice. For critics opposed to ecclesiastical jurisdiction in principle, this evident intellectual vigor could only have been disquieting. The new literature suggested a determination to state a positive case for ecclesiastical jurisdiction.

THE SCOPE OF INSTANCE LITIGATION

The second subject requires consideration of the nature of civil litigation brought before the ecclesiastical courts. Here there was not simply retention of most aspects of ecclesiastical jurisdiction. There was actually expansion in the scope of actions cognizable in the ecclesiastical forum. Whether this

---

[32] See Baker, *Monuments of Endlesse Labours*, pp 56–76; P Stein, 'English Civil Law Literature', in *Ins Wasser geworfen und Ozeane durchquert: Festschrift für Knut Wolfgang Nörr* (Cologne et al. 2003), pp 979–92.

[33] See Coquillette, *The Civilian Writers*, pp 71–96; Coing, 'Das Schrifttum der englischen Civilians'.

was the result of a conscious 'competition for jurisdiction' between court systems – something that is widely thought to have animated judges and lawyers in earlier eras – is (for me) an open question. There is little actual evidence to prove that lawyers thought that way. It is undeniable, however, that the livelihood of the judges and lawyers who practiced in the church's courts depended in some measure upon the fees collected in the causes submitted to them. More litigation led to greater rewards. And it is also true that new areas of litigation were 'opened up' during this era. These were natural sources of increased legal activity and for optimism about the future. None of them was a complete innovation. They built on what had gone before, but they were sources of expansion in the scope of activity in the courts all the same. Five examples demonstrate what happened.

Alimony Awards

The first is the creation of alimony. Alimony was the payment one spouse, almost always the husband, was required to make to the other when they were divorced or separated. Usually, the obligation continued for a number of years, often until the husband or wife's death. Although texts from the Roman law did provide texts that might have been used to support something like alimony payments, they themselves were not parts of the Roman law inherited by the medieval church. Medieval practice in the ecclesiastical courts had not provided for the payment of alimony after a *de facto* marriage had been declared dissolved.[34] It was limited to payments made while the suit for divorce was in process. When couples had been fully divorced on the grounds of an existing impediment to the marriage – the prohibited degrees of affinity and consanguinity, for example – no provision was made for one spouse to support the other. Apparently the reason was simply that there had never been any valid marriage between them. But the denial went further; no alimony was payable when the couple was separated by judicial decree where cruelty or adultery could be proved – the divorce called *a mensa et thoro*.

Beginning in Elizabeth's reign, this stern regime came under challenge. Observing that the existing regime offered 'slender relief for distressed wives',

---

[34] See Dig. 25.3.1–9 (dealing with children) and the texts cited in Ayliffe, *Parergon*, v. 'Of Alimony, and the Nature of it'; Classical Roman law itself apparently restricted the rights of the divorced wife to the recovery of her dowry (Dig. 24.3.2); see J F Gardner, *Women in Roman Law & Society* (Bloomington, IN 1986), pp 97–116 and P E Corbett, *The Roman Law of Marriage* (Oxford 1930, reprint 1969), pp 122–34.

the judges, first in the courts of High Commission,[35] then in the ecclesiastical courts themselves, began to make alimony available to those 'distressed' women who were fully divorced.[36] And it was not a trifling matter or a token payment. One ecclesiastical lawyer's notebook from the 1630s stated that under most circumstances the award should amount to at least a quarter of the man's annual income.[37] Another stated that the Chancery would make available a writ *ne exeat regnum* to prevent a husband's flight to avoid its payment.[38] This must have appeared to be a positive development to most contemporary observers. But it did not seem positive to everyone. Complaints were made in Parliament that the availability of alimony was causing wives to act in 'disobedient and contemptuous' ways towards their husbands. Worse, some concerned observers complained that alimony had had the effect of unleashing women 'of strong and enlarged sexual appetites' upon an unsuspecting masculine population. This had led (they said) to a general decline in morals. Some opponents of the ecclesiastical law also saw this expansion as an act of aggression, extending the boundaries of ecclesiastical jurisdiction beyond its traditional limits. Alimony awards required the payment of money. On that account, they were open to objection of the common lawyers on the grounds that it exceeded the proper limits of spiritual jurisdiction. It became accepted practice nonetheless. It served a legitimate purpose, and it expanded the place of ecclesiastical jurisdiction in the country's legal life.

Augmentation of Tithes Owed to Vicars

A second example of jurisdictional expansion is more esoteric, but was probably regarded as more significant at the time: the revival of the legal action called *causa augmentationis vicarii*. This revival requires a word of explanation. During the twelfth century, many parish churches were given to monastic houses by laymen whose ancestors had founded and endowed the churches. The gift was an act of piety and also a response to the medieval church's attempt to eliminate lay control over ecclesiastical property. Most

[35] This subject is dealt with at greater length in my *Roman Canon Law in Reformation England*, pp 77–79; on the clerical and civilian lawyers in the branches of the High Commission, see R Usher, *Rise and Fall of the High Commission* (Oxford 1913, reprint 1968), pp 82–84, 250–53.

[36] 'Abstract of his maieste's High Commissioners ecclesiasticall' (York, 17th century) HC.MISC. 1614/10, n 8.

[37] Nottingham University Library, MS. A 43, 5th folio from the end: '[I]udex solet allocare uxori tertiam vel ad minus quartam partem annui valoris bonorum immobilium'.

[38] See Sir John Reade's Case (*c*.1676), in 'Lawyer's Commonplace Book', BL, Add. MS. 72544(A), f 314.

of the monasteries that received these churches did not wish to have their monks serve there, however, so they appointed vicars to do so. The revenues (mostly tithes) were divided between the vicar and the monastery according to a formula arrived at during the appropriation (that is what the process was called) and approved by the diocesan bishop. Such appropriations, however, always made the formula subject to change if the revenue allocated to the vicar proved inadequate over the course of time. That was always the true purpose of the tithe, and where negotiation failed, legal actions happened from time to time called by the name just given – the *causa augmentationis vicarii*. It seems not to have been common during the Middle Ages,[39] however, perhaps because of the relative stability in agricultural prices.

When the monastic houses were suppressed under Henry VIII, the lands came into the hands of laymen, who collected the same revenues the monks had once taken. They were in effect landlords, as the monks had been. Both regarded those rents as their right. During the sixteenth century, however, the value of money and consequently the worth of the tithes received by the vicars in these parish churches declined precipitously. This left the vicars, the parochial clergy, worse off materially than they had been.[40] In the years around 1600, however, the bishops did attempt to extend their care to the parochial clergy; their courts entertained actions allowing vicars to sue the laymen who held the tithes. This was to treat a consequence of the Dissolution of the Monasteries as changing the share each received – of course in favor of the clergy.[41] The subject elicited a learned work by Sir Thomas Ryves (d. 1652), called *The Poor Vicar's Plea for Tithes*.[42] His argument was that the law had always required that a 'congruent portion' of the tithes should be reserved for the parochial incumbents. What 'congruent' meant could vary the amount

---

[39] I did find one cause so styled, Hythe c Prior and Convent of Bruton (Bath & Wells 1478), Act book D/D/Ca 1, p 176.

[40] R O'Day and A Hughes, 'Augmentation and Amalgamation: Was There a Systematic Approach to the Reform of Parochial Finance, 1640–60?' in R O'Day and F Heal (eds), *Princes & Paupers in the English Church 1500–1800* (Leicester 1981), pp 167–93. The fullest treatment of the general subject is C Hill, *Economic Problems of the Church: from Archbishop Whitgift to the Long Parliament* (Oxford 1956, reprint 1963).

[41] See Precedent Book (Buckingham c.1600), MS. D/A/X/4, ff 275–78: 'Libellus quando vicarius cuiusdam ecclesie agit contra rectorem eiusdem ecclesie pro portione congrua et competente'. None of these causes dealt with the property in the monarch's hands, and I found no record of the matter coming up in the Court of Augmentations or its successors in W C Richardson, *History of the Court of Augmentations 1536–1554* (Baton Rouge, LA 1961).

[42] Printed in London in 1620; Ryves was a learned civilian and the treatise was as much an exploration of the canon law on the subject as it was a call for fair treatment of a competent parochial clergy.

due to the two holders of tithes, and in 1600 this meant enlarging the sum owed to the vicar.

This was the same situation that later led to the creation of Queen Anne's Bounty (2 & 3 Ann. c 20, 1703). In the 1600s, of course, there was no such source of funds, and this led some of the clergy to invoke a remedy that was for them merely a reassertion of a beneficent rule established in the earlier centuries. They could have cited occasional cases from the records of the medieval ecclesiastical courts in support.[43] To the laymen involved at the time, however, it would have seemed a dangerous new invasion of settled property rights they had held for a hundred years and more. Some complied. Some resisted. All of them must have complained about this outdated assertion of ecclesiastical right. The pages of the English court records under the Stuarts contain examples of these disputes,[44] and from the perspective of the laity involved, they must have seemed like naked attacks on settled property rights. Perhaps they were, but from the limited perspective of the lawyers on both sides of these disputes, which is the subject of this chapter, it seems fair to say that many of the civilians would have profited from the increase in numbers of these once infrequent instance causes. Little doubt they would have felt that what they were doing was fully justified.

Jactitation

A third example has to do with boasting, called jactitation in juridical parlance of the time and still mentioned in some modern legal works.[45] During the early seventeenth century, the English ecclesiastical courts sought to expand the scope of their jurisdiction to include jactitation beyond its medieval form. The term itself did not mean everyday braggadocio. It meant claiming a legal right one did not have, most conspicuously (and successfully) in the church's traditional jurisdiction over marriage. If one person, say Titius, claimed to have entered into a valid marriage contract with another, say Bertha, whereas in fact he had not done so, Bertha's chances on the marriage market would be diminished. Who would want to marry her if he would face the complications caused by the claim to her as his wife made by Titius? In consequence, Bertha

---

[43] E.g., Vicar of Shorne c Abbot and Convent of Bermondsey (Rochester 1441), Act book DRb Pa. 1, f 195.

[44] E.g., Wall c Smith et al. (Salisbury 1640), Act book D1/39/1/54, ff 21v, 48, 66, styled 'negotium augmentationis vicarii de Stapleford'. The proper forms for these causes were included in precedent books of the times; e.g., (Buckingham), MS. D/A/X/4, ff 275–78.

[45] See, e.g., D Greenberg (ed), *Stroud's Judicial Dictionary of Words and Phrases*, 7th edn (London 2006), p 1416.

was accorded a right to sue Titius for having boasted publicly of the prior marriage contract's existence, one he claimed had already taken place. It was called a *causa jactitationis matrimonii*. If successful, it established that Bertha was free to marry whom she pleased without fear of Titius' claim. Never frequent in court practice, this jurisdictional reach was nonetheless well established in England.

During the late sixteenth and seventeenth centuries the lawyers who controlled practice before the courts of the church sought to expand upon it. The result was that greater numbers of claims related to boasting of different kinds are found in the court books. Some of the expansion was connected with the *ex officio* side of ecclesiastical jurisdiction. John Hawkes, for instance, was brought before the diocesan court at Winchester for having 'most imprudently' boasted that he had sexually 'contaminated' a woman named Dorothy Moore seven times in a single night.[46] Whether his boast were true or false is not revealed in the surviving record. There was no reason for including that. It was the boast that was the offense.

More importantly, other examples went further in substantive coverage. The idea must have occurred to civilians that the legal concept behind this cause of action need not be limited to marriage; it could cover boasting of many kinds. So we find *causae jactitationis decimarum* and *causae jactitationis testamenti* – that is, actions begun against persons for having boasted falsely that they possessed a legal right to tithes or to an inheritance. Some quite unusual forms of this remedy found their way into the church's courts.[47] That the causes based on this theory were a way of avoiding writs of prohibition is certainly possible. If the underlying cause of action was based on a verbal boast rather than what the boasting had been about (which might have been a secular subject), there would have been little reason for intervention by the common law's judges. This might be so even if the boast itself concerned a secular subject like lands or chattels. Whatever the motive, it could be said that the ecclesiastical offense was only about spoken words.

In fact, actions based on these expanded definitions of what actionable boasting might cover never became fully established. Except in the law of marriage, they seem to have attracted resistance of litigants and common lawyers right from the start. It could not be honestly claimed that they belonged

---

[46] Ex officio c Hawkes (Winchester 1589), Act book 21M65/C/B 60, f 54 ('valde imprudenter gloriando se illam septies per noctem contaminasse').

[47] E.g., Executors of Wellingham c Waterman (Hertford 1632), Act book AHH 5/11, f 2v ('causa iactitationis non solutionis legati'; see also Precedent book (Buckingham late 16th century) MS. D/A/X/4, f 302 ('libellus in causa jactitationis beneficii'); Precedent book (Suffolk, 17th century), MS. E 14/11/2, n 129 (a libel in a 'causa jactitationis jurisdictionis').

within the competence of the spiritual forum inherited from the Middle Ages and they concerned subjects very far removed from the world of the spirit. From the perspective of the first forty years of the seventeenth century, however, the possibility that their existence would allow the church to enlarge its reach to cover many new subjects would have appeared threatening to many observers. Where would it end if the church's judicial system could subject all such 'boasters' to its jurisdiction? What limits were there to this intrusiveness? This would have been hard to predict. It might have looked promising for ecclesiastical lawyers in the years before the Civil War than it turned out to be in fact, but it would also have been a cause for alarm among enemies of ecclesiastical jurisdiction.

Faculty Jurisdiction and Pews

A fourth example relates to seating within churches. We take pews for granted today, but their introduction and extent were something new in the sixteenth century. The practical beginnings of the exercise of faculty jurisdiction by today's ecclesiastical courts in England are also to be found in these years. A faculty, meaning a permission granted by authority to do an act, is needed to permit some alterations in a church or its contents, including the creation or removal of pews.[48] The subject became a contentious matter raised in the English consistory courts because of the erection by individuals of seats and pews in many churches during this period. They had not been a common feature of religious life in the Middle Ages.[49] Starting slowly in the fifteenth century and becoming more common in the sixteenth, they began to appear in English churches. Some of this development was authorized by permissions issued directly by diocesan tribunals.[50] To judge by the court records, however, much of it seems to have been the product of what might be called private initiative. Prominent local families paid to have permanent pews erected in the churches where they worshipped. The longer sermons characteristic of Protestant worship may have suggested their need and encouraged the trend.[51] For whatever reason, the practice occurred, sometimes with the permission of the incumbent or other officer of the church, sometimes without. In the

---

[48] M Hill, *Ecclesiastical Law*, 2d edn (Oxford 2001) § 7.01.

[49] A Heales, *History and Law of Church Seats or Pews* (London 1872, reprint 1998), pp 1–15; J C Cox, *Bench-Ends in English Churches* (Oxford 1916), pp 17–27.

[50] See, e.g., D M Smith, *Guide to the Archive Collections in the Borthwick Institute of Historical Research* (York 1973), p. 59; Marchant, *Church under the Law*, p 26.

[51] Cox, *Bench-Ends*, p 24.

court records this development seems often to have been allowed as a matter of grace, indifference, or respect for the family involved.

The pertinent point is that no generally agreed upon system for granting rights to church seats existed, and not everyone agreed about either the desirability or the legality of the practice. In 1633 Archbishop Laud, for instance, wrote to the King describing the cathedral church at Salisbury as having been 'pestered with seats'. He had given orders to have them removed, and solicited the King's help in securing their enforcement.[52] Did the Archbishop have the authority to issue that order? Did all bishops or the incumbents of parish churches? The churchwardens? At one time or another, all of them apparently made an attempt to assert this authority, most likely at the behest of those who wished to construct a pew.[53] A consequence was that contention over pew rights came before the ecclesiastical courts with increasing frequency in the sixteenth and seventeenth centuries. The result was normally denominated a 'causa sedilis'.[54] When they were brought before one of England's consistory courts, whether by rival claimants or as *ex officio* challenges to a pew's right to exist, the holders of the pew commonly claimed to have been given a valid faculty or else defended their possession of a pew by asserting rights based upon local custom or lawful prescription.[55] Disputes between rival claimants to the same pews – some of which apparently led to some use of force within the pews themselves – also came before the courts from time to time.[56] They were sometimes said to have been causes of disturbance to the congregations and even (it was said) the source of danger to the souls of those involved.[57] In assessing the impact of this development in the professional lives of England's

---

[52] G Ornsby (ed), *Correspondence of John Cosin* (Surtees Society 52, 1869), p xxix.

[53] E.g., Wardens acting *ex officio* c Rawlings (Hereford 1638) Act book HD/4/1/98, s.d. 8 May (objecting that 'a new pew or seate [had been] erected and lately built larger than the old one'); see also Heales, *History and Law*, p 90.

[54] Or more elaborately a 'causa sedendi in quodam sedili in ecclesia de Leke', in Backlough c Mawkyn (Lichfield 1531), Act book B/C/2/3, f 1571 (1531). See also the many examples of contention in A Flather, *The Politics of Place: a Study of Church Seating in Essex, c.1580–1640* (Leicester 1999).

[55] E.g., Hyde c Clerke et al. (Lichfield 1525), Act book B/C/2/1, ff 7v and 8 (asserting possession 'temporibus solitis et consuetis'); Cardy c Brees (Chester 1558), Act book EDC 5/19/11 (asserting family rights 'a tempore cuius initii sive contrarii memoria hominum non existit'); Ex officio c Crowe (Ely 1607), Act book EDR B/2/26, f 14 (that he sat there for twelve years and the churchwardens never displaced him). *Bl. Comm.* vol II, *429, described them as similar legally to heirlooms, descending 'by custom immemorial (without any ecclesiastical concurrence) from the ancestor to the heir'.

[56] E.g., Kelk c Warson (Canterbury 1614), MS. Z/5/8, f 270 (ten years' occupancy against a recent and unwelcome act of entering the pew by 'a maiden of thirteen or fourteen years').

[57] E.g., Cardy c Brees (Chester 1588), Act book EDC 5/17/11 (stressing the disturbance to the divine service and also the 'periculum' to the soul of the disturber).

advocates and proctors, one can safely say that it opened up a new source of work and income for them. More important in the long run, of course, was its role in the development of faculty jurisdiction, a matter still within the partial control of the church's tribunals.

The Duplex Querela

A fifth example of advance in the courts related to disputes about the *ius patronatus* and the admission of men to clerical benefices. Its exercise depended upon holding a right of presentation – meaning the power to nominate an incumbent of a parish church or some other ecclesiastical benefice upon the death or resignation of the holder. Normally called an advowson in English law, its exercise allowed its holders to present the man they had selected to the diocesan bishop for institution and induction into the relevant benefice. This right was widely dispersed in England and it was treated as a property right in the common law. It could be inherited or conveyed. Patrons, who might be individuals or corporations such as a monastic house or a Cambridge college, held the right through purchase or inheritance – in other words, through something that might come into dispute. This system existed throughout most of Latin Christendom. It was recognized and regulated in the canon law itself.[58]

In England, the settlement of disputes about who held rights of advowsons had long been a matter of dispute – in fact from the twelfth century during the reign of Henry II. The Constitutions of Clarendon (1164) declared that all disputes 'concerning advowsons and presentation to churches [were to be] treated in the court of the lord king'.[59] This became the accepted rule. The royal courts provided writs of *Darrein presentment* and *Quare impedit* to make it effective; they were used to determine who had the right to present.[60] Their existence had never meant, however, that the bishops were to have no part in decisions about whom to admit. If a man presented to a benefice could not read or if his presentation had been the product of a simoniacal bargain, the bishop could refuse. It has widely been accepted in the academic literature on this subject that a bishop in most such situations had to settle such

---

[58] P Landau, *Jus Patronatus: Studien zur Entwicklung des Patronats im Dekretalenrecht und der Kanonistik des 12. und 13. Jahrhunderts* (Cologne 1975).

[59] D Douglas (ed), *English Historical Documents: Volume II 1042–1189* (London 1968), n 1.

[60] See J Tate, 'Glanvill and the Development of the English Advowson Writs', in J Witte, Jr, S McDougall, and A di Robilant (eds), *Texts and Contexts in Legal History: Essays in Honor of Charles Donahue* (Berkeley, CA 2016), pp 129–44.

a matter before the King's justices,[61] but in fact throughout the Middle Ages occasional entries in the church courts' records show that they could turn up there, showing that most such disputes were handled by special commissions when the possibility of a dispute arose.

What occurred in the years after the Reformation in England was the growth and regularization of this process within the courts of the church itself. This was accomplished by the creation of a remedy called the *Duplex Querela*. The term *duplex* seems to have been chosen in part because the ecclesiastical remedy was a rough match to that which was available to patrons in the royal courts.[62] The difference was that it was available to the men who had been presented to a benefice, allowing them to assert their own rights, independently of the jurisdiction over advowsons that belonged to the patrons and were heard in the common law courts.[63] It turns out that some of the same issues raised in the royal courts were also raised in the church's courts – Who was the rightful patron, how had the right accrued to him, and so forth? – this in addition to questions about the canonical eligibility of the candidate. These causes began to appear during Elizabeth's reign in act books,[64] and also in the formularies used by advocates and proctors.[65] They became accepted parts of ecclesiastical jurisdiction. The bishops and their officials involved in these disputes normally protected themselves against later action in the royal courts by taking a bond to be held harmless from the party who prevailed in the spiritual forum.[66] The details of how this dual process worked itself out in practice remain to be investigated, and it will not be a simple subject to master. For the present subject, what is apparent in the records is that English ecclesiastical lawyers would easily have regarded the existence of the *Duplex querela* as a promising step forward.

---

[61] The standard treatment of the subject, a good one, remains W R Jones, 'Relations of the Two Jurisdictions', pp 102–32.

[62] See Ayliffe, *Parergon*, v. *Duplex querela*; Wiltshire Record Office, MS. D5/24/18, f 47v (discussing the extent of intervention by others with an interest in the benefice).

[63] See, e.g., In re William Cockson (York 1596), Chanc.AB.13, ff 84v–86 (styled a cause 'pro inductione Willelmi Cockson clerici in actualem et corporalem posessionem vicarie ecclesie parochialis de Ilkley'); Welch c Hathcote (Lincoln 1604), Act book DIOC/Cj 15, ff 49, 58 (described as a *causa beneficialis* involving the rectory of Compton Parva).

[64] E.g., Prentice c Asheton (York 1575), Chanc.AB.10, f 9; Porter c Caren (Winchester 1593), Act book 21M 65/C/2 28, s.d. 27 October; Paston c Clement (Lichfield 1596), Act book B/C/2/31, s.d. 16 March.

[65] E.g., manuscript formularies: (Chichester *c*.1561), MS. Ep I/51/1; (Bath & Wells *c*.1600), MS. D1/45/1, f 1700v; (Suffolk *c*.1600), MS. E 14/11/4, f 159.

[66] E.g., LPL, MS. 1590 (*c*.1620), f. 37v.

THE SCOPE OF *EX OFFICIO* JURISDICTION

This chapter's third subject of investigation, *ex officio* prosecutions, deals with efforts made to discipline men and women for violating the penal laws of the church. Proctors and advocates did not normally profit financially in an immediate sense from this jurisdiction. Except in special circumstances, lawyers were excluded by law from representing defendants in criminal cases. It should be remembered, however, that these special circumstances actually existed with some regularity in practice. English proctors appeared in them as a consequence. For instance, if a cause was begun *ex officio promoto*, as often happened, proctors might be admitted under the theory that a contest between two persons was more directly involved than a criminal matter,[67] and in fact this took place with apparent regularity. It put the prosecution into private hands, sometimes a party who had been defamed, for example, or at least someone other than the law itself. In cases like these, proctors might appropriately be appointed to assist defendants. The lawyers would thus have benefitted incidentally from an expansion in ecclesiastical jurisdiction to cover new subjects. It also seems probable that experienced proctors gave informal advice to defendants summoned to answer for misconduct even where no such special circumstances existed. Familiarity with the course of proceeding in the courts would have made their advice valuable. However, this subject must remain largely invisible. Rarely was it recorded in the relevant act book, but the result – appearance by a proctor in a criminal matter – did occur often enough in the records to at least make it probable and worthy of note.

Taking a longer view, one may object that treating this as a sign of progress is a mistake. Public prosecution for offenses against morality was an irksome business. Nowadays it may appear to have been a useless nuisance, though its necessity seems to have been accepted as a matter of course in earlier centuries. Our ancestors thought that punishment of sexual offenses was a good thing.[68] In its favor, it can also be said that ecclesiastical jurisdiction probably did sometimes serve as a means of promoting harmony within local communities. Quarrels were ventilated and sometimes settled. But this was not the law's primary purpose, and the church's efforts were not a huge success in achieving it. What the evidence from act books does show clearly is that, just as was true on the instance side, the ecclesiastical courts were very far from

---

[67] E.g., Ex officio c Palmer (Norwich 1593), Act book ANW/2/31, f 11, a cause brought for 'scolding' in which the defendant's proctor sought dismissal on the ground that the presentment was 'nimis generalis et vaga'. See also Ritchie, *The Ecclesiastical Courts of York*, pp 155–57.

[68] Ingram, 'Reformation of Manners in Early Modern England', 47–88.

moribund during the first third of the seventeenth century. On the *ex officio* side, they would in fact have appeared to be thriving in the years before the Civil War. Or at least busy. On that account they gave legitimate cause for alarm among opponents of the courts and for optimism among the lawyers whose careers were spent in them. Three examples follow.

The first was improvement in the machinery by which *ex officio* causes were handled. Visitations – the process by which court officials surveyed the conduct of men and women in every parish in order to ferret out what was going wrong – were held more regularly and organized more efficiently than they had been. The duty of the churchwardens – the representatives of each parish – to report and record what was amiss was itself more rigorously enforced.[69] Records of disciplinary action were more scrupulously kept, at least to judge by the records that have survived. And, of course, the several courts of High Commission – one in each diocese – were strengthened as a way of backing up the efforts of the ordinary courts to secure religious uniformity.

The second was a modest substantive expansion in what counted as an unlawful act to be prosecuted before the ecclesiastical courts. Habitual drunkenness, pre-marital unchastity, inappropriate behavior in the churchyard, and what is called 'attempting the chastity' of a maiden all began to appear in the pages of the courts' act books. Some of these new tasks for the courts came about because of Parliamentary statutes – the licensing of schoolmasters, for example. And some of them were simply the consequence of a growth in religious dissent. But, taken all together, the expansion amounted to a threat that ordinary peoples' lives would be more closely regulated than they once had been.[70] Who knew where it would stop?

The third was the prosecution of people who mattered. England in 1600 was not an egalitarian society, and most of the men and women who had traditionally been brought before the courts to answer for unlawful conduct were not among the elite. This changed in the seventeenth century. Influential men were called before the ecclesiastical tribunals for a variety of offenses based on their religious views and for their opposition to the ceremonial movement of the Church of England under the Stuarts. A general example consists of the Puritan clergy – the 'grave and learned' men whom Archbishop Laud and his

---

[69] E.g., Ex officio c Eastword and Holden, Churchwardens of New Church (Chester 1606), Visitation book EDV 1/14, f 158, a prosecution 'for concealinge matters presentable'.

[70] The professional literature of the time gives some hints, as for example the opinion of Dr. Talbot, a civilian, who is recorded as thinking that the courts might entertain a prosecution for 'breeding or raising a difference' between a man and wife; see Worcester, MS. 794.093, BA 2470, f 76v. So far as I have found, this never became established in practice.

predecessors required to conform or be deprived.[71] From the immediate perspective of the officials of the courts, all this appeared to be for the best. In this area, their jurisdiction was expanding; and their self-confidence was growing. It should of course be said that the ravages of the inflation of the currency that occurred in the sixteenth century depressed the purchasing power of many proctors. Their fees seem not to have risen accordingly. No one has yet been able to calculate what their fees would buy. In terms of the scope of their jurisdiction, however, they did have some reasons for optimism.

This conclusion is not just the imagination of a present-day enthusiast. Mark Tabor, registrar of the court of the archdeaconry of Wells, spent the years of his forced retirement during the English Civil War annotating some of the works of practice he had used before 1640. Today they are in the Wells Cathedral library.[72] In them, he committed to paper his lament for the fate of the courts of the Church – they had all been swept away in the 1640s. But, looking back, he admitted that he could see some reason for the attacks made upon them. God had punished him (and presumably his fellow lawyers) for the 'greed and presumption' that had captured their ambitions and distorted their behavior in the years before the Civil War. Indeed, he admitted, there had been overreaching among almost all the civilians.[73] The too common acceptance of substantial money payments for commuting public penances, for example, had become a common practice.[74] Now they suffered for having encouraged it.

With things as they were, Tabor and other civilians had few options but to repent at leisure. The content of his lament was, of course, a common reaction to disaster in earlier centuries; but Tabor had been present and active in the courts. He knew what 'greed and presumption' had meant on the ground. For historians, his reaction was only a negative way of putting what the records of the ecclesiastical courts demonstrate: a strengthening and potential expansion of the criminal jurisdiction of the English ecclesiastical courts that occurred in the fifty years or so before the 1640s.

---

[71] See, e.g., J Fielding, 'Arminianism in the Localities: Peterborough Diocese, 1603–1643', in K Fincham (ed), *The Early Stuart Church 1603–1642* (Stanford, CA 1993), pp 93–113.

[72] See his copy of Clerke, *Praxis in curiis ecclesiasticis*, ff 149–53, 160–72.

[73] This is evident elsewhere; e.g., Ex officio c Cornish (London 1636) Act book DL/C/B/043/M50 9064/20, f 45v (taxation of expenses (costs) even though the defendant had successfully undergone canonical purgation).

[74] E.g., Ex officio c Gifford (London 1636), Act book DL/C/B/043/M50 9064/20, f 32 (£6, 13s. 4d. for commuting a public penance of a man who admitted having fathered an illegitimate child).

CONCLUSION

In the run-up to the Civil War, the authors of the Remonstrance sought to portray themselves as high-minded opponents of the dangerous 'vexations' visited upon honest men and women that had resulted from the practices of the ecclesiastical courts.[75] Of course, that status is what many controversialists claimed at the time. It was common form. However, what the evidence from the records of the ecclesiastical courts shows is that this was not all form. The ecclesiastical courts were in fact acting with energy. Their reach was expanding. Their opponents therefore had legitimate reasons for describing the activities of the courts as dangerous inventions. The Parliamentary or Puritan or Constitutionalist side – call it what you like – had a real grievance, not an imaginary or spurious one, against the agents of spiritual jurisdiction. They could not share the indifference of modern historians towards the church's courts. They did not know the outcome, and they feared the worst.

Should one therefore ascribe the coming of the English Civil War to the activity of the ecclesiastical courts? Surely not. But the ecclesiastical courts did play a part in creating resistance to the church and to the episcopal system of government they supported. The court records show more than gasping signs of life among the civilians on the eve of the English Civil War. They show an established system of courts seeking to protect and indeed to expand the church's jurisdiction. Not only that, they seemed in some measure to be succeeding. If the efforts of English ecclesiastical lawyers described above had been successful, it would have meant – at least in the short term – a quite considerable expansion in the role of ecclesiastical jurisdiction in English life.

The effort failed. It would all come crashing down. The courts, the English civilians, and the bishops got their comeuppance. They all suffered twenty years of isolation and deprivation. What would happen to their fortunes in the years immediately following the restoration of episcopacy in the 1660s remains to be investigated in detail.[76] But that was in the future. In the 1630s, an eclipse in the profession of ecclesiastical law would have seemed far from inevitable to the lawyers whose careers were spent in England's ecclesiastical courts.

---

[75] See articles 51, 63, 85, 132 of the Grand Remonstrance, in Gardiner, *Constitutional Documents*, pp 214, 216, 218, 223.

[76] J Spurr, *The Restoration Church of England, 1646–1689* (New Haven, CT and London 1991), pp 209–19; Outhwaite, *Rise and Fall*, pp 78–82; M G Smith, *The Church Courts, 1680–1840: From Canon to Ecclesiastical Law* (Lampeter 2006); P Polden, 'The Civilian Courts and the Probate, Divorce, and Admiralty Division', in W Cornish et al. (eds), *Oxford History of the Laws of England*, vol XI (Oxford 2010), pp 692–714.

To them, the prospect of additional and purposeful activity in their tribunals may actually have appeared more likely. It took a civil war and years afterwards to find out what the future would hold.

It is also worth restating that it would take two centuries for their profession to disappear. That is a long time, and in the 1630s, the English civilians had reasons for optimism. The reverse was the reaction of the authors of complaints stated in the Grand Remonstrance and the Root and Branch petition. To them the assertions of ecclesiastical authority to which they objected were injustices that were all too present. The civilians were acting to protect what they had and even to expand the scope of their jurisdiction. For the system's critics, complaints about ecclesiastical jurisdiction were not the product of fantasy or idle nostalgia. They were natural reactions to current events.

PART II

The Profession Illustrated

5

Roger of Worcester (d. 1179)

Except among a small coterie of specialists in the medieval canon law, the contribution of English ecclesiastical lawyers to the formulation and growth of the law of the church has never loomed large.[1] There is an apparent reason for this. English canonists never played a role comparable to that of the leading lights from the Continental universities. Even admitting this, the contribution to this great work that was in fact made by English lawyers was not negligible. Some of it should be made visible.

The case for recognizing the English contributions is particularly strong for the twelfth century. A once common view, stated forcefully by Maitland and Brooke, held that during the pivotal era between the completion of Gratian's *Decretum* in the 1140s and the compilation of the Gregorian Decretals in 1234, the leaders of the English church lagged behind their Continental brethren in knowledge of, and perhaps even respect for, the canon law.[2] Why else should they have required so much correction at the hand of Pope Alexander III? The preponderance of papal letters addressed to English bishops so conspicuous in the Decretals reflects their need for instruction and correction.

In fact, however, something like the reverse has now been shown to be a more accurate explanation. The large number of decretals sent to England actually shows that twelfth-century Englishmen played a particularly creative part in the movement forward of the *ius commune*. Indeed they were in the van. Of this, there are few better examples than the subject of this chapter, Roger, the bishop of Worcester from 1164 until his death in 1179.

---

[1]   E Rathbone and S Kuttner, 'Anglo-Norman Canonists', (1949/51) 7 *Traditio* 279–358.
[2]   F Maitland, *Roman Canon Law in the Church of England* (London 1898), pp 122–24; Z Brooke, *The English Church and the Papacy* (Cambridge 1952), p 214.

ROGER'S LIFE AND CAREER

The youngest son of Robert, Earl of Gloucester, Robert was born c.1133. He was brought up in the company of his cousin, who would become King Henry II, while Henry was in the care of his uncle Earl Robert. Meant for the church, Roger studied in the schools in Paris, though we cannot be sure about the subject. Thomas Becket did later once apply the term *iurisperitus* to him, at least in an oblique way,[3] but it is not certain that the archbishop meant this to refer to an academic qualification. As a bishop, Roger was also commonly addressed as a man familiar with the intricacies of the law,[4] but again this may reflect only the kind of knowledge that comes from dealing repeatedly with worldly matters.[5]

As bishop of Worcester, he inevitably became involved in the dispute between Henry II and Thomas Becket, somehow managing to retain the good will of both men. Even so, he spent most of the years between 1167 and 1172 in France, ostensibly for the purpose of study.[6] Upon his return to England after the Settlement of Avranches (1172), his work as diocesan bishop earned high praise among his contemporaries. Nigel of Canterbury called him 'famous for holy living, faith and nobility'.[7] Gerald of Wales described him, together with Bartholomew, bishop of Exeter, as 'twin candelabra illuminating all Britain'.[8] Thomas Becket professed his admiration for Roger, albeit in slightly ambiguous circumstances.[9]

If this were the sum of Roger's life and career, he would have no particular importance to England's place in the history of ecclesiastical law, except perhaps to shed some light on the reaction of a sensible participant in the 'Becket controversy'. In fact, it was to this subject that the entry in the first *Dictionary*

---

[3] Epistles I, no 179, in *Materials for the History of Thomas Becket*, Rolls Series 67:5 (1875–85), p 345.

[4] E.g., A Morey and C Brooke (eds), *Letters and Charters of Gilbert Foliot* (Cambridge 1967), p 190, no 145.

[5] The most recent opinion on this subject holds that it would be 'surprising' and in fact 'improbable' to suppose that Roger had no formal legal training. See M Cheney, D Smith, C Brooke, and P Hoskin (eds), *English Episcopal Acta 33: Worcester 1062–1185*, (Oxford 2007), pp xlviii–xlix.

[6] M Cheney, 'Roger (c 1134–1179), Bishop of Worcester', in *Oxford Dictionary of National Biography* (2004–12).

[7] See T Wright (ed), *The Anglo-Latin Satirical Poets and Epigrammatists of the Twelfth Century*, Rolls Series 59:1 (1872), p 198.

[8] Giraldus Cambrensis, 'Vita St Remigii' c 28, in *Opera*, Rolls Series 21:7 (1877), p 57.

[9] Letter No. 88 (1166), in A Duggan (ed), *Correspondence of Thomas Becket* 1, (Oxford 2000), pp 356–57; the letter was coupled with a request amounting to a demand for aid in Becket's controversy with the King.

of National Biography devoted almost its entire entry. More recent scholar-ship – in particular the careful work of Mary Cheney – has allowed us to take a fuller and more balanced look at the whole of Bishop Roger's career.[10]

ROGER AS A PAPAL JUDGE DELEGATE

Roger's work as an ecclesiastical lawyer is most visible in the sources as a papal judge delegate. The twelfth century witnessed a dramatic increase in the number of disputes appealed to the papal court. Even quite trivial causes were brought there. These causes, however, were rarely decided in Rome. Most were sent back to be heard where the parties and the witnesses lived. Local judges were appointed to act, according to forms and instructions worked out at the papal court. Many English clerics carried out this role, but few as often as Roger of Worcester. An estimate made forty years ago put the number at between sixty and seventy instances in which he was appointed or addressed as one of the papal judges delegate,[11] and Mary Cheney's more energetic efforts have pushed that number to something close to 130.[12] Considering the survival rate of documents from the mid-twelfth century, 130 is a large number. Of course, by itself the number proves little about Roger's expertise in law. Legal training was not a prerequisite for service as a papal judge delegate.[13] Prominent men were likely to have been appointed, whatever their qualifications. Here, however, when coupled with Pope Alexander III's high opinion of Roger's probity and knowledge,[14] the frequency of delegation to him does suggest that he was regarded as a particularly able judge.

The rise of this system of delegated jurisdiction is most commonly used to show the centralization of power in the hands of the Roman pontiffs in the twelfth century. It does show that, no doubt. But understanding the nature of that system and the way it worked in practice is more important as evi-dence of how the canon law grew, and Roger of Worcester's part in it shows this with particular clarity. The outlines of the story are familiar. By the mid-twelfth century, the study of Roman law had established itself in the nascent

---

[10] M Cheney, *Roger, Bishop of Worcester 1164–1179* (Oxford 1980).

[11] J Sayers, *Papal Judges Delegate in the Province of Canterbury, 1198–1254* (Oxford 1971), p 10. Other frequent judges delegate during this period were Gilbert Foliot, bishop of Hereford and later London, and Bartholomew, bishop of Exeter.

[12] Cheney, *Roger of Worcester*, pp 317–73.

[13] See, e.g., Hostiensis, *Summa Aurea*, Lib I, tit *De officio et potestate iudicis delegati*, no 3.

[14] Giraldus Cambrensis, 'Vita St Remigii', p 345; perhaps he exaggerated, but the statement about Alexander's opinion of Roger cannot be entirely without substance. See also D Knowles, *The Episcopal Colleagues of Archbishop Thomas Becket* (Cambridge 1951), pp 22–23, 51–52.

European universities. Gratian's *Decretum* had also been completed and was being taught in the Schools. They were both signs of progress towards a mature *ius commune*. However, the former could not serve as a statement of the law of the church; too many of its texts were out of line with spiritual principles regarded as vital to proper rule of the church. The *Decretum* too was not sufficient for a working system of law. It was not meant to be. It was a school book, useful in teaching legal skills and in stating general principles of canon law, but of lesser utility for dealing with the questions of law and procedure that arose almost daily in the dioceses of the Western church. Think, for example, of the law of elections or the law regulating appointments to ecclesiastical benefices. The *Decretum* contained too many contradictory texts and too few fixed directions to guide the course of litigation. That remained to be done.

It was done. Many things contributed to the evolution of a workable system of canon law – the creation of a system of consistory courts, the enactment of constitutions in church councils, the work of generations of canonists and commentators. But the regular use of delegated jurisdiction was the primary contributor during the twelfth century, and Roger of Worcester's role shows the advances in canon law it made possible with particular clarity. He was not simply a recipient of orders from Pope Alexander III. Much of the law was new, and Roger was active in framing the legal issues, sometimes suggesting one solution or another on the basis of his own experience. Mary Cheney speaks of 'interplay' between the two men in deciding what to do.[15]

Exchanges of views seem to have arisen out of Roger's own experience in dealing with difficult questions – the abuses associated with the appropriation of parish churches to monastic houses, for example. The monks had sometimes imposed such unrealistic monetary burdens upon the vicars they appointed to serve their parochial churches that the vicars could not sustain the responsibilities of hospitality or fulfill the duties of their office. Roger consulted the pope about the problem, and the papal response, requiring that a *congrua portio* be assigned to the vicar, at length found its way into the Gregorian Decretals.[16]

Similar dilemmas recurred in the correspondence between the two men. Another decretal letter that ended in a statement of the general law of the church forbade the imposition of annual pensions on benefices without the consent and supervision of the diocesan bishop.[17] It was an attempt to

---

[15] M Cheney, 'Pope Alexander III and Roger, Bishop of Worcester, 1164–1179: The Exchange of Ideas', in S Kuttner (ed), *Proceedings of the Fourth International Congress of Medieval Canon Law* (Vatican City 1976), pp 207–27, at p 227.

[16] X 3.5.12. For an example of Roger's concern, see Acta, no 229 (1164 x 1179), in *English Episcopal Acta* 33, pp 154–55.

[17] X 3.39.8.

preserve parochial revenues for spiritual purposes. Roger had applied to Rome for instructions and support in one such matter – he needed help in dealing with local opposition on the part of monastic houses. And he seems to have played an active role in formulating what would become the general law of the church.

What Mary Cheney called a 'veil of obscurity' surrounds many of the causes dealt with by Roger as judge delegate,[18] but when that veil is lifted, we see a process beginning with a statement of the difficulties and possible solutions; the consultation produced a working out of the most realistic solution. The difficulties of securing the appearance of litigants, for example, led gradually to the development of a law of expenses imposing progressive fines for delay on parties who refused to come before a competent judge.[19] It was worked out by consultation and experiment. Of course it was not a perfect remedy. But it was better than the alternatives.

In these situations, the Pope had the final say. No matter his esteem for Roger, Alexander did not always follow the desires of the English bishop. When Roger suggested ways of curbing some of the appeals that were being made to the papal court in matters of little significance, for example, Alexander replied that 'it was necessary to defer to appeals made on trivial questions, ... no less than in those concerning greater matters'.[20] The right to appeal was a matter of principle for Alexander, but the number and the abuses it fostered were problems that would continue to fester. The title, De appellationibus, in the Decretals was one of its longest and it was followed by similar titles in the Liber sextus (1298) and the Clementines (1317).[21] The routine delegation of causes appellatione remota never worked very well to stem appeals, and 'trivial matters' can be hard to define. One man's trivial cause is another's question of principle. That Roger chose to raise the problem speaks of its difficulty as well as his practical mindedness. Even his failures give evidence of that quality.

ROGER AND DECRETAL COLLECTIONS

One of the results of the interest in canon law among the English clergy was the collection of papal decretals, and it is this habit of preservation that best explains the preponderance of English sources in the Gregorian Decretals,

---

[18] Cheney, 'Exchange of Ideas', p 221.
[19] X 2.14.5; the ins and outs of this process can be traced in P Torquebiau, 'Contumace', in R Naz (ed), Dictionnaire de droit canonique 4 (Paris 1935–65), pp 506–21; see generally Nörr, Romanisch-kanonisches Prozessrecht, pp 72–77.
[20] X 2.28.11. The Pope here seems to have followed the Roman law on this point. See Cod 7.62.20.
[21] X 2.28.1–73; Sext 2.15.1–12; Clem 2.12.1–7.

not a need for correction of the English clergy. These decretals, stating some of the most recent legal rules, called out for collection and organization. Roger had a hand in the process, although it is rarely possible to ascribe any specific collection to one individual or another. At any rate, three of the early surviving decretal collections had a connection with the see of Worcester, and in the judgment of specialists, a connection between them and Roger's initiative seems highly probable.[22]

The connection is important. It was through the process of collecting papal decretals and arranging them in a usable form that the law of the church was advanced. The papal chancery made no systematic record of the letters sent to the far corners of Europe. True, there were earlier collections, but much of what was being done was new. If not legislation, the instructions to papal judges delegate entered areas where decision was needed. As the number of letters of justice coming from the papal court increased, the result was a 'forest' of decretals – stating the law in particular cases, but unusable without organization. That was the function served by the English collection of papal decretals. Once arranged by subject matter, they passed into general circulation, eventually ending as the *Quinque compilationes antiquae* and then the Gregorian Decretals edited by Raymond of Peñafort.[23] It was neither accident nor policy that English decretals figured so prominently in the process. It was a result of the English work of collection. In this activity, Roger took a part. His work as a judge delegate was both a means of and a spur to the process. It made them more widely available. We cannot penetrate into the details of this process, but that he played a role in its encouragement is so likely it would be foolish to allow academic caution to reject it out of hand. By all accounts Roger was a practical man. In his time, this was probably the most practical step for an ecclesiastical lawyer to take.

6

Gilbert Foliot (d. 1187)

For the Ford Lectures in 1955, Professor C R Cheney chose as his topic the government of the English church during the period between two famous archbishops of Canterbury, Thomas Becket (1162–70) and Stephen Langton (1207–28). He expressed the hope in his introduction that 'future historians of the twelfth-century church may discover the way in which a bishop went to work in those days'.[1] A dozen years later, an important step towards achievement of that goal appeared. It was the publication of a handsome edition of the letters and charters of Gilbert Foliot, bishop of London from 1163 until his death in 1187.[2] Foliot is best known among historians as the leading opponent among the English bishops of archbishop Thomas Becket in the latter's struggle with King Henry II.[3] That dispute, which began over the jurisdictional competence to try and punish clerics accused of having committed a crime, divided *regnum* and *sacerdotium* then, as it sometimes divides medieval historians even today. However, it is not the subject of the greatest prominence in Foliot's letters. Nor is that dispute the subject in these letters of the greatest relevance to the history of the profession of ecclesiastical law in England. What is depicted in Foliot's letters is the world as it was in the century before the publication of the Gregorian Decretals, the creation of formal consistory courts in England, and the emergence of the practice of canon law in courts as a distinct profession.[4] Indeed both Foliot's letters and his career take us back

---

[1] C R Cheney, *From Becket to Langton: English Church Government 1170–1213* (Manchester 1956), p 8.

[2] Morey and Brooke, *Letters and Charters of Gilbert Foliot.*

[3] See Knowles, *The Episcopal Colleagues*, pp 37–49; and also the sources collected in T Jones (ed), *The Becket Controversy* (New York 1970).

[4] A treatment of this later development can be found in Winfried Trusen, 'Die gelehrte Gerichtsbarkeit der Kirche', in H Coing (ed), *Handbuch der Quellen und Literatur der neueren Europäischen Privatrechtsgeschichte* (Munich 1973), vol I, pp 467–83.

to the time when the classical canon law was first being formulated and then put into place throughout the Western church. That great change had begun, most overtly with the composition of the *Concordia discordantium canonum*, traditionally ascribed to a Master Gratian in Bologna and dated c.1140,[5] but it had a considerable distance to travel. It led to the creation of a working system of ecclesiastical law and to what some critics would come to criticize as the 'lawyerization' of the church.

LIFE AND CAREER

Gilbert Foliot himself was born into a Norman family established in England before 1100.[6] Among those he counted as his relations were several prominent men, including two who had served as bishops of London and of Winchester, and also Miles Foliot (d. 1143), constable of Gloucester and earl of Hereford. Little is known about Gilbert's upbringing and education, but it certainly included university study – first in the liberal arts and then in both Roman law and theology. The editors of his letter collection concluded that his study of the latter occurred in Bologna, and that certainly is possible, though it rests only on a balance of probabilities.[7] There is no conclusive evidence for it. Whatever the place and date of his education were, we do know that sometime around 1130 he chose to become a monk at Cluny. It was not an unusual choice for a man like Foliot in those days, and it had a lasting effect. He retained some of the norms of monastic life even to the end of his own. However, the cloister at Cluny did not hold him for long. Promotion and worldly position came rapidly. He became prior of the Cluniac house in Abbeville, and in 1139 he was made abbot of the Benedictine monastery at Gloucester. Following that, he became bishop of Hereford in 1148, and in 1162–63 bishop of London. He survived the Becket crisis, continuing conscientious service in his London see, although Foliot's later years were marked by a serious decline in his health. He went blind at some point, but even this malady did not prevent him from carrying out his episcopal duties as best he could. He died on February 18, 1187. Only a few years previously, Walter Map had written in Foliot's praise

---

[5]　The dating of the *Decretum* and the ascription of its texts to Master Gratian have been thrown into doubt by the publication of A Winroth, *The Making of Gratian's Decretum* (Cambridge 2000), but that subject has only the slightest importance for the subject of this essay.

[6]　C N L Brooke, 'Gilbert Foliot', in www.oxforddnb.com/, accessed October 17, 2017.

[7]　Morey and Brooke, *Gilbert Foliot and his Letters*, pp 59–69, including their conclusion, at p 68, that the evidence linking Foliot with Bologna is 'tolerably strong; but it falls well short of demonstration'.

that his accomplishment had been to 'light up the dark places in God's law ... straightening the winding paths' in it.[8]

FOLIOT AND THE CHURCH'S LAW

Distancing themselves from the laudatory views of Walter Map, the modern editors of Foliot's letters describe his career as worthy of scholarly attention chiefly because he was 'a mirror of his age'.[9] It was a time before the emergence of a professional group of canon lawyers.[10] That may be all that can be said with certainty. However, his letters do in fact add to what is known about the state of the church's law during the twelfth century. He acted frequently as a papal judge delegate, although he seems not to have taken an active part in the formation and collection of papal decretals as did his contemporary, Roger, bishop of Worcester. His letters also show that he frequently faced legal problems. Often involved in disputes that called upon his knowledge of ecclesiastical law, his letters tell us how he sought to solve them. They show at least three things of interest to historians who take an interest in that subject.

First, they add valuable evidence to the question of the timing and extent of Gratian's work's penetration into the law of the church north of the Alps. This has long been a subject of uncertainty.[11] There is little dated evidence. Foliot himself was too young to have come into contact with Gratian's text as a student, but his letters themselves show that he did make some use of its contents in the course of his career. The clearest example comes from a letter of his from 1169 to King Henry II.[12] Actually it comes from a mistake in that letter; Foliot quoted a text found in the *Decretum* (C. 24 q. 3 c. 16), but attributed it to a Pope Sixtus II rather than its actual author, Pope Felix II. However, the ascription to Sixtus is correct for the immediately prior canon (c. 15) in the *Decretum*. Either the copyist or Foliot himself must, therefore, have taken the quotation from Gratian's work, rather than from another source.

---

[8] IV, c. 5 in M R James, C N L. Brooke, and R A B Mynors (eds), *Walter Map De Nugis Curialium* (Oxford 1994), pp 312–13.

[9] Morey and Brooke, *Foliot and his Letters*, p 1.

[10] Brand, *Origins of the English Legal Profession*, 143 (speaking of 'evidence for the study of canon law in England ..., [but not for the existence of] a distinctive or distinctively professional group').

[11] See M Hartmann, 'The Letter Collection of Abbot Wibald of Stablo and Corvey and the *Decretum Gratiani*' (2011–12) 29 *Bulletin of Medieval Canon Law*, n.s. 37–40; P Landau, 'Gratian and the Decretum *Gratiani*', in W Hartmann and K Pennington (eds), *History of Medieval Canon Law in the Classical Period, 1140–1234* (Washington, DC 2008), pp 48–49.

[12] *Letters*, n 201.

A few of Foliot's other letters quote language found in the *Decretum* word for word, or at least almost word for word. They furnish additional evidence to support the probability of his active use of it.[13] However, it is also clear that at least for Foliot, Gratian's text had not assumed the authority within the law of the church that would later be attributed to it. Gratian came to be known as the father of the canon law, but no one would guess it from these letters. Where Foliot used the *Decretum*, he appears to have treated it as a source of texts, not as an authority in itself. Authoritative texts from the past are, of course, exactly what it contained, and it was a school book not a code. And that is how he made use of it.

Foliot himself seems also to have regarded the *Decretum* in a different light than he did Roman law. Unlike Roman law, which he cited and acknowledged as having come from a specific part of the Codex or Digest, a part to which he gave its proper name,[14] Foliot never identified a text he cited as having come from the *Decretum*. He simply used the texts he found there. For him, it appears to have served as a source book, rather than an authoritative statement of the church's law. The editors of Foliot's letters have added many footnote references to specific texts from the *Decretum* with the introductory symbol 'Cf.', but all this means is that a subject of one of the letters was covered in Gratian's text, not that Foliot himself was making use of it. Occasionally, this can mislead us. One example comes from a letter dealing with a difficult question in marriage law; the editors provide a footnote to the *Decretum*, but the text of the letter itself mentions instead the absence in the case of any *deductio in domum*, showing that Foliot himself thought about the matter in civilian terms.[15] He often failed to use or cite the *Decretum* where he had a choice, even on a subject as canonical as marriage. None of this means that he spurned the canon law or the authority of the popes. He cited the authority of

---

[13] Ibid., n 22 (use of language from C. 3 q. 6 c. 4) and n 203 (use of language from C. 11 q. 3 c. 63). See also J Taliadoros, 'Law and Theology in Gilbert of Foliot's (c. 1105/10–1187/88) Correspondence' (2005) 16 *Haskins Society Journal: Studies in Medieval History* 77–94.

[14] E.g., *Letters*, n 110 (1150/59), identifying the texts 'in septimo Codicis' to deal with a technical question relating to the possibility of appeal from a papal rescript issued *appellatione remota*. Other examples: nn 95 (1150); 176 (1165/67); 158 (1165). A review of the understanding of Roman law's place in canonical jurisprudence during this period is K Pennington, 'Roman Law at the Papal Curia in the early twelfth century', in Uta-Renate Blumenthal, A Winroth and P Landau (eds), *Canon Law, Religion & Politics: Liber Amicorum Robert Somerville* (Washington, DC, 2012), pp 233–52.

[15] *Letters*, nn 162 and 164 (1172). A similar example is found in n 96 (1150) dealing with the burden of proof in litigation; the operative language quoted comes from the *Codex Justinianus* rather than the *Decretum*. Foliot's usage is very like that found in the work of Vacarius (d. c.1200), see his comments on the subject, printed in F W Maitland, 'Magistri Vacarii Summa de Matrimonio' (1897) 12 *LQR* 133–43, 270–87.

'the sacred canons and decretal letters' respectfully and more than once.[16] He was also a frequent papal judge delegate. It simply signals that the law he had learned as a student was Roman law, not canon law.[17] If it is true, as Maitland once suggested, that 'taught law is tough law' this makes an excellent example of what he meant.[18]

Second, Foliot's letters demonstrate the existence of an apparently wide-spread ignorance of the church's law among his fellow countrymen, including those on the episcopal bench. Foliot was not shy about pointing this out to them. Historians once supposed that the reason so many of the decretal letters preserved in the Decretals and earlier decretal collections were addressed to English recipients was that England was then a backwater in matters of canon law. They needed instruction. No one believes that today – the reason for the preponderance is found in the assiduity of English clergy in putting together collections of decretal letters. The collectors took what they knew first hand: letters sent to English recipients. Foliot's letters suggest, however, there might be something in the now discredited view. Historians sometimes speak of the canon law in the twelfth century as 'a uniform system of jurisprudence',[19] but that is not what appears in Foliot's letters. What we do not know is whether a similar ignorance of the canon law may have prevailed in other parts of Europe. It seems likely, but it is hard to be certain.

At any rate, Foliot's collected letters contain several that scold and correct recipients for their ignorance of some basic legal principles. For example, in a dispute over rights in a chapel to which Foliot was a party, he had received a letter on behalf of his opponent asking for the delivery of *apostoli* in the cause.[20] 'What is this confusion of matters?' Foliot replied. *Apostoli* were letters delivered by the judge in a cause appealed from his ruling. They were not produced by one of the parties – a blunder he was quick to point out. In another dispute over the effect of a local interdict, Foliot reminded the bishop of Winchester that the power of a bishop extended no further than his own diocese.[21] In a third, he reminded the men acting for the King that an appeal to the Roman court had the effect of suspending the execution of a sentence of excommunication.[22] These were all elementary aspects of the

---

[16] *Letters*, nn 22 (1143); 248 (1163/71).
[17] See J Taliadoros, 'Law and Theology', 77–94.
[18] F W Maitland, 'English Law and the Renaissance', in H Cam (ed), *Selected Historical Essays of F. W. Maitland* (Boston, 1957), p 142.
[19] See, e.g., Knowles, *Episcopal Colleagues*, pp 50–51.
[20] *Letters*, n 243 (1164–79); see also n 66 (1145/48) on the law of prescription.
[21] *Letters*, n 22 (1143); see also n 148 (1163/64) on the nature and consequences of a peremptory exception.
[22] *Letters*, n 203 (1169).

church's law, and at least as Foliot saw it, too many recipients of his letters seemed to have been confused about them. Most frequent of such reminders about proper procedure were his letters reminding the recipients of the need for proof before sentence.[23] Many judges, among them some of his colleagues in the clergy, were acting hastily without having the adequate proof required by both Roman and canon law. Of course, we have only Foliot's opinions in these letters, not the answers of the recipients. Almost certainly there was another side. All the same, it is impossible to dismiss entirely the force of this evidence from a legally trained bishop.

Third is a point with intellectual ties to the second. There were good reasons for some of the ignorance among his colleagues about which Foliot complained. The procedural side of the canon law was itself quite undeveloped when Foliot became a bishop. What there was came mainly from Roman law sources. Those sources did contain a mine of procedural rules and institutions, but they were inadequate to solve some pressing twelfth-century problems. The Codex and Digest made no mention of sentences of excommunication, for example, and the canon law on the subject was itself quite uncertain in 1150. Borrowing civil law to deal with problems raised by subjects like this had to be by analogy. Canonists responded to the problem in different ways. One was by the composition of new *ordines judiciarii* to meet this and other procedural needs.[24] Another was by the use of precedents set out in papal rescripts that had been used within the system of delegated papal jurisdiction. For good reasons, the title *De appellationibus* in the Gregorian Decretals (X 2.28.1–73) turned out to be one of its longest. A third, the path which is most prominently on display in Foliot's letters, was that of caution. Settlement and agreement among the disputants were the paramount goals. This was not out of line with canonical thought of the time,[25] and it seems to have characterized Foliot's approach.

There are many examples of that cautious approach in Foliot's letters, but few of greater interest than those that contain his reaction to the problem put to him by Roger, bishop of Worcester, in the 1160s. The problem was what should be done about the arrival in England of a group of allegedly heretical weavers.[26] Citing a text from Roman law, several texts from the Bible, and the example of St. Augustine, he replied by urging that they be kept in

---

[23] *Letters*, nn. 9 (1129–48); 96 (1150); 201 (1169).

[24] See Fowler-Magerl, *Ordines iudiciarii and Libelli de ordine iudiciorum*, pp 16–28; Landau, 'The Origin of Civil Procedure'.

[25] William of Drogheda, *Summa aurea*, c. 152, p 181: 'Spectat etiam ad eum ordinem iuris observare … [et] pacis compositioni semper debet intendere'.

[26] *Letters*, nn 157 and 158 (1165).

custody and subjected to efforts of persuasion. If this course failed, the weavers might be subjected to stripes, but not to death. Above all, he urged that the whole question should be debated and decided at a meeting of the bishops. In time, procedural law dealing with heresy would be the subject of a substantial body of canon law,[27] but in Foliot's time that lay in the future. Better to go slowly than to rush precipitously ahead and make a mistake. His response also reminds us once again that in the twelfth century, there was no body of consistory courts with the power to deal with questions like that posed by the allegedly heretical weavers. Foliot could not have recommended a canonical trial before his consistory court as a possibility. A century later he would have had that choice.

CONCLUSION

Foliot's references to the resources of the *ius commune* were cautious and incomplete, but still quite assertive. This appears to have been characteristic of the years before the publication of the Gregorian Decretals and the organization of a court-based system of ecclesiastical jurisdiction. Professor Brundage described it as the century before the 'Professionalization of the Canon Law'.[28] Part I of this book was written to follow that theme into legal practice. Although Foliot's reputation among historians is tied to the acrimony in his opposition to the actions of Archbishop Thomas Becket, for students of the profession of ecclesiastical law in England, it should also be remembered for what it stated and what it foretold about the coming of the classical canon law to England.

[27] X 5.7.1–16; Sext. 5.2.1–20; Clem. 5.3.1–3.
[28] J Brundage, 'Legal Learning and Professionalization of Canon Law', in H Vogt and M Münsteer-Swendsen (eds), *Law and Learning in the Middle Ages: Proceedings of the Second Carlsberg Academy Conference on Medieval Legal History 2005* (Copenhagen 2006), pp 5–28; see also Brand, *Origins*, 143.

7

William of Drogheda (d. 1245)

To include a man whose name identifies him with Ireland in a book devoted to English civilians may seem a stretch, but so William of Drogheda has normally been treated, and not without good reason. Everything that is known today about his life and work took place in England. He held the benefice of Grafton Underwood in Northamptonshire and he sought to be buried (together with his parents) in the priory church at Monk Sherborne in Hampshire. He was a teacher of law in Oxford, an association called to mind to the present day by the existence of 'Drawda Hall' in the High Street. Nothing but his name places him across the Irish Sea.

WILLIAM OF DROGHEDA'S REPUTATION

At least when compared with many other English ecclesiastical lawyers, William's life and career have not been neglected by historians. His name and work figure among those mentioned in the standard encyclopedic guides to the history of the canon law.[1] What has survived of his principal contribution to the development of the procedural law of the church, the *Summa aurea*, was published in a scholarly edition by Ludwig Wahrmund in 1914,[2] and several treatments touching upon William's career and historical importance have also appeared over the years.[3]

---

[1] E.g., J F von Schulte, *Die Geschichte der Quellen und Literatur des canonischen Rechts* (Stuttgart,1875), vol II, p 113.

[2] 'Die Summa aurea des Wilhelmus de Drokeda', in *Quellen zur Geschichte des römisch-kanonischen Prozesses im Mittelalter* (Innsbruck, 1905–31), vol 2:2, pp 1–432 [hereinafter abbreviated as Wahrmund, *Summa*].

[3] E.g., F de Zulueta, 'William of Drogheda', in J van Kan and F de Zulueta (eds), *Mélanges de droit romain dédiés à Georges Cornil* (Paris 1926), vol II, pp 641–57; J Sayers, 'William of Drogheda and the English canonists', in Peter Linehan (ed), *Proceedings of the Seventh International Congress of Medieval Canon Law* (Vatican City 1988), pp 205–22.

English legal historians have made use of Drogheda's career and work for their own purposes. The greatest among them, F W Maitland, invoked the *Summa aurea* to show that the claims to power of the medieval papacy were fully acknowledged in England in the early thirteenth century.[4] H G Richardson relied upon the text of Drogheda's treatise to assess the extent of civilian influences on the thirteenth-century treatise on English law known as *Bracton*.[5] More recently, Jane Sayers relied on his work to help provide information about the ways in which the jurisdiction of papal judges delegate was exercised in England during the early thirteenth century.[6]

Accounts of William's career have often been enlivened by comments assessing the quality of Drogheda's work and character – most of them distinctly negative. Hermann Kantorowicz, for instance, felt moved to single out the *Summa aurea* as 'one of the worst products of medieval legal literature' of which he was aware.[7] An earlier and equally learned German critic agreed: 'There is little good that can be said of it'.[8] Maitland himself added a more directly personal criticism; some of the suggestions Drogheda made for use by ecclesiastical lawyers, he thought, were 'none too honest'.[9] It has been easy to think it no great loss to the legal profession that Drogheda was murdered by one of his servants in 1245.

There are, however, good reasons for pausing before dismissing Drogheda's contribution to ecclesiastical law. The writers who lived nearer to his own time held a more favorable opinion of him. Joannes Andreae (*c.*1270–1348), the most famous canonist of the fourteenth century, described Drogheda's work as praiseworthy and productive.[10] Alberico Gentili (1552–1608), the great Italian jurist, who himself found a home in Oxford after being driven from the land of his birth, also praised the merits of his predecessor's work.[11] A late-thirteenth-century compiler of a basic collection of works on the procedural

---

4 'William of Drogheda and the Universal Ordinary', in *Roman Canon Law in the Church of England* (London 1898), pp 107–116.

5 'Azo, Drogheda, and Bracton' (1944) 59 *EHR* 22–47. See also H Kantorowicz, *Bractonian Problems* (Glasgow 1941), pp 27–36.

6 Sayers, *Papal Judges Delegate in the Province of Canterbury*, pp 54, 71, 109, 222, 232–33.

7 *Bractonian Problems*, p 29.

8 M A Bethmann-Hollweg (1795–1877), *Der Civilprozeß des gemeinen Rechts in geschichtlicher Entwicklung* (Bonn 1864–74), vol VI, p 126: 'Von der Schrift selbst ist nicht viel Gutes zu sagen'.

9 *Roman Canon Law*, p 110.

10 See Joannes Andreae, *Proemium* to Willelmus Durantis, *Speculum iudiciale* (Basle, 1574), v. *plurimis* [p 4 circa medium]: 'Secundum sit Gulielmus de Droreda [sic] Anglicus qui legens Oxoniae satis commendabilem et copiosum libellum composuit de iudiciorum ordine'.

11 See his *Laudes academiae Perusinae et Oxoniensis* (Hanover 1605), cited in Maitland, *Roman Canon Law*, p 108, n 2.

law of the church thought highly enough of Drogheda's *Summa* to include it with the admired works of Geoffrey of Trani and Tancred of Bologna.[12] The existence of these opinions at least suggests the possibility of a more positive assessment of Drogheda's work than he has received from modern historians. So does the recent discovery of two additional manuscripts of the *Summa aurea*, one from across the Channel in Bruges.[13] Four of the previously known six manuscripts were also located in Continental archives.[14] Evidently, he had a following outside England.

Other recent scholarship has also opened the door to a fresh look at the evidence. Substantial work, both books and articles, devoted to the development of procedural law in the *ius commune* has now been done,[15] and a useful research paper on the nature and sources of Drogheda's treatise has been written. It is a valuable, though unfortunately still unpublished, paper by Professor Rudi Lindner of the University of Michigan.[16] Arriving at a more balanced judgment of Drogheda's merits as a jurist is easier than it was one hundred years ago.

THE *SUMMA AUREA*

Drogheda planned for a treatise divided into six separate parts. They were to be devoted to: 1) jurisdiction, the parties and preparation for trials; 2) from the *litis contestatio* to the sentence; 3) sentences and their consequences; 4) appeals; 5) matrimonial causes; and 6) criminal prosecutions and canonical elections. These six subjects were specifically named in his Prologue.[17] However, if he completed more than the first of these before his untimely death, none of them has come down to us. We must use what there is to estimate what there might have been. Luckily, it is sufficient for us to form a good idea of the intent and the place of the work in the larger history of the law of the church. Five features of the work deserve particular attention. All of them require us to consider the date of its composition. It was written in the 1230s, almost contemporaneously with the appearance of the Gregorian Decretals in 1234.

---

[12] See Worcester Cathedral Library, MS F 74, fols 75–170v.

[13] See J Sayers, in *Oxford Dictionary of National Biography*, v. Drogheda.

[14] See Wahrmund, *Summa*, pp ix–xi.

[15] See Nörr, *Romanisch-kanonisches Prozessrecht*; Fowler-Magerl, *Ordines iudiciarii and Libelli de ordine iudiciorum*; Y Mausen, *Veritatis adiutor: la procédure du témoignage dans le droit savant et la pratique française (XIIe–XIVe siècles)* (Milan 2006).

[16] With characteristic modesty, he gave his paper the title: 'William of Drogheda: A Few Notes'. I thank Professor Lindner for his generosity in sharing it with me.

[17] Wahrmund, *Summa*, Proem (pp 6–7).

Its Use of Roman Law

Like most works of the *ius commune*, the text of the *Summa aurea* was filled with citations to legal authorities. Later on, a similar effort would have included citations to the great commentators – Bartolus or Panormitanus, for example. In the first half of the thirteenth century, however, references were more commonly limited to the texts of the Roman and canon laws, sometimes without even mentioning the *glossa ordinaria* that accompanied the texts. The great treatises lay in the future. In Drogheda's work, Professor Lindner has established the dominance of citations to the *Corpus iuris civilis*. There were citations to the Gregorian Decretals and Gratian's Decretum, even a very occasional mention of another jurist.[18] By Lindner's count, however, there were 4.7 times as many citations to Roman law texts as there were to canonical texts.[19] This preponderance takes the reader back to the days when the canon law was very much the junior partner to the elder of the two laws. Vacarius, a teacher of Roman law, had been the dominant figure in England. Even the law of marriage, which increasingly fell within the church's jurisdiction, was built mostly from the Roman law, except occasionally where a specific ecclesiastical decision asserted the necessity of altering the law.[20] Drogheda's approach to law in this treatise makes a sharp reminder of the civil law's initial dominance in the formation of the *ius commune*. That dominance was overcome, but only gradually.

Its Procedural Focus

The extent of the attention that was commonly paid to procedural law during the twelfth and thirteenth centuries is also a point of importance. The proliferation of *ordines iudiciarii* and works similar to Drogheda's responded to a need. Part of the need was caused by the character of the classical texts. The Roman jurists had not separated procedure from substantive law. The procedure used at the time the texts in the Digest were written was also quite different from that which had come to prevail by Justinian's time. Applicable texts were scattered throughout the Digest and Codex. They had not been put into titles of their own,[21] and there was a consequent need for more usable presentations.

---

[18] Ibid., tit 28, a reference to the *glossa ordinaria* of Bernard of Parma; see also Sayers, *Papal Judges Delegate*.

[19] He was described as 'primarily a legist' in de Zulueta, 'William of Drogheda', p 655.

[20] See L J M Waelkens, 'Medieval Family and Marriage Law: From Actions of Status to Legal Doctrine', in J W Cairns and P J du Plessis (eds), *The Creation of the* Ius Commune: *From Casus to* Regula (Edinburgh 2010), pp 103–25.

[21] P Stein, *Roman Law in European History* (Cambridge 1999), pp 57–59.

Drogheda responded to it. Another part of the need for procedural works was caused by new ways of thinking about settling disputes and trying criminals.[22] Ordeals were being abandoned. Regular courts of law were coming into existence. The search for workable rules of evidence was underway. The compilation of written records of court proceedings was required.[23] Drogheda's work should be understood in the context of these fundamental developments in Western law. His contributions were overtaken in due course – notably by the elephantine treatise compiled by Willelmus Durantis (1231–96), the *Speculum iudiciale*. Filled with forms and miscellaneous information, some of it seemingly compiled at random, it became the standard resource of ecclesiastical lawyers. That was one reason Drogheda's *Summa aurea* was not printed before modern times, but if seen in context, it should be admired as one part of a great and largely successful development in the law.

Its Prolixity

Drogheda has been criticized for disorganization and loquaciousness in the presentation of his material.[24] At one point, even the usually even-tempered Professor Lindner described him as 'a windbag'. That characterization is not without support in the treatise. For example, the *Summa aurea* contains forty-three different forms for the appointment of proctors,[25] and the Prologue is excessive in discursiveness even by the elastic standards of the time. Some of the many libels for which forms are given – for instance one complaining against an impeder of the complainant's use of a privy – cannot have been in common use.[26] It is hard to explain, much less to justify, the multiplication of forms found in the treatise. What can be said in partial mitigation is that the treatise was written at a time when jurisdictional boundaries were more fluid than they later became. It was also a period open to development in the received law.[27] There was room for experiment, and Drogheda seized the opportunity. He may have gone too far, but he could have believed full

---

[22] A Tardif, *La procédure civile et criminelle aux XIIIe et XIVe siècles* (Paris 1885), pp 1–4; J P Lévy, *Le problème de la preuve dans les droits savants du Moyen Age* [Recueils de la Société Jean Bodin 17] (1965), pp 137–67.

[23] Most particularly by the enactment by the Fourth Lateran Council (1215) of the constitution *Quoniam contra falsam* (X 2.19.11).

[24] E.g., de Zulueta, 'William of Drogheda', p 646.

[25] Wahrmund, *Summa*, tits 99–141.

[26] Ibid., tit 245.

[27] See T Wetzstein, 'Prozeßschriftgut im Mittelalter – einfürende Überlegungen', in S Lepsius and T Wetzstein (eds), *Als die Welt in die Akten kam: Prozeßschriftgut im europäischen Mittelalter* (Frankfurt 2008), pp 1–27.

discussion with illustrations would be useful, and this would not necessarily have been obvious self-deception. He was also not the only author who could be charged with verbal excess. In attention to the virtues of clarity and conciseness, he stands somewhere between the economical Tancred of Bologna[28] and the truly unstoppable Durantis.

Its Scholasticism

A large part of the *Summa aurea* is taken up by *Quaestiones*, a standard method of presenting information in the thirteenth century. Gratian had used it, and Thomas Aquinas honed it into a repetitive art form in the *Summa theologiae*. In Drogheda's work, to take one example, Titles 400–426, which deal with judicial treatment of papal rescripts of justice, is divided into twenty-six separate *quaestiones*. Some are quite short, but most of them are divided into statements of an affirmative opinion, followed by a contrary opinion, ending with Drogheda's solution. So, for example, it was asked: if a papal rescript contained a *suggestio falsi*, could the judge proceed to hear and determine the cause nonetheless. Authorities for and against were presented. Then the jurist 'solved' the problem, in this case by distinguishing between judges with ordinary jurisdiction and judges with delegated jurisdiction. In other words, the *quaestio* and the *solutio* came out of the Schools. We cannot lay blame at Drogheda's door for this feature of his work, though it is far from certain that his solution to this problem carried the day and it is true that most of the medieval jurists did not adopt this artificial way of presenting the subject. It is also worth noting that some (though not all) of the 'none too honest' tips to which Maitland took exception resulted from the scholastic habit of advancing arguments pro and con.[29]

Its Practicality

Despite its connection with the Schools, the *Summa aurea* was not a purely academic effort. Drogheda himself took an active role as a lawyer in the *forum externum*, and his treatise was filled with observations about what commonly happened in courts and with advice about how to proceed in them. For instance, he advised advocates to make sure they received their professional fee before the end of a proceeding.[30] He tackled this touchy subject with good

---

28 See his 'Ordo iudiciarius' in Bermann, *Libri de iudiciorum ordine*, pp 89–316.
29 E.g., Wahrmund, *Summa*, tit 64, dealing with the multiplication of legal actions based on a single wrong.
30 Ibid., tit 95.

sense, not allowing himself to get caught up in speculation about how to deal
with the ancient prohibition forbidding lawyers from demanding any payment
for their services.[31] Similarly, Drogheda advised his readers to avoid the use
of the civilian *aestimatio* of damages in the spiritual forum.[32] To do so, he
noted, would risk the introduction of a royal writ of prohibition that would
bring the case to an unnecessary halt. This was the identical advice given
two centuries later under similar circumstances by William Lyndwood.[33] If
Drogheda sometimes went too far in this concern for practicality, as he did
in advising lawyers to use deliberate and unnecessary delay in litigation as a
tactic to wear down any opponent who had a meritorious case,[34] one can only
concede that Maitland's estimate was not wholly wrong. In its better side, however, it provides an early example of one of the continuing admirable features
of the profession of ecclesiastical law in England – a preference for success in
result over purity in theory.

---

[31] Cod. 2.13.15.
[32] Wahrmund, *Summa*, tit 65.
[33] Lyndwood, *Provinciale*, p 314, v. *perjurio*.
[34] Wahrmund, *Summa*, tit 66.

8

John de Burgh (d. 1398)

Knowledge of the law of the church has always existed outside the world of practicing lawyers, and the uses to which the canon law was put in earlier centuries were so varied that only casting a wide net can do justice to the subject's history. Of this there are few better examples than that of John de Burgh. Author of what his entry in the *Oxford Dictionary of National Biography* (*ODNB*) describes as 'a very influential work of pastoral theology entitled *Pupilla oculi*', Burgh knew his canon law. The description in the *ODNB* is not inaccurate. However, it does not do justice to the author's knowledge of the church's laws or to his place in securing the law's application. The *Pupilla oculi* digested complex and sometimes confusing legal texts, providing usable summaries of their meaning, adding learned authorities to support them, and giving advice about how they could be put to use. It was widely used.

The starting point for understanding the work's importance must be a recognition of the rudimentary nature of the formal education required of the parochial clergy during the Middle Ages. 'Precious little' is how the foremost student of the subject summed up the quantity of learning candidates were obliged to acquire before they were ordained.[1] No time spent at a university was necessary. No training in the law of the church was required. With Burgh's treatise in hand, however, the men charged with the administration of parochial life might still learn the basic rules of the canon law and put them into practice. It was training on the job, no doubt. It may have slighted the law's

---

[1] L Boyle, 'Aspects of Clerical Education in fourteenth-century England', in *Acta Vol IV: The Fourteenth Century*, Center for Medieval and Early Renaissance Studies, SUNY (Binghampton, NY 1977), reprinted in L Boyle, *Pastoral Care, Clerical Education and Canon Law, 1200–1400* (London 1981), IX, pp 19–32. See also J Shinners and W Dohar (eds), *Pastors and the Care of Souls in Medieval England* (Notre Dame, IN 1998), pp 33–38; J Goering, 'The Changing Face of the Village Parish: The Thirteenth Century', in J Raftis (ed), *Pathways to Medieval Peasants* (Toronto 1981), pp 323–33.

nuances. But it was a vast improvement on ignorance, and that is the reason that Burgh's contribution counted for as much as it did.

BURGH'S LIFE AND CAREER

Many aspects of Burgh's life remain unknown – even to the date of both his birth and his death. We know only a few things with any certainty.[2] A native of Lincolnshire, he entered the University of Cambridge and had proceeded MA by 1370. He then remained at the University for eighteen years. Elected to the normal two-year term as chancellor of the university in 1384, by that year he had received a doctorate in theology.[3] Whether he studied the Roman and canon laws during that long time span is uncertain, but it would not have been unusual for a student in the arts or theological faculties to have done so,[4] and this common practice may explain the familiarity Burgh had acquired with the *ius commune* by the time he left the university in 1388. Moreover, he himself would have witnessed legal skills being put to use. He served as proctor of the university in 1370, and as chancellor he would have presided over a court governed by the civil law. In these offices, Burgh would have had the opportunity to learn to use the legal texts and the works of commentators on them.

Burgh's move out of university circles was certainly something he desired. During the decade before he left he sought to obtain a benefice by petitioning Pope Gregory XI,[5] and by 1388 he had become rector of Collingham in the diocese of York. Retaining that benefice when he added another, he became vicar of Newark in the same diocese ten years later. For all we know, he lived out his life as a country parson in the north of England. Even that conclusion, however, rests simply on assumptions based on the offices he held. We know nothing of his activities there, not even the circumstances or the place of his death. No known monument to him remains to us. What marks him out as worthy of attention is the composition of the *Pupilla oculi*, which took place before he left Cambridge.

---

[2] See J Goering, 'Burgh John (*fl.* 1370–1398)', in *Oxford Dictionary of National Biography*, Oxford University Press, 2004, www.oxforddnb.com/view/article/2912, accessed July 14, 2015.

[3] A Emden, *Biographical Register of the University of Cambridge to 1500* (Cambridge 1963), p 107.

[4] J Mullinger, *The University of Cambridge from the Earliest Times to the Royal Injunctions of 1535* (Cambridge 1911, reprint 1969), pp 140–43; D Leader, *History of the University of Cambridge, Vol 1: The University to 1546* (Cambridge 1988), pp 200–01.

[5] See entry in 'Notes on Cambridge Clerks petitioning for Benefices, 1370–1399' (1943–1945) 20 *Bulletin of the Institute of Historical Research*, 83.

THE PLACE OF THE *PUPILLA OCULI* IN THE LITERATURE
OF THE *IUS COMMUNE*

Burgh's treatise belongs within the broad category of medieval pastoral manuals meant for use by the clergy.[6] They are sometimes described as *Summae confessorum* because of their utility in the internal forum of auricular confession.[7] Most of them sought to summarize the church's penitential and sacramental laws so that they could be understood and applied in practice, as Burgh's work did.[8] The utility of these works was not limited to confession, however. They were used to good advantage, for example, in preparing sermons,[9] and they provided instructions for the clergy on how to live up to legal standards. It would not be off the mark to describe them as vehicles by which the medieval church's doctrines and laws were taken from the schools and brought into parishes. Their authors mostly eschewed the juristic speculation and debates that were familiar (and appropriate) parts of university education. Whenever Burgh did allude to disagreements found in the texts or to debates among the commentators, he did so briefly and also stated briefly his own view of which was the better opinion.

The title of Burgh's work – an odd one today, though no stranger to the literature coming out of the European schools – meant 'apple of the eye', as in 'He kept him as the apple of his eye' (Deut 32:10). Its title made a connection with a previous work that had provided Burgh's starting point: the *Oculus sacerdotis* of William Paull (or William Pagula, as he was called by the scholar who had the most to do with bringing Paull's work to the attention of modern historians, Leonard Boyle).[10] Boyle downplayed the contributions made by Burgh's work, apparently regarding it as a derivative work, and perhaps a needless one at that.[11] However, the view of most scholars (myself included) is

6 An instructive essay is J Goering, 'Leonard E. Boyle and the Invention of *Pastoralia*', in R Stansbury (ed), *Companion to Pastoral Care in the Late Middle Ages (1200–1500)* (Leiden and Boston, MA 2010), pp 7–20.

7 Examples with discussion are found in A Van Hove, *Prolegomena ad codicem iuris canonici* (Mechelen and Rome 1945), pp 512–17.

8 The most recent and complete treatment related to Burgh is H Kelly, 'Penitential Theology and Law at the Turn of the Fifteenth Century', in A Firey (ed), *A New History of Penance* (Leiden and Boston, MA 2008), pp 239–317.

9 See, e.g., S Wenzel (ed and trans), *Fasciculus Morum: A Fourteenth-Century Preacher's Handbook* (University Park, PA 1989).

10 See L Boyle, 'The *Oculus Sacerdotis* and Some Other Works of William of Pagula' (1955) 5 *Transactions of the Royal Historical Society*, 5th series, 81–110, reprinted in his *Pastoral Care*, No IV. See also J Baker, 'William Paull', in *Monuments of Endlesse Labours*, pp 9–15.

11 For Boyle's views, see '*Oculus Sacerdotis*', pp 84–87. His opinion was also shared by Cardinal Gasquet; see his *Old English Bible and other Essays* (London 1897), pp 195–198.

that the *Pupilla oculi* is a distinct improvement on its predecessor.[12] The topics are more economically arranged. They are easier to find. Their exposition is clearer. And its statements of the church's law are better established by textual references. Whether either of the two men would have regarded the other as a rival or as a co-worker, we can only speculate. They did not meet. Paull died in 1332. However, the verdict of the marketplace supports Burgh's higher reputation. Although both works are found in many manuscript copies from the Middle Ages, including a handsome 'showpiece' manuscript of Burgh's work,[13] only the *Pupilla oculi* reached print. Paull's treatise did not. Burgh's work was printed several times in the first quarter of the sixteenth century, including editions published both in England and on the Continent (Paris, Rouen, and Strasbourg).[14]

In common with Paull's treatise, the conclusions in Burgh's text rested on recognized authorities. He cited legal sources for every topic he covered, though without the accumulation of authorities found in many of the canonical treatises from the later Middle Ages. Normally the *Pupilla oculi* provided only one relevant text for each conclusion. They came from a range of sources. The Bible and works by theologians appeared often; also Church fathers such as St. Augustine and more recent theologians like Thomas Aquinas. Burgh also cited Roman law texts occasionally,[15] though the religious nature of his subject discouraged frequent reference to them. The majority of his references were to the *Corpus iuris canonici* – from Gratian's *Decretum* to the *Extravagantes* – and also to the best known of the commentaries on them. He referred repeatedly to the works of Hostiensis, Innocent IV, Joannes Andreae, and Raymund of Peñaforte. He also did not neglect the provincial constitutions of the province of Canterbury. They had an immediate impact on parochial life in England, and he was right to refer to them.

---

[12] See H Davis, 'The Canon Law in England' (1914) 34 *Zeitschrift der Savigny-Stiftung für Rechtsgeschichte, Kan. Abt.* 349–50; W Pantin, *The English Church in the Fourteenth Century* (Notre Dame, IN 1962), pp 213–14; J Hughes, *Pastors and Visionaries: Religion and Secular Life in late Medieval Yorkshire* (Woodbridge 1998), pp 193–94; Kelly, 'Penitential Theology', pp 243–44.

[13] Kate Harris, 'The Patronage and Dating of Longleat House MS 24, a Prestige Copy of the *Pupilla Oculi* illuminated by the Master of the *Troilus* Frontispiece', in F Riddy (ed), *Prestige, Authority and Power in late-medieval Manuscripts and Texts'* (York 2000), pp 35–54.

[14] The entry in the ODNB states that it was printed at least four times before 1500, but I think this must have been a slip. See, e g, *British Museum General Catalogue of Printed Books*, vol 30 (London 1955), p 98, listing editions published in 1510, 1514, 1516, 1518, and 1521; the last edition to which I have seen a reference was published in London in 1590.

[15] E.g., Pt VIII, ch 15, lit B (citation to Dig. 25.4.1).

THE CONTENTS OF THE *PUPILLA OCULI*

Burgh divided his work into ten Parts of unequal length.[16] They were: I) The Sacraments in General; II) Baptism; III) Confirmation; IV) The Eucharist; V) Penitence and Sentences of Excommunication; VI) Extreme Unction; VII) Holy Orders; VIII) Marriage and Matrimonial Causes; IX) Tithes, Sanctuary, Last Wills and Testaments, Clerical Residence, and Similar Matters; and X) Practical Theology, including the Ten Commandments, the Seven Deadly Sins, and Works of Mercy. Each Part was then divided into separate chapters, and within each chapter separate letters were assigned to subjects as they were discussed. Thus, in the copy printed in Paris in 1521, the treatment of the rules regulating clerical residence with women is found in Part VII, Chapter 10, Letter L. A serviceable index in this edition also helped an uninstructed clerical reader to find the specific subjects he required.

What most immediately strikes a modern reader of Burgh's treatment of his subjects is the economy and clarity of his exposition. Compare, for example, his treatment of the prohibition mentioned against clerics living together with women with the fuller coverage in the Decretals. Burgh's text gives a reason for the rule (avoidance of the temptation to commit the sin of adultery) and a statement of one of its exceptions (women related to a cleric in close degrees of consanguinity). But that is about all. The same subject was dealt with at great length in the formal texts of the canon law, and Burgh provided a reference to two of them in his own treatment of the subject (Dist. 37 c. 27 and X 3.2.9). However, he did not go into detail. It was not a classroom exercise. Nor was it a preparation for litigation. It was an exposition of the basic law on the subject and a plain statement of the reasons supporting it.

Burgh's treatment of clandestine marriages contains a good example of his normal approach. Under the medieval canon law, an agreement made by words of present consent was a true and indissoluble marriage. A secret marriage, even if entered into without ceremony or witnesses, bound the contracting parties in conscience. Without doubt, it was an awkward law in practice – 'no masterpiece of human wisdom', as Maitland once described it.[17] Here, however, is what Burgh told his clerical readers. Make an investigation of your own, he wrote, and if the spousals were not celebrated *in facie ecclesie* but were contracted publicly before others, they could not be dissolved by the mutual agreement of the parties. The matter must be referred to a court for decision. If, however, they were contracted entirely secretly, they could be

---

[16] For example, Pt VI contains only two chapters; Pt VIII has eighteen.
[17] Pollock and Maitland, *History of English Law*, vol II, p 368.

dissolved without a judgment of the church.[18] Practical advice, one might call it, although Burgh supported it only by a reference to one commentator on Peter Lombard's *Sentences*.

Among the matters covered by Burgh's treatise is a lengthy treatment of Magna Carta.[19] Inclusion of the Charter in a religious treatise may seem surprising today, but in the context of its own times, it fitted. Led by Archbishop Stephen Langton, the bishops had taken a hand in its formulation in 1215, though just how strong a hand it was remains a matter of uncertainty. Successive archbishops had later issued sentences of excommunication against any person who infringed the Charter's provisions.[20] Among those subjected to these sentences were all persons who acted against Clause One's promise of the freedom for the English Church, but the sanction was not limited to them. The sanction of excommunication extended to all. As Professor Cheney put it, by the start of the fourteenth century, 'Magna Carta had come to stay, and the English hierarchy was committed to safeguarding it.'[21]

CONCLUSION

'Neither English university produced a lawyer of international reputation during the Middle Ages'.[22] That has been the verdict of most historians of the canon law, and the example of John de Burgh does not disprove it. No mention of *Pupilla oculi* appears in today's standard works on the history of the canon law.[23] However, what Burgh sought to accomplish he achieved. His work provided the means by which basic rules of law for the administration of a medieval parish and the conduct of a Christian life could be found and put to use – no mean accomplishment.

---

[18] Pt VIII, ch 2, lit L: 'Si autem secrete contracta fuerint sine iudicio ecclesie dissolvi possunt secundum Richardum super iiii, dist. xxvii'.

[19] Pt V, ch 22 is devoted to it.

[20] E.g., Wilkins, *Concilia*, vol II, pp 240–42: 'Sententia excommunicationis per Robertum Cantuariensem archiepiscopum lata contra ... infringentes articulos chartarum, scilicet Magnae Cartae' (1298); see also D Carpenter, *Magna Carta* (London 2015), pp 422–23.

[21] C Cheney, 'The Church and Magna Carta' (1965) 65 *Theology* 265–72 at 272.

[22] Leader, *History of the University of Cambridge*, p 199.

[23] He is mentioned only in H Hurter, *Nomenclator literarius theologiae catholicae theologos* (Innsbrook 1903–13), vol II, pp 714–15.

9

Adam Usk (d. 1430)

The study of the Roman and canon laws at a university in medieval England – and indeed in later centuries – could lead eventually to high office in church or state.[1] With luck, even the episcopal bench was an attainable goal for talented civilians who had chosen to follow their study with entry into holy orders. Perhaps it was inevitable, therefore – certainly it was natural – that failure to attain the episcopate, or at least something close to it, could lead to ever more feverish efforts to secure benefices and finally to disappointment and bitterness among able men who had been denied promotion. Equally, however, the experience could lead to humility and acceptance in the face of misfortune. Of both these consequences there are few better examples than Adam Usk. His career and his writings are full of fascination for anyone who takes an interest of the history of the law of the English Church. The famous *Chronicle* he wrote opens windows on that subject,[2] as it does on many of the events surrounding the deposition of King Richard II and the difficult years that followed the accession of King Henry IV.

ADAM'S LIFE AND CAREER

He was born in the village of Usk in Monmouthshire, and attracted early the patronage of Edmund Mortimer, earl of March and lord of Usk, who sponsored his entry to Oxford University and supported him while he was a student there.[3] The exact chronology of his academic career is

---

[1] R Storey, *Diocesan Administration in Fifteenth-Century England*, 2d edn (York 1972), pp 13–18; R Davies, 'The Episcopate', in C Clough (ed), *Profession, Vocation, and Culture in Later Medieval England* (Liverpool 1982), pp 51–89 at 64–65.

[2] C Given-Wilson (ed and trans), *The Chronicle of Adam Usk 1377–1421* (Oxford 1997).

[3] *Chronicle*, pp 158–59.

uncertain.[4] Like his support from the Earl, we know about many of the steps
he took at Oxford only because he mentioned them as asides in the *Chronicle*
he later compiled. We do know that he was listed as a Bachelor of Law in
1388, and had become *Doctor utriusque iuris* by 1390.[5] Prior to leaving Oxford
to serve as an advocate in the Court of Arches, a step he took in 1395, he had
also held what he himself described as a chair in civil law there.[6] The move to
London was a normal next step for any aspiring civilian. There his work at the
Court of Arches brought him into contact with Thomas Arundel, archbishop
of Canterbury, who supported him and whom he supported in his account of
the archbishop's tribulations and exile that occurred in Richard II's 'Revenge
Parliament' of September 1397.[7] After Thomas died in 1414, Adam described
the Archbishop as 'the light and delight of church and clergy and the unshake-
able pillar of the Christian faith'.[8] On a mundane level, Adam had him to
thank for the bestowal of at least three benefices and, as he ruefully recalled
later, of the promise of even more.[9] He was, he said, 'hoping to be promoted
to greater things'. These hopes were not to be fulfilled. Among the reasons for
this, Adam blamed prejudice against the Welsh. It was the most prominent
factor.

There may have been more than simple prejudice involved, however. At
the very least, Adam sympathized with the outbreak of Owen Glendower's
revolt in the fall of 1400, and he may have done more.[10] Whatever the reasons,
in early 1402 Adam left England for the Roman court. There he hoped to be
able to take advantage of his talents as a lawyer, and in this goal he succeeded.
Having passed what he described as 'a rigorous examination' of his legal knowledge administered by the Cardinal who was to be the future Pope Innocent
VII, he was named papal chaplain and one of the Auditors of Causes in the
Apostolic Palace.[11] Within a week, he noted with satisfaction, 'thirty major
causes' had been handed to him for decision. However, Adam fared less well

---

[4] The standard course of study is well described in Brundage, *The Medieval Origins of the Legal Profession*, pp 248–71.

[5] The slightly conflicting evidence for the steps and their dates is stated and discussed in Professor Given-Wilson's Introduction to *Chronicle*, pp xiv–xvii; see also in his 'Usk, Adam (c.1350–1430)', in ODNB (2004); online edn, Jan 2009, http://oxforddnb.com/, accessed June 16, 2016.

[6] *Chronicle*, pp 152–53, 250–55; see also Logan, *The Medieval Court of Arches*, p 221.

[7] See Margaret Aston, *Thomas Arundel: A Study in Church Life in the Reign of Richard II* (Oxford 1967), pp 368–69 and 378.

[8] *Chronicle*, pp 246–47.

[9] The best record of the benefices he received is contained in A Emden, *Biographical Register of the University of Oxford to A.D. 1500* (Oxford 1959), vol III, pp 1937–38.

[10] Introduction, *Chronicle*, p xxiii.

[11] *Chronicle*, pp 154–55.

with the other ambition that had spurred his decision to leave England – the attainment of the bishopric. This was, his modern biographer tells us, something 'he clearly regarded as his due'.[12] He concluded that he stood a better chance for securing it in Rome than he had in London. But it was not to be. Despite several near misses, no miter came his way. He left Rome in 1406, and after fruitless wandering, intrigue with some of Glendower's supporters, and deprivation of virtually all his English benefices, in March of 1411 he received the King's permission and returned to take up his career again as an advocate in London. He still hoped for promotion after his return, but he spent more time in Wales and may even have contemplated entry into a monastic house there. He died in 1430 and was buried in the parish church at Usk, where his grave was marked by an epitaph in Welsh. It remains in the church today, attached to its fifteenth-century choir screen.[13] His will, making his kinsman Edward ap Adam his executor, was proved on March 26, 1430.[14] All of the twenty-one legatees named in it were Welsh.

ADAM AS A LAWYER

Adam's *Chronicle* and his role in political events in England have deservedly claimed the lion's share of the attention historians have paid to him. It is indeed an interesting account, containing both great events and a focus on the author's personal experiences that is unusual for the times.[15] It also includes a compelling description of life in the Eternal City. Adam was fascinated by the papal ceremonies, but repelled by the venality of the papal court. 'Everything was for sale' there, he recalled.[16] For present purposes, the *Chronicle*'s most important feature is the material it contains that aids us in tracing the place of ecclesiastical law in English history. Most of it has attracted little or no notice among the many historians who have used the *Chronicle*. But its contents repay focusing briefly on that subject.

Probably the best example of the utility of taking this approach comes from Adam's account of the most dramatic event recorded in it – the deposition of Richard II. Finding legal justification for this step was no easy matter. Adam's *Chronicle* records that the solution the leaders hit upon was to put the question to a group of doctors (of law) and bishops. He himself was one of

---

[12] See Introduction, *Chronicle*, pp xxiii–xxiv.
[13] See J Morris-Jones, 'Adam Usk's Epitaph' (1921) 31 *Y Cymmrodor* 112–34.
[14] It is printed; E Owen, 'The Will of Adam of Usk' (1903) 18 *EHR* 316–17.
[15] E Jacob, *Essays in the Conciliar Epoch* (Manchester 1963), pp 24–25.
[16] *Chronicle*, pp 160–61.

them.[17] They obliged, basing their conclusion on the decree of Pope Innocent IV issued at the Council of Lyons that had declared the deposition of the Emperor Frederick II. That decree had been included in the *Liber sextus*,[18] and its wording, including some of what appeared only in the *glossa ordinaria* or in other canonical commentary on the decree, duly appeared – first in the decree of deposition and then in the abdication that Richard II was obliged to read before Parliament.[19] Among other things, he was obliged to confess himself a *rex inutilis*, subject to removal from his throne under one current reading of the canonical authorities.[20] Traditionally historians have paid little attention to the use that was made of the canon law on this occasion, and it is undeniable that the armed revolt led by the future Henry IV was counted most in securing the result.[21] Even so, as the careful research of Gerard Caspary has established, one lesson taught by the incident was that it was 'considered normal to state the terms of the problem in the vocabulary of canon law'.[22] It provided the legal justification. That is how Adam perceived it and also how he presented it.

As one might expect from his primary profession, reference to authorities found in the *ius commune* came naturally to Adam. This habit of mind appears throughout his *Chronicle*. He described a legal representative as a *procurator*, not an attorney.[23] For him, treason was *laesio maiestatis*, and the penalty for failing to prove a formal accusation in law was *pena talionis*.[24] His references to legal questions involving oaths come from the titles *De iureiurando* found in the Roman and canon laws.[25] Of course, these terms were not unknown to English common lawyers, and occasionally they used them. Still, their preponderance in Adam's *Chronicle* points to the importance of his training in

---

[17] *Chronicle*, pp 62–63.
[18] Sext 2.14.2.
[19] *Rotuli Parlaimentorum* (London 1783), vol III, ff 416–17.
[20] On the development of this concept, see E Peters, *The Shadow King: Rex Inutilis in Medieval Law and Literature, 751–1327* (New Haven, CT 1970).
[21] See, e.g., G Lapsley, 'The Parliamentary Title of Henry IV', 44 (1934) *English Historical Review* 423–49, reprinted in G Lapsley, *Crown Community and Parliament in the later Middle Ages*, in H Cam and G Barraclough (eds) (Oxford 1951), pp 272–340, at 288–91, 310–21; G Harriss, *Shaping the Nation: England 1360–1461* (Oxford 2005), pp 488–95.
[22] G Caspary, 'The Deposition of Richard II and the Canon Law', in S Kuttner and J Ryan (eds), *Proceedings of the Second International Congress of Medieval Canon Law* (Vatican City 1965), pp 189–201, at 201. Some notice is taken, however, of Adam of Usk's account and Caspary's contribution in what is now the authoritative work on the reign: N Saul, *Richard II* (New Haven, CT and London 1997), pp 418–19 and also in M Bennett, *Richard II and the Revolution of 1399* (Stroud 1999), pp 175–76.
[23] *Chronicle*, pp 24–25.
[24] Ibid., pp 242–43; 122–23.
[25] Ibid., pp 120–21. See Dig. 12.2.1–42; X 2.24.1–36.

the civil law and perhaps to a civilian's belief in their continued relevance in England.

This habit of making explicit reference to the *ius commune* carried over into many of the subjects Adam chose to raise alongside his narrative of the great events of his day. For instance, he interrupted his account to describe three disputes over heraldry heard in the Court of Chivalry in 1401. Here there was a special reason: Adam himself had been counsel in one of them. He recorded that its outcome turned upon the law of possessory interdicts found in Roman law, and a dispute about its fit with the facts of the dispute occasioned what he described as 'tumultuous argument'.[26] Likewise, he described more than a few incidents from his career where he himself had been consulted on points of civil and canon law. For instance, the prior of Charterhouse near London had asked him whether a monk who voluntarily starved himself to death should be accorded Christian burial or should instead be treated as a suicide.[27] Unfortunately Adam did not leave even a hint of what his answer had been. Thankfully, the monk had not died. Adam was, however, more forthcoming about the results that followed objections raised in the 1414 Parliament against 'the several excesses, extortions and omissions' alleged to have marred the exercise of English church's jurisdiction over last wills and testaments.[28] Here he provided detail about the reforms that were adopted in Convocation after the King had determined that the subject should be dealt with there.[29]

The *Chronicle* included several direct references to the canon and Roman laws. Adam did not think them out of place. He was not above citing the texts of the *Corpus iuris canonici* in ways that showed his lawyerly skill in their manipulation.[30] He also used them quite broadly in his narrative. In a discussion with envoys from the duke of Bavaria over the current election of an Emperor, for example, he reminded them of the exclusive right of the pope to judge the qualifications of the candidate elected, a right that was asserted in a text from the *Liber sextus* and endorsed by the commentary of Joannes Andreae.[31] Nothing came of it, however. The bishop of Hereford had quickly told him to be silent – a rebuke he also recorded. Similarly, Adam thought it relevant to cite a text from the Roman law's Codex in support of a dispute in Parliament about habitual royal largess. The Commons had objected to overly generous grants of Crown land. Adam seized upon the civil law's text

---

[26] *Chronicle*, pp 132–35.
[27] Ibid., pp 126–27.
[28] Ibid., pp 250–51.
[29] They are more fully set out in Wilkins, *Concilia*, vol III, 358–68.
[30] See *Chronicle*, pp 96–97, dealing with the law of costs in the ecclesiastical forum.
[31] Sext 2.14.2; Joannes Andreae was responsible for the *glossa ordinaria* on the texts of the Sext.

for an answer: subjects should not be allowed to 'impose restraints upon the king's natural benevolence'.[32] He was also not at all hesitant about citing the canon law as relevant to the treatment of the clergy in the temporal forum. The imprisonment of bishops was the issue of the day. Adam brought forward relevant texts from the Gregorian Decretals and the Clementines to prove its illegality and to condemn its occasional use in English practice.[33]

CONCLUSION

A significant though perhaps obvious point about Adam's life and career ought to be made in closing. He made a career as an ecclesiastical lawyer in England, France, and Italy; even in the highest ecclesiastical court in Europe. Everywhere, he had found clients who were willing to pay for his expertise. He did not himself make much of this aspect of his life in the *Chronicle*; indeed he mentioned it as a cause of regret. It was a necessity, something forced on him by his long-continued failure to secure a bishopric. Nonetheless, what might be called the international dimension of one Englishman's career remains impressive, even surprising. The legal connections between England and the Continent evident in Adam's career of course point to a time before the sixteenth-century break with the papacy, and they also point to the strength and ubiquity of the European *ius commune*, a strength that outlasted that break. What we must regret, therefore, is the loss of the records of the Court of Arches in London from the time when Adam was a practicing advocate there. They would have told us more about his career, and they would also have advanced what we know about the history of the *ius commune* in England.

---

[32] *Chronicle*, pp 82–83; the text was Cod. 10.12.2.
[33] *Chronicle*, pp 92–93; the texts were X 5.12.6 and Clem. 5.8.1.

10

Richard Rudhale (d. 1476)

A book devoted to notable English civilians ought to make room for at least one student of the law whose subsequent career was spent outside the academy and outside the law courts. Attention is particularly appropriate if the candidate made regular use of his training in law. The life of the English church and nation has been touched in many ways by the contributions of law graduates who made 'conventional' careers – rising to become deans or bishops or serving in more humble positions. It is quite remarkable how many of them there have been over the centuries. Medieval lawyers seem actually to have formed the majority of the graduates who became deans, archdeacons, and residentiary canons in English cathedrals, even in some of the smaller dioceses.[1] At Chichester, for example, the modern edition of Le Neve's *Fasti* shows that fully twenty-one of the twenty-nine university graduates who qualified as members of the cathedral chapter during the fifteenth century were lawyers by training.[2] At Salisbury cathedral, a slightly larger establishment, the equivalent figure for the same period is fifty-three lawyers as against twenty-one theologians and others.[3] For the diocese of Hereford, where Richard Rudhale had his career, during the same period fully twenty of the holders of dignities came equipped with a law degree, whereas only fourteen held degrees in theology or some other subject.[4]

[1] Other historians have made the same observation; e.g., D Lepine, *Brotherhood of Canons Serving God: English Secular Cathedrals in the later Middle Ages* (Woodbridge 1995), p 161.

[2] This includes the deans, archdeacons, precentors, chancellors, and treasurers. There were, however, also twenty-two men for whom no university degree could be given. See J Horn (ed), *Le Neve, Fasti Ecclesiae Anglicanae 1300–1541, VII Chichester Diocese* (London 1964), pp 4–14.

[3] The list includes deans, subdeans, archdeacons, precentors, chancellors, and treasurers; for thirty-two holders of these offices, no degree was listed. See J Horn (ed), *Le Neve, Fasti Ecclesiae Anglicanae 1300–1541, III Salisbury Diocese* (London 1962), pp 3–21.

[4] The list includes deans, archdeacons, precentors, treasurers, and chancellors; for twenty-five holders no degree was listed. See J Horn (ed), *Le Neve, Fasti Ecclesiae Anglicanae, 1300–1541, II Hereford Diocese* (London 1962), pp 3–14.

If the preponderance in the numbers of these lawyers attracts the immediate interest of modern ecclesiastical lawyers, it cannot fully satisfy a natural curiosity about the careers of these men. We rarely know much about the details involved. Did they lose contact with the law, as modern graduates often lose touch with the subject they read at university? Or did they carry that learning into their careers, as many (though not all) modern law graduates do if they enter the world of commerce or manufacture? In other words, can we tell whether the graduates made use of the church's law in performing duties outside strictly legal work? Did it matter?

The career of the man who is the subject of this chapter suggests positive answers to those questions. Richard Rudhale was archdeacon of Hereford from 1446 to 1476. Rudhale was not a practicing advocate or judge. He left no treatise or other scholarly writing. However, the evidence shows that he brought legal knowledge to bear on several aspects of the religious life of the land, just as surely as a modern law graduate who spends his career in industry or commerce may contribute meaningfully to England's economy or political life.[5] As is often true today, the study of the law provided him with a leg up.

RUDHALE'S LIFE AND CAREER

Rudhale first appearance in the historical record comes from the same place in which he ended his life – Hereford Cathedral. From a local family resident near Ross-on-Wye, Rudhale was ordained acolyte by Bishop Thomas Spofford in December of 1434.[6] At the time he was a student in the law faculty at Oxford, and he must already have been marked out for a successful career. He had received a degree as bachelor of canon and civil law by 1435,[7] this after having been created apostolic and imperial notary public the preceding year.[8] Rudhale then chose to take part in what was already something close to an

---

5 K Edwards, *English Secular Cathedrals in the Middle Ages*, 2d revised edn (Manchester 1967), pp 322–25.

6 A Bannister (ed), *Registrum Thome Spofford, episcopi Herefordensis, A.D. MCCCCXXII–MCCCCXLVIII* (C & Y Soc. 23, 1919), p 317.

7 For information on his offices and benefices, see Emden, *Biographical Register of the University of Oxford*, III, p 1603. Fundamental for his work in the diocese of Hereford is D Lepine, '"A Long Way from University": Cathedral Canons and Learning at Hereford in the Fifteenth Century', in C Barron and J Stratford (eds), *The Church and Learning in Later Medieval Society: Essays in Honour of R. B. Dobson* (Donington 2002), pp 178–209, at 191–95.

8 See H Emanuel, 'Notaries Public and their Marks Recorded in the Archives of the Dean and Chapter of Hereford' (1953) 8 *National Library of Wales Journal* 147–62, at p 162.

English tradition, one that would only grow over the next two centuries. He crossed the Channel to continue academic study of law at the University of Padua.[9] There he incepted as Doctor of Decrees (i.e. canon law) in 1443.[10] He returned to England and was admitted as an advocate in the Court of Arches in London later that same year, but this must have been more a matter of form and future choice only, for he was also installed as canon treasurer of Hereford Cathedral. He succeeded to the archdeaconry of Hereford in 1446.[11] In that position he remained, all the while accumulating a succession of lucrative benefices and other offices which today seem bewildering in their amplitude but which were then quite normal in the career of a successful clergyman.[12] From 1458 until his death in 1476, for example, he served as a sub-collector of the papal *camera*, charged with administration of part of the revenues derived from English dioceses.[13] At the same time he acted as warden of St Mary's chantry in the church at Newton-in-the-Isle in the diocese of Ely, and several times he acted as vicar-general in spirituals to his bishop, an office that brought him into contact with legal questions.[14] Rudhale advanced no further than the office of archdeacon, but for many years he led an obviously busy and apparently useful life in the diocese. Appropriately (and at his own request), after his death in 1476 Rudhale was buried in the Cathedral church within the quire, although today the only physical monument left to preserve his memory is an impressive brass placed on the wall of the southeast transept.[15]

---

[9] See generally J Woolfson, *Padua and the Tudors: English Students in Italy, 1485–1603* (Toronto 1998), pp 10–38; R Mitchell, 'English Students at Padua, 1460–75' (1936) 8 *Transactions of the Royal Historical Society*, 4th ser, 101–117, at 117.

[10] G Zonto and J Brotto (eds), *Acta graduum academicorum Gymnasii Patavini* (Padua 1969–2008), vol I, pt 2, pp 1626–27 [nos 143–44]. His name, however, does not appear among the English students noted in G Andrich, *De natione Anglica et Scota iuristarum Universitatis Patvinae ab anno MCCXXII* (Padua 1892).

[11] Horn, *Le Neve, Fasti Ecclesiae Anglicanae 1300–1541, II Hereford Diocese*, pp 6 and 11.

[12] See Edwards, *English Secular Cathedrals*, pp 39–49.

[13] See *Calendar of Entries in the Papal Registers Relating to Great Britain and Ireland, Papal Letters* (London 1893–1960), vol X, p 361; vol XI, pp 367 and 681.

[14] E.g., A Bannister (ed), *Registrum Johannis Stanbury, episcopi Herefordensis, A.D. MCCCCLIII–MCCCCLXXIV* (C & Y Soc. 25, 1920), pp 71–82 (canonical elections); ibid., pp 127–31 (heresy); A Bannister (ed), *Registrum Thome Myllyng, episcopi Herefordensis, A.D. MCCCCLXXIV–MCCCCLXCII* (C & Y Soc. 26, 1920), pp 14–16 (compurgation).

[15] P Heseltine and H Stuchfield, *Monumental Brasses of Hereford Cathedral* (London 2005), pp 22–23. A picture of the brass is found in R Swanson and D Lepine, 'The Later Middle Ages, 1268–1535', in G Aylmer and J Tiller (eds), *Hereford Cathedral: A History* (London and Rio Grande, OH 2000), p 66. The text is given in A Winnington-Ingram, *Monumental Brasses in Hereford Cathedral*, 3d edn (Hereford 1972), pp 8, 17.

RUDHALE'S LAW BOOKS

What sets Rudhale apart from many of his contemporaries is the collection of works on the canon and civil laws that he annotated and ultimately gave to the cathedral library. The books – at least nine of them – are still there.[16] During his lifetime, he made regular use of them, and the annotations he made in them demonstrate the continuing utility of the Roman and canon laws for a career spent outside the consistory courts. They are not the notes of a student. He may have acquired some of these volumes as a student in Padua and brought them back home with him, but his notes are those of an archdeacon fully involved in the life of the church in Hereford. Four features of these books and his annotations in them are of particular interest for understanding the history of the profession of ecclesiastical law in England.

First, the books include a judicious selection of the old and the new, including both established works of authority and the most recent works from Rudhale's own time. One of the former is a thirteenth-century copy of the *Summa Codicis* by Azo of Bologna (d. 1230), purchased by Rudhale as a student in 1441.[17] Remembered by jurists through centuries from the tag 'Chi non ha Azzo non vada al palazzo' (roughly, 'Don't go to court without a copy of Azo'), and the likely source of some of the civilian learning found in the English treatise now known as *Bracton*,[18] Azo's commentary was just the sort of thing one might buy as a student and later carry into practice. It was a standard source of learning. One of the latter, the new type of juristic literature, is the *Singularia in causis criminalibus* of Ludovicus Pontanus (d. 1439), also known as Romanus.[19] The author was part of the later medieval movement which remained faithful to Bartolist traditions even while enlarging their scope. Their effort was designed to meet criticism that the jurists were somehow 'out of touch' with society's needs.[20] The work's title accurately describes the miscellaneous nature of the information found in it, but the many works written (and later published) under similar titles proved useful for raising and solving

---

[16] R Mynors and R Thomson, *Catalogue of the Manuscripts of Hereford Cathedral Library* (Woodbridge 1993), p xxiii (hereinafter *Catalogue*). References to the manuscripts are given herein by the letters and numbers found in this *Catalogue*.

[17] P.V.14; its ownership from 1271 to Rudhale's purchase is traced in *Catalogue*, p 102.

[18] F Maitland, Introduction, *Select Passages from the Works of Bracton and Azo*, SS 8 (London 1895), pp ix–x; K Güterbock, *Bracton and his Relation to the Roman Law* (Philadelphia, PA 1894), pp 51–55.

[19] O.IX.4.

[20] Van Hove, *Prolegomena ad Codicem iuris canonici*, p 521.

many practical legal problems not adequately covered in the older literature.[21] Rudhale was one among many users.

Second, much of Rudhale's attention, at least as shown in his annotations, centered around matters that came his way as archdeacon. He was enough of a 'theorist' to take note that the Kings of both France and England were not subject to the commands of the Roman emperor,[22] but most of his marginal comments concerned practical questions of ecclesiastical administration. He signaled the relevance of a treatment of the law of prescription in Innocent IV's commentary on the Decretals, for example, as being of particular relevance to the rights of archdeacons.[23] As he saw it, Innocent's treatment stood 'pro iure archidiaconali'. Very likely, in dealing with the related theme of custom's force in canon law it was no accident that another of his marginal notes made reference to the commentary of Guido de Baysio (d. 1313). He was commonly known as 'Archidiaconus'.[24] And many of the subjects about which Rudhale chose to comment were those that would naturally have come before an archdeacon, as for example, the question of when a cleric could be deprived of his benefice for having committed a crime or other act of clerical irregularity.[25]

Third, Rudhale's annotations give repeated evidence of that hardy though oft lamented feature of English church life: discord within cathedral chapters. Legal argument often came into these quarrels. Rudhale was not a man to let an injury or slight to his position as archdeacon of Hereford pass without protest, and he used the canonical manuscripts he owned to buttress his position. In the margins of one of them we see him calling attention to the opinion of Innocent IV on a point of evidence law. It was, he recorded, useful 'against Pede', meaning Richard Pede, Dean of Hereford between 1463 and 1481.[26] In the margin of another manuscript, he cited the opinion of Joannes Monachus (d. 1313) on a text from the *Liber sextus* as standing 'against Master Grene and for Richard Rudhale'.[27] Grene was his predecessor as prebendary of Bullinghope, and the dispute dealt with Grene's pretended right to alienate

[21] I have sought to describe briefly the contemporary place of such works in the Introduction, Helmholz, *Three Civilian Notebooks*, pp xlix–l.

[22] P.VI.7, f. 87v: 'Nota rex Francie non subiicitur imperatori. Idem de rege Anglie ut notat Host[iensis]' (a reference to X 4.17.13).

[23] P.VIII.10, f. 131: 'pro iure archidiaconali' (discussion of X 2.26.15, dealing with the establishment of prescriptive rights).

[24] P.VIII.10, f. 51: 'Pro hac glossa nota bene Arch' xii d, c illud (Dist. 12, c. 4).

[25] O.IX.4, f. 173v: 'Nota pro Mauricio de Wynter contra Symondes'.

[26] P.VIII.10, f. 113v: 'Contra Pede' (referring to X 2.20.37). Similar is O.VII.5, f. 51v: 'Nota contra Pede'.

[27] O.VII.5, f. 139v: 'Contra Mag. Grene et pro Ricardo Rudhale'.

some part of the property rights attached to the prebend. Less self-interested perhaps, but no less combative in spirit was Rudhale's notation, placed besides one of the texts in Justinian's Institutes, that its authority was directly opposed to one of the opinions of Richard Rotherham, the man who had held a canonry in the cathedral just prior to Rudhale's arrival to take up the same office.[28] Unfortunately, he did not record just what specific interests were at stake.

Fourth and more pleasant to contemplate for a modern student of ecclesiastical law, Rudhale's annotations show how well he had mastered one the great techniques of the Schools, using it to good effect in administering his archdeaconry. This was the ability to take a text from the Roman and canon laws and reason from a principle discerned within it in order to determine a question that could never have occurred to the author of the text. It was a technique taught in the Schools, and a necessary one if the ancient texts were to serve current needs. The texts in the Decretals and the Digest could not be changed, but the understanding of their potential application might be widened. One example among many must suffice. The question was whether an erroneous lifting of a sentence of excommunication was effective to relieve the person from attendant canonical penalties. It was not simply a theoretical question, because even if it were unjust, reversing the absolution would ordinarily require having recourse to the judge who had granted it, and circumstances might make this difficult. Rudhale did not find the answer to his question within the title on excommunication in the Gregorian Decretals (X 5.39.1–60). He found it within the Roman law of *precarium*. A title in the Digest dealt with the subject – roughly speaking the revocable delivery of possession of a chattel – and one text within it (Dig. 43.26.22) seemed to hold that, even if the delivery was made in error (but not through fraud), the possessor nevertheless held a legally recognized property right in the chattel, one entitling him to legal protection by interdict. The same underlying principle, it seemed to Rudhale, should apply to a grant of absolution from a previous sentence of excommunication.[29] The grant stood until reversed. Obviously, here was a man for whom legal training had not been a waste.

---

[28] O.VIII.7, f. 50: 'Nota contra opinionem domini Rotherham'.
[29] P.VIII.10, ff 14v, 18: 'Nota absolutio tenet iniusta ut hic, … et melius ff. De precario l. fi.' (Dig. 43.26.22).

11

Daniel Dun (d. 1617)

Historians habitually assess the importance of members of learned professions by what they wrote. Unless a man or woman took part in a dramatic historical event, what they accomplished seems almost not to count. This approach must come naturally to historians; it is how they themselves are judged. A moment's reflection, however, shows how inadequate a test of a lawyer's importance it is. Most lawyers do not write treatises. They act. They represent clients in court; they give advice; they administer organizations; and they serve governments. Lawyers may have a large influence on human affairs even if they leave no treatise behind.[1] For historians to ignore this fact of professional life may cause them to misjudge the importance of ecclesiastical lawyers like the subject of this entry, Sir Daniel Dun. Dun never published a treatise, yet he was responsible for real accomplishments at a critical moment in the history of ecclesiastical law in England. He rose to high office, and he influenced the course of affairs in Church and State. Luckily, the evidence about his career is thick enough to provide a fair means of evaluating his place as an ecclesiastical lawyer.

DUN'S LIFE AND CAREER

The circumstances of Dun's birth are not free from doubt. We do not know its exact date, though 1545 is a likely estimate.[2] Nor are the origins of his family

---

[1] H Thieme, 'Le rôle des *Doctores legum* dans la Société allemande du XVIe siècle', in *Individu et sociétè à la Renaissance* (Brussels 1967), pp 159–69. This same point is made in an only slightly different context by Robert Franklin, 'Sir Richard Steward and the Crisis of the Caroline Regime', in S Green and P Horden (eds), *All Souls under the Ancien Régime* (Oxford 2007), p 39.

[2] R Houlbrooke, 'Dun [Donne], Sir Daniel (1544/5-1617)', *Oxford Dictionary of National Biography*; online edn 2008, www.oxforddnb.com/, accessed December 20, 2013. See also Levack, *The Civil Lawyers in England*, pp 226–27.

certain. There are indications that he came originally from a Welsh family, as was the case for many of the civilians, but he was the son of Robert Dun of London, a common lawyer of Gray's Inn. Even this is not entirely sure, however. There are also indications that he came from a family of East Anglian bondsmen. Professor Diarmaid MacCulloch discovered a record of a Daniel Dun's manumission in the Patent Rolls for 1576.[3]

By that year, he was already a fellow at All Souls College, having been admitted in 1567.[4] Of his prior schooling and the exact nature of his studies little is known, but at Oxford he was admitted BCL in 1572 and DCL in 1580. In the latter year he was elected Principal of New Inn Hall, a center for academic jurists, as All Souls was also. Later that same year he moved to London, where he received a commission from the Archbishop of Canterbury to serve as an advocate in the Court of Arches, and on January 22, 1582 he was admitted to a place in Doctors' Commons.

Thereafter his career took off. He had been named official principal for the archdeacon of Essex by 1585, and before the end of the decade, he had received commissions to serve as auditor of causes in the Archbishop's Court of Audience and then as Dean of the Arches. Think of it – Dean of the Arches at such a young age. After that, professional honors and responsibilities came thick and fast. He was admitted an honorary member of Gray's Inn in 1599. He became a master in the Court of Requests in 1602 and a master in Chancery two years later. He was serving regularly as a judge of the High Court of Admiralty by 1609, and he was MP for Taunton in 1601, then in the same capacity for Oxford University during the Parliaments of 1604 and 1614. Knighted in 1603, in part for his skill in concluding the Treaty of Bremen, he did not cease to serve as a judge in the English courts where the European *ius commune* applied. Dun died in September of 1617, having been active in his profession almost to the end. He was not quickly forgotten, however. A bust of Dun was commissioned by the fellows of All Souls College in 1750. It was one of the twenty-four placed high in the gallery of the Codrington Library as one of 'the most eminent members of the College'.[5] It is still there to be seen (at a considerable distance), a fitting memorial to the successful career of an English civilian.

---

[3]   *Calendar of Patent Rolls, Elizabeth I*, vol VII, nos 705–06; see D MacCulloch, 'Bondmen under the Tudors', in C Cross, D Loades, and J J Scarisbrick (eds), *Law and Government under the Tudors* (Cambridge 1988), pp 91–110, at p 92.

[4]   See All Souls College, Oxford, MS Statuta collegii Omnium Animarum, f 178, where he was listed as a jurist of London.

[5]   A Wood, *History and Antiquities of the Colleges and Halls in the University of Oxford*, J Gutch (ed) (Oxford 1786), vol IV, p 284.

If there can be little doubt about Dun's professional success and contemporary eminence, legitimate doubt could be raised as to his contributions to the history of the ecclesiastical law in England. No one doubts that he was an able practitioner who rose to the top of his profession. But was he anything more? The fellows of All Souls certainly thought so more than one hundred years after his death, and their opinion is supported by other evidence. Dun never wrote a treatise. However, he did make significant contributions to the profession of ecclesiastical law in at least three respects: in preserving its learned traditions; in improving practice in the courts of the church; and in resisting encroachments on ecclesiastical jurisdiction by some aggressive litigants and common lawyers.

PRESERVATION OF THE LAW OF THE CHURCH

The era when Dun grew up was a time of threat to the traditional law of the English church. The jurisdiction of the church's courts was not overturned at the Reformation, but a thoroughgoing reformation of its law was promised from the 1530s, and the Commission appointed to compile a reformed law finally produced the *Reformatio legum ecclesiasticarum* in 1552.[6] It turned out to be a proper code, and it would have set the ecclesiastical law on a new and different course. This did not happen, however, because it never received the approval of King and Parliament. It stood thereafter as a silent critic of the existing law. Dun resisted that criticism. He was a leader among the ecclesiastical lawyers whose knowledge of the traditional *ius commune* kept its learning alive and even vigorous. In time, the *Reformatio* itself faded from the scene. Proof of Dun's effort to preserve the learned traditions of his profession is buried in manuscript reports of causes heard in the ecclesiastical courts, but it is impressive when brought to light.

An illustrative example appears in his intervention in a dispute between the Archbishop of York and the Dean and Chapter of Durham over their respective rights in the bishop's powers *sede vacante*.[7] Like many such cases, the outcome depended on the law of proof and the difference between petitory and possessory claims. Dun's analysis of the relationship between these two and the consequences that followed began with the two basic texts from the *Corpus iuris canonici*, one from the Gregorian Decretals (X 2.12.5), the other from the

---

[6] Its most recent edition is G Bray (ed), *Tudor Church Reform: The Henrician Canons of 1535 and the Reformatio Legum Ecclesiasticarum* (Church of England Record Society, vol VIII, 2004), 166–743.

[7] Taken from Helmholz, *Three Civilian Notebooks*, no 8, at p 15.

Clementines (Clem. 2.3.1). He gave them a broad reading – extending them beyond their immediate subject (causes involving benefices) to include other rights incident to ecclesiastical offices. This was fully in accord with traditional civilian ways of reasoning *De similibus ad similia*. He buttressed his interpretation with authoritative medieval commentaries by Panormitanus (d. 1445), and Joannes ab Imola (d. 1436). He then added references from the abundant *Consilia* literature, citation to collections of opinions written by Paulus de Castro (d. 1441), Jason de Mayno (d. 1519), Joannes Franciscus de Ripa (d. 1535), and Marianus Socinus, Jr. (d. 1556). He concluded by citing the most recent specialized treatments of the subject then available – now quite obscure works by Fabius Accorombonus (d. 1559), Ludovicus Bologninus (d. 1508), Berengarius Fernandus (d. *c.*1574), Hormanoctius Deti (d. *c.*1531), Claudius Marmerius (*fl.* 1557), and Joannes Antonius Rubeus (d. 1544). These Italian jurists were sixteenth-century authors of *Repetitiones* on the subject. Very likely, Dun's references to them came from a collection of scholarly opinions on the subject in which they were published together.[8] Whatever his immediate source was, however, their citation shows that he and his fellows kept abreast of developments in the contemporary *ius commune*. Dun made no mention of arguments based on the English common law. He cited nothing of the comparable differences between common law writs of right and the possessory assizes. For him, the relevant authority came from the *oceanus iuris* of European law. In his determination to preserve the learned traditions of his profession he was not alone, but he was one of its leaders.

IMPROVEMENTS IN THE ECCLESIASTICAL COURTS

The English civilians are sometimes regarded as instinctive defenders of the old order, and Dun's desire to preserve traditional learning supports that characterization. However, it is too one-sided a description to capture the complexity of his attitude. He, along with his fellow civilians, recognized that faults existed in the church's courts. Whatever their merits, the actual exercise of ecclesiastical jurisdiction left much to be desired. A manuscript now at Lambeth Palace written in Dun's hand spelled out some of them: overlapping jurisdictions, frivolous appeals, excessive fees and costs, unnecessary delays in litigation, and failures to follow procedural requirements.[9] Most of

---

[8] Probably *Repetitiones in iure civili variae* (Lyon 1553); see Lipenius, *Bibliotheca realis iuridica*, vol II, pp 264–65, where these authors are listed under this title.

[9] For examples of these alleged failings, see 'Statuta omnia et singula', Lambeth Palace Library, MS 1748 (1590), said to be in Dun's hand, and with Dun's signature at the bottom of f. 1; and LPL, MS Reg Whitgift (1602), f 135 (letter from the Queen dealing with common complaints).

these complaints were not new, but perennial complaints are not necessarily unjustified complaints, and in a series of statutes enacted for the courts during Dun's service in the Court of Arches, measures were taken to remedy some of them.[10] It would not be right to attribute these measures to Dun alone, but that he stood behind them and encouraged their enactment seems self-evident from the manuscript evidence.

Dun was a practical man. He carried that characteristic into practice. An early seventeenth-century civilian's notebook records him as saying that in doubtful cases arbitration was to be preferred to litigation. Even judges would be well advised to serve as arbitrators where doubt about the law or the facts existed.[11] Contemporary accounts confirm that he himself acted on that view.[12] Dun also attempted to sort out vexed questions relating to the jurisdiction exercised by the archbishop of Canterbury, in the end defending the archbishop's courts as 'easy of access and fortified by the expertise of men learned in the law'.[13] Most intriguing of the practical expedients connected with Dun is a collection of reported cases from London's ecclesiastical courts during his tenure as Dean of the Arches. It is now Tanner MS. 427 in the Bodleian Library – identified by Sir John Baker as a possibly unique source in its attention to the arguments made in the courts.[14] This useful and practical experiment did not subvert traditional learning. Other reports of arguments and decisions in the spiritual tribunals were compiled during the Stuart era, but it was not until the eighteenth century that they became normal.

INDEPENDENCE OF THE ECCLESIASTICAL COURTS

Dun's career coincided with what most civilians regarded as new and unwarranted interference in their independence by the common lawyers. Writs of prohibition purporting to restrict the scope of ecclesiastical jurisdiction were becoming a familiar part of their life as judges. Dun, like most other civilians, did not resist prohibitions directly, but he did not wish to surrender the church's right to its independent place in the English legal system. He regarded prohibitions as acts of power, not statements of the law.

Dun's touchiness on the subject was exemplified by an incident that took place while he was sitting as a judge in the court of Admiralty.[15] Greene, a

---

[10] Wilkins, *Concilia*, vol IV, pp 328–35 (1587), pp 352–56 (1597), pp 417–24 (1605).
[11] MS. 794.093/2470 'Collectanea B', f 16, Worcester Record Office, 'The Hive', Worcester.
[12] See *Clarke v Blage* (1615), *Acts of the Privy Council 1615–1616* (London 1925), pp 215–16;
[13] All Souls College, MS 226, fols 210–17.
[14] J H Baker, *English Legal Manuscripts*, vol II (covering Lincoln's Inn, the Bodleian Library and Gray's Inn) (Zurich and London 1978), p 150.
[15] *Bruistone v Baker* (1615), 1 Rolle 315, 81 Eng Rep 511.

messenger, sought to deliver a writ of prohibition to him. Not pleased by the intrusion, he told Greene to take it and hand it to the registrar. Greene refused, saying that the writ was directed to Dun as the judge, not to any subordinate. Hard words followed. Dun is reported to have threatened to commit Greene to prison and have his writ thrown after him.[16] He carried out at least the former threat,[17] and when Greene's counsel later had him released by a writ of habeas corpus, the question arose as to whether any action should be taken against Dun himself. The counsel sought a writ of attachment against him. This, however, was refused. Dun, the report continued, 'was known as a man of good fame', and beyond doubt Greene had behaved 'sawcilie' in delivering the writ. Sir Edward Coke himself reached this conclusion, remarking that it had not been 'bon manners' to act as Greene did.

The full report of this case makes an important but often neglected point about the larger history of the relationship between what we now call church and state. It took place in a small world. Dun and Coke knew each other. They had sat together as judges by commission.[18] The common law judges sometimes called upon the civilians, Dun among them, to appear and advise them about the contents of foreign and canon law.[19] The history of writs of prohibition undoubtedly includes a clash of ideas, but it took place in a world where personal relations counted. That Dun supported what we would now call 'the losing side' should not cause historians to ignore the contemporary importance of that aspect of his career. He may have left no treatise behind, but his 'publication record' makes a poor measure of his place in the history of ecclesiastical jurisdiction in England.

[16] Ibid., 'Sir Daniel dit que il fuit pluis sawcie, et dit que s'il nollet issint faire, il voilet luy committer & throw the prohibition after him'.

[17] Ibid., 'et puis il commit le dit Greene al prison'.

[18] Case of the Spanish Ambassador (1614), *Acts of the Privy Council 1615–1616* (London 1925), pp 74–75.

[19] E.g., *Penson v Cartwright* (1614), 2 Bulst 207, 80 Eng Rep 1071; Petition of Beale, Yates, et al. (1616), *Acts of the Privy Council*, pp 611–14.

12

Clement Colmore (d. 1619)

Clement Colmore, chancellor and official principal of the diocese of Durham from 1582 until his death in 1619, has attracted little attention among chroniclers of the English church. No entry for him appears in the *ODNB*. He was not included in Coote's *Sketches of English Civilians*. Nor does his name figure in ecclesiastical histories of the period. There has been a single exception. Colmore came to the notice of Brian Levack, author of an admirable study of the English civilians during the run-up to the Civil War in 1641. After giving his readers basic biographical details, Professor Levack compiled a list of the offices and benefices his subject held. It turned out to be quite a long list, and he concluded by describing Colmore as 'the fourth-wealthiest clergyman of the entire diocese'.[1] Of course, the greater part of that fortune would not have been the fruits of judicial office. It would have come from the lands he held and the benefices he enjoyed.[2] Still, he was rich – perhaps too rich to be taken for a model civilian. However, Colmore also has a quite different claim to fame among English ecclesiastical lawyers, one not discussed by Professor Levack. He was the compiler of a large manuscript Notebook, one filled with useful information about the realities of legal practice in the ecclesiastical courts during the reigns of the early Stuarts.[3]

COLMORE'S LIFE AND CAREER

Born in Birmingham, the second son of William Colmore and his wife Joan, the daughter of Henry Hunt of Tamworth, Colmore matriculated at Brasenose

---

[1]   Levack, *The Civil Lawyers in England*, p 67.
[2]   Colmore's career was noted as an example of a common pattern in R O'Day, *The English Clergy: The Emergence and Consolidation of a Profession 1558–1642* (Leicester 1979), p 157.
[3]   The manuscript is now kept in the University of Durham's Palace Green Library (or at No 5, The College, on my last visit) as MS DDR/EJ/CCG/2/1. All further references marked as 'MS' below are to this manuscript.

College, Oxford and proceeded BA in 1570 and MA three years later. Then, moving to the civil law faculty at Cambridge, he proceeded BCL in 1580 and DCL in 1581. His appointment as judge in the most important ecclesiastical court in the diocese of Durham then followed, almost immediately upon receipt of the latter degree. It was not then an unusual career move for a promising graduate of one of the civil law faculties in England. Colmore did also later take a step towards admission at Doctors' Commons in London,[4] but his motives for doing so remain uncertain, and little seems to have come of this effort. He remained in Durham, holding the same judicial office until his death in 1619. Act book entries from the period have survived that show him presiding.[5] Twice married, he was the father of ten children. He was proud enough to have listed all of them, together with their baptismal sponsors, in the Notebook. Colmore also served as a JP for Durham, and he took part in an English delegation to meet with the Scottish King in 1594 in an effort to find remedies for the troubles that were endemic to the region. When he died, his will was proved at York. He was buried in Durham cathedral in accordance with his own wishes 'between my two wives'.[6] He had enjoyed a successful but not an exceptional career.

COLMORE'S NOTEBOOK

Although Colmore himself might not have claimed any special distinction for it, to historians his most notable contribution to understanding the law of the post-Reformation English church is the double folio Notebook he compiled. Its 386 folios are a mine of informative material. They include opinions of counsel in disputed matters, forms for use in the ecclesiastical courts, comments about current events and legal problems, an alphabetical dictionary of terms and concepts found in the civil and canon laws, and many reports of cases heard in the ecclesiastical courts of the Northern province. It is not a unique survival. Several such notebooks from the period remain, and a much larger number must once have existed.[7] By comparison with most of the survivors, however, Colmore's is particularly full and informative.

---

[4]   See Squibb, *Doctors' Commons*, p 205. His name was not mentioned in Coote, *Sketches of the Lives and Characters of Eminent English Civilians*.

[5]   See, e.g., the Durham court's Act book for 1608–1610, DDR/EJ/CCA/1/7, f 9v, describing him as vicar general as well as official principal.

[6]   G Armytage (ed), *Baptismal, Marriage, and Burial Registers of the Cathedral Church of Christ ... at Durham 1609–1896* (Harleian Society, vol XXIII, 1897), p 83.

[7]   Some of these are described in Helmholz, *Roman Canon Law in Reformation England*, pp 121–57.

Perhaps most valuable are the first of the contents mentioned above: opinions of counsel. They are scattered throughout the Notebook. One from Henry Swinburne dealt with rights to erect and maintain pews; one from Thomas Talbot covered a dispute over payment of tithes, and two from Richard Hudson dealt with clerical dues and a question of testamentary law.[8] Colmore even added an opinion or two of his own.[9] They all contain both questions of fact and law. An example of their character is found in the first entry in the Notebook, an opinion of Henry Swinburne dealing with the law of defamation.[10] Exactly who the parties were or who the person seeking Swinburne's opinion was we are not told. However, the facts of the case and the legal point at issue were stated clearly. The question was: Were words spoken in response to a verbal provocation actionable under the church's law? According to Swinburne, the answer depended on the intent with which they had been uttered. The specific words involved – 'Thou liest like a bawde' – had been spoken to the plaintiff 'in defence of [the speaker] and her maid'. Swinburne's opinion did not invoke the *mitior sensus* doctrine. He concluded instead that unless the speaker had uttered them with a malicious intent, they were not actionable. His reason: their primary intent had been to deny a prior accusation against the defendant or her maid. In his opinion, the determinative question – whether malicious intent had been present in the cause – could be settled by the defendant's compurgatory oath.

Of equal interest and of much greater frequency in the Notebook are his reports of cases heard in the ecclesiastical courts. How they had come to Colmore's attention is not entirely clear. Some, probably even the majority, must have come from his own court. He probably implied that by giving them familiar titles (such as 'Master Barker's Case' at f 229), or identifying subjects that had come before him (such as 'administration of the goodes of James Suerties his kinsman intestate' at f 165v). Some concerned clearly local questions, such as the effect of a verbal devise of property held by burgage tenure in the city of Durham (f 140) or the status of parochial taxation in a parish within the diocese of Durham (f 218) A few included the formal sentence that Colmore had himself given (e.g., 'Master Dent's Case' at f 153). However, at least some of his cases came from elsewhere, such as Carlisle (Skelton c Saunderson at f 160) or London (Bevers' Will at f 232v), and occasionally no location at all

---

8   They are found at MS, fols 217-217v (Swinburne); f. 218 (Talbot), and fols 210–11, 235 (Hudson). For biographies of Talbot, see Levack, *Civil Lawyers*, at p 274; for Hudson, see Squibb, *Doctors' Commons*, p 165.

9   MS, fols 235–36.

10   MS, f 2. Another example is found in Derrett, *Henry Swinburne*, pp 29–31. See also Baker, *Monuments of Endlesse Labours*, pp 59–60.

can be recovered from his notes. The English civilians across the realm shared professional information, and some of the cases that interested Colmore may have been the product of that sort of exchange.

Information about the realities of practice in the ecclesiastical courts are a particularly valuable addition to the Notebook. The frequency of testamentary matters is noteworthy. It not only confirms Brian Outhwaite's conclusions about the lasting importance of that aspect of the English church's jurisdiction,[11] it also helps to reveal some of the realities of practice that have not been clear to historians. One of them illuminates the details involving the Northern province's preservation of the child's right to a portion of his parent's estate, the so-called *legitim*.[12] Another involves the dominant role in the decision of cases played by the complex law of evidence drawn from the fonts of the European *ius commune*.[13] A third involves a question not answered by the formal law – the priority and order in which debts and legacies were to be paid by executors under the ecclesiastical law of the time.[14]

COLMORE'S INTERESTS AND CONCERNS

The particular topics that interested Colmore are evident throughout the Notebook. He did not hide them. He had no hesitation in recording the names and numbers of his own family, and he was not shy about expressing his own attitudes and opinions. Three general conclusions about those attitudes stand out as of particular interest to historians of the English Church's law.

The first is his habitual reliance on the traditional sources of authority in the church's law – the texts and commentaries found in the storehouses of the *ius commune*. When a disputed question in a case on the law of tithes arose, it was to the interpretation of the Gregorian Decretals and the treatise by Petrus Rebuffus (d. 1557), *De decimis*, that Colmore turned.[15] In a marriage case where a question about the level of proof that had to be established came up, it was around the opinion of the great canonist, Nicolaus de Tudeschis, called Panormitanus (d. 1445), that the discussion in the Notebook

---

[11] See Outhwaite, *The Rise and Fall of the English Ecclesiastical Courts*, pp 33–39.

[12] MS, fols 235–36 (dealing with the requisite size of the estate, the problems raised by inter vivos transfers, and the ambiguous status for jurisdictional purposes of leases of land).

[13] MS, f 223 (difficulties of proof raised by objection that witnesses to the exchange of matrimonial consent heard the spoken words imperfectly and slightly differently).

[14] MS, f 254v. (According to the entry the debts were to be paid with the following priority: Debts to the crown, debts provable by official records; debts evidenced by a specialty; servants' wages, rents and similar obligations, all others.)

[15] Slingsbie c Urpath, MS, f 211 (reference to X 2.26.7 and Rebuffus' treatise ad Quaest 13, nos 64 et seq).

revolved.[16] Similarly, one defendant's refusal to take what common lawyers called the 'ex officio' oath was supported by the authority of the *Consilia* of Joachim Mynsinger (d. 1588), not by authority drawn from the common law.[17] English statutes enacted in Parliament did come into play in some of the cases Colmore recorded – the Edwardian statutes on the law of tithes for instance – but cases heard in the royal courts virtually never did.[18] When a show of learned authority was needed, he used the commentaries on the civil and canon laws – the opinions of jurists like Panormitanus, Philippus Decius (d. 1536), Dominicus de Sancto Geminiano (*fl. c.*1450), Philipus Franchus (d. 1471), Willelmus Durantis (d. 1296), and William Lyndwood (d. 1446).[19]

The second point of special interest that comes from perusal of the Notebook – one slightly at odds with the first – is Colmore's interest in the English common law. He raised repeated queries about it, often seeking ways around rules when they restricted the scope of ecclesiastical jurisdiction. He worried about the future on this account, but his interests were broader than self-protection. An instance of simple curiosity occurs at a point in the Notebook where he raised the question of whether the common lawyers meant the same thing by 'the equity of a statute' as civil lawyers did by 'the mind of a statute'.[20] His answer was tentative – 'So it seems', he concluded. He did not say how he reached that conclusion, but the similarity in the use made of both concepts must have made their rough equivalence obvious. An example of his search for ways around the common law's restrictions occurred when he was confronted by a writ of prohibition from the royal courts. The writ's words prevented him from proceeding in the case before him. However, he asked, could he nonetheless remit the case to the archbishop's court, where it might continue? He concluded that he could, since the writ only forbade him from proceeding in the case, and 'I am so far from proceeding in the cause that I utterly rid my hands of it'.[21] Many examples of a source of interest caused by disagreements between common lawyers and the civilians came from testamentary law. To Colmore, statutes and judicial decisions seemed to be interfering with orderly process of administering estates. Did the statute

---

[16] Clesasbye c Collingwood, MS, fols 231–31v (reference was to his *Commentaria ad* X 2.24.36). The entry is enlivened by the remark, at f 121v, that one of the lawyers involved in the case 'offered to laie 100s. to 4d. [that] Panormitanus had no such place'.

[17] Harrison c Brigges, MS, f 258 (reference to his *Responsa iuris sive consilia decades sex*, Dec 1, no 22.

[18] Master Dent's Case, MS, fols 153–53v (dealing with 2 & 3 Edw VI, c 13).

[19] Skelton c Saunderson, MS, f 160 (an opinion of Colmore's dealing with the law of proof).

[20] MS, f 137v. The Roman law on this point is at Cod. 1.14.5 and DD ad id.

[21] Swifte c Johnson, MS, f 125.

28 Hen. VIII, c. 5 inhibit probate judges from requiring litigants to provide sureties for faithful performance of legitimate orders? He concluded that it did not. Rightly understood, the statute left the judge free to do 'as he might have done before the making of this act'.[22] That was not, however, the conclusion towards which the common law judges were tending. The future therefore seemed uncertain to him.

The third point of particular interest in the Notebook is an aspect of law practice that will be familiar to modern lawyers, although it often surprises others. Despite the huge number of precedents that exist in today's case law, it often happens that lawyers find no clear answer in them. They produce no definitive solution. We share this experience with Colmore. He often faced questions he could not answer. Who was entitled to administer the estate of a man who had died intestate, when his widow had died after him without having sought to claim the right to do so? Should it be her children or should it be someone related to the deceased husband? The Notebook raised the question, and immediately after stating it, Colmore added the word 'Solutio' followed by a blank space.[23] He hoped an answer would soon be evident. When it did, he would fill in the blank. In the end, however, he had to leave it blank. No answer was forthcoming. No doubt this indecision was exacerbated by the actions of contemporary common lawyers, who had thrown many long-settled jurisdictional questions into doubt. But his uncertainty was not limited to contentious cases. It recurred throughout the Notebook. Were Colmore alive today, it might be a comfort to him to know that something like the same situation remains common four centuries later.

[22] MS f 138v.
[23] Hudson's Case, MS, f 255.

13

Arthur Duck (d. 1648)

In the long history of the ecclesiastical law in England, Dr Arthur Duck is one of the better-known civilians. He makes an appearance in most accounts of the Church's history during the reigns of the early Stuart monarchs.[1] Chancellor of the diocese of Bath and Wells and later of London, Master in Chancery, King's advocate in the Court of Chivalry and member of Parliament, Duck has long enjoyed the reputation of an effective administrator in troubled times. The extent of his enthusiasm for Archbishop Laud's plans to strengthen the Church has been a matter of occasional dispute,[2] but his integrity and the quality of his services to Crown and Church have not been doubted. Duck can claim an entry in the *ODNB*, and he is mentioned in works that discuss the civil law's place in English life.[3] His career and character are noted in most standard works of reference.[4]

---

[1] C Carlton, *Archbishop William Laud* (London 1987), pp 106–07; J Davies, *The Caroline Captivity of the Church: Charles I and the Remoulding of Anglicanism 1625–1641* (Oxford 1992), pp 181, 229, 279; K Fincham, *Prelate as Pastor: the Episcopate of James I* (Oxford 1990), p 180; Stieg, *Laud's Laboratory: the Diocese of Bath and Wells in the Early Seventeenth Century*, pp 171–73; G Aylmer, *The King's Servants; the Civil Service of Charles I, 1625–1642* (New York 1961), p 386; Hill, *Economic Problems of the Church*, p 180.

[2] Compare H Trevor-Roper, *Archbishop Laud 1573–1645* (London 1963), p 355 ('strong supporter of the Archbishop'), with T Webster, *Godly Clergy in early Stuart England* (Cambridge 1997), pp 206–07 ('incomplete commitment to Laudianism'). See also D Cressy, *Travesties and Transgressions in Tudor and Stuart England* (Oxford 2000), pp 193, 326.

[3] T Scrutton, 'Roman Law Influence in Chancery, Church Courts, Admiralty, and Law Merchant', in *Select Essays in Anglo-American Legal History* (Boston, MA 1907), vol I, pp 215–16.

[4] P Stein, 'Duck, Arthur (1580–1648)', in *ODNB*, http://oxforddnb.com., accessed August 27, 2014. See also E Heward, *Masters in Ordinary* (Chichester, 1990), pp 124–25; Squibb, *Doctors' Commons*, p 170; Levack, *The Civil Lawyers in England*, pp 225–26; Coote, *Sketches of the Lives and Characters of Eminent English Civilians*, p 72.

Despite the attention paid to him, it remains true that Duck has not been sufficiently appreciated for the great work of scholarship that put him in the front ranks of English civilians. This is his account of the comparative history and contemporary status of the Roman and canon laws in European lands: *De usu et authoritate iuris civilis in dominiis principum Christianorum* (1st edn 1654). Often reprinted and translated into more than one language,[5] it was an impressive work of legal scholarship when it was published, and it remains impressive to this day.

DUCK'S LIFE AND CAREER

Born and brought up in Devon, Duck first followed a path laid out by his elder brother, Nicholas, entering Exeter College, Oxford, in 1595. By then, his brother had left the university without taking a degree. He became a common lawyer (at Lincoln's Inn). Arthur made a different choice, and his academic career was not a short one. In this respect it was similar to that of many prominent civilians. He migrated to Hart Hall, proceeding MA in 1602. In 1604 he was elected a fellow of All Souls, taking the BCL in 1607 and the DCL five years later, the second after having completed an extended trip to European centers of learning. He became sub-warden of All Souls in 1610, later writing a Life of the College's founder, Archbishop Henry Chichele.[6]

Like most English civilians, Duck moved away from academic life even while he retained a toe-hold in it. In 1614, he was admitted as an advocate at Doctors' Commons in London. Already a favorite of the bishop of Bath and Wells, Arthur Lake, Duck became his chancellor in 1616. The bishop paid him the compliment of solemnizing his marriage with Margaret, daughter of Henry Southworth, a London merchant. It was a happy union, producing nine children, of whom unfortunately only two girls survived to maturity. Margaret's life was itself celebrated in Samuel Clarke's *Collection of the Lives of Ten Eminent Divines*, published in 1662.[7]

Once begun on this sound footing, Duck's career was marked by success, including the accumulation of offices in church and state. Besides those already mentioned, he served on one of the courts of High Commission; he acted as a commissioner for admiralty in Dorset and Middlesex, and he served

---

[5] The English translation of 1699 in its second section included only the author's account of the Roman law in England, omitting treatment of Continental lands.

[6] *Vita Henrici Chichele archiepiscopi Cantuariensis sub regibus Henrici V et VI* (Oxford 1617); the work was translated into English in 1699.

[7] She was not one of the ten divines; the entry devoted to her life followed in the second part of Clarke's work. In it the lives of four women were described.

as visitor for schools and poorhouses in the diocese of Canterbury. He was also regularly consulted on public questions of moment.

Of course, most of this edifice came tumbling down with the coming of the Civil War. The ecclesiastical courts over which he presided ceased to exist in anything but name. Duck was not excluded entirely from public life, however. In fact he was made a Master in Chancery in 1645, but even so, it was a time of limited horizons for civilians, and with the assistance of Gerard Langbaine, provost of Queen's College, Oxford, he turned his attention to the work that was to stand as his great contribution to comparative law and legal history. Duck put to good use what might have been years of enforced idleness.

DUCK'S GREAT WORK

De iure et authoritate iuris civilis is not a huge volume – 478 octavo pages of text, plus a short list of its contents and an index in the pocketbook edition published at Leiden in 1654.[8] By the standards of civilian treatises from the same era, it is quite modest in size. The footnotes to the edition, which are extensive, appear in tiny print and in the highly abbreviated form of citation used at the time. The text itself is divided into two separate books. The first, much shorter than the second, opens by describing the origins, the separate parts, and the nature of the *Corpus iuris civilis*. It then adds chapters devoted to post-Justinianic developments – to the feudal law and the *Libri feudorum*, to the contributions of the canon law, and finally to a general analysis of legal reasoning and decision-making within the *ius commune*. All this information was well worth knowing then, just as it remains worth knowing today that the author believed that the Roman law was a permanent gift of God to all peoples.[9] That understanding, not unusual among civil lawyers of the time, opens a window on their approach to legal problems.

It is the second book, however, that contains Duck's most valuable contribution to legal literature. He followed a regular method. He first provided a description of the broad course of legal development in the several European kingdoms, principalities, and cities. Then it added examples. The range of the sources from which Duck drew conclusions in this second book is impressive, even astonishing. He began with Germany, noting that the seat of Roman empire had been translated there.[10] He covered the law of the Germans in

---

[8] I have used A Duck, *De usu et authoritate iuris civilis Romanorum in dominiis principum Christianorum*, Lib II, ch 2 §§ 15–16 (Leiden 1654). An Elsevier book, its modern technical description is: 13 cm (24mo in half-sheets). All subsequent references to it are made to book, chapter and section.

[9] Lib I, ch 2 § 4: 'leges autem condere orbi terrarum proprie Romanis a Deo concessum est'.

[10] Lib II, ch 2 § 3.

detail and with a grasp of the relevant literature. To take only one example, in discussing the law and practice of inheritance in cases of intestacy in Saxony, he devoted two subsections to the comparative authority of Saxon and Roman laws as they had been worked out in practice. Here Duck drew upon nine separate learned works, few if any of which will be familiar to modern students of legal history.[11] They were Johannes Schneidewein (Ointomos), *In Institutionum imperialium commentarii* (1595), Johannes Sichardus, *Commentarius ad Codicem* (1586), Ernestus Cothemannus, *Consilia et Responsa iuris* (1609), Dominicus Arumaeus, *Discursus academicus ad Auream Bullam* (1617), Antonius Colerus, *Sectiones de iure imperii Germanici* (1613), Matthaeus Stephanus, *Constitutiones publicorum iudiciorum Caroli* VI (1616), Albert Krantz, *Viri in theologia et iure pontificio celeberrimi … [de]Wandalia* (1575), Anon, *Ius provinciale ducatus Prussiae* (1624), and one more I have so far been unsuccessful in identifying.[12] Particularly noteworthy are the number and breadth of these treatises. It is typical of the learning characteristic of Duck's approach. Subsections like these followed – with different though equally learned sources.

What did Duck use the information in these references to accomplish? Roughly speaking, they allowed him to go inside the German legal development we now call 'the Reception' of Roman law. As Duck portrayed it, 'Reception' was far from a mechanical process, and it was not accomplished at a stroke. He recounted, for example, both its successes and the resistance to it in Saxony. The old law still governed many questions of succession. As the passage from Schneidewein's commentary on the *Institutes* cited by Duck described it, the requirement of Saxon law that a nephew be of the blood of an intestate in order to inherit from him had been retained in contemporary practice. By contrast, on the subject of inheritance by illegitimate children, the Roman law had won out. Here, he recorded that 'Saxon law' had been superseded. Because of its 'wickedness'; it had been displaced by the *ius commune*.[13] Tellingly, Duck noted that even in many of the situations where the Saxon law had been retained, it was being interpreted according to principles drawn from the learned laws. This process of interpretation meant a great deal in fact. Some of the cities in northern Germany had all but abandoned the letter of their old laws by means of applying rules of interpretation drawn

---

[11]   Lib II, ch 2 §§ 15–16.

[12]   This was a commentary on the Digest by 'Brust'.

[13]   Schneidewein, *In Institutionum imperialium commentarii*, tit. *De haereditibus ab intestato*, ch 1 § 20, 'Sed in hoc casu sicut in multis aliis, jus saxonicum propter eius iniquitatem non observatur sed restringitur secundum ius commune', also citing a case from a German court in support.

from civilian traditions.[14] The picture was not uniform. There was variety, and many areas had gone only part way in the process of 'Reception'. Duck dealt with both.

Something of the same patience with diversity animated Duck's treatment of the law applied to Italian cities and principalities, the subject that followed. Here he was faced with a mass of statutes, *consilia* and *decisiones*, and other works of local *praxis*. He mastered this literature, drawing upon it selectively to describe the laws of Rome, Venice, Florence, Milan, Lucca, Genoa, Urbino, and Mantua,[15] as well as larger areas like the Piedmont, Savoy and the kingdom of Naples. Duck tells us that in all these places the strength of the *ius commune* had been tested and sometimes overtaken by the enactment of local statutes. Unlike Germany, the starting point in Italy had been the inherited Roman law, but it too had been subject to change. In describing the resulting situation, Duck again had a mass of literature at his disposal – for example the *Decreta seu statuta vetera Sabaudiae ducum et Pedemonti principum* (1586) by Johannes Nevizianus, the various descriptive works by Pierre d'Avity (d. 1635), and many legal works such as the one devoted to practice in the Milanese courts compiled by Julius Caesar Ruginelli (d. 1628).[16] By the time Duck wrote, the production of such works – perfectly suited to the interests of a comparative lawyer – had grown to the point where one or more of them existed for almost every legal center in Europe. They contained a kind of balance between municipal law and the *ius commune*, and Duck assessed the relative importance of both in each geographical area he discussed. His principal theme throughout, however, was the enduring strength of the civilian heritage shared by virtually all European cities and provinces. Local statutes were rightly interpreted according to principles found within Roman law; if a city's statutes punished an action without qualification, for example, they would nonetheless be read to require malicious intent in accordance with requirements supplied by the *ius commune*.[17] Italy was not the sea of undifferentiated Romanism we sometimes imagine it to have been, but its many parts were united by the common heritage of Roman law it was Duck's aim to describe.

---

[14] Lib II, ch 2 § 17: 'Ista vero statuta Saxonica, Lubecensia, Culmensia et alia quaecunque Germanica, secundum jus civile Romanorum intelliguntur et ab eo interpretationem recipiunt'.

[15] Lib II, ch 3 §§ 1–33.

[16] Lib II, ch 3 § 25. The second work was *Le monde, ou la description générale de ses quatre parties* (1637); the third was *Liber singularis practicarum quaestionum rerumque iudicatarum* (1610).

[17] Ibid. § 29: '[P]uta si de homicidio agat statutum, intelligendum est secundum ius commune, modo cum dolo commissum sit'.

Duck's discussion of French law followed.[18] As he described its history, the reign of Roman law there had been impeded by several obstacles: the French kings' traditional insistence that they were sovereign in their realm, the division of the kingdom into the *pays de droit écrit* and the *pays des coutumes*, and the lasting prestige of the Salic law. These forces never meant, however, that Roman law was confined to a small corner of French legal life. Even in the north, it had influenced customary law; parts of that law were in fact of Roman origin; Roman law supplied the relevant law where the customs were silent or ambiguous, and it had inspired royal interventions to improve the administration of justice throughout the realm. The French law of restitution, for example, had arisen from royal and professorial efforts – a product ultimately of the *ius commune*.[19] 'And thus', Duck concluded, 'the Roman law became the Gallic law'.[20] It is probably superfluous to add that his treatment of this subject was based upon a full (and fully referenced) familiarity with the works of French jurists. Finding them requires an effort for modern readers. To support the conclusion just stated, for instance, he cited Bernardus Antumnus, *Conference du droit françois avec le droit romain* (1629); Stephanus Paschasius, *Les recherches de la France* (1596), and Guilliemus Ranchinus, *Variae Lectiones* (1597).

A chapter like this one can only illustrate a few of the details; it cannot do justice to the scope of Duck's research into the history of European legal systems; it does not reach most English developments. It must be enough to add only that the chapters that followed took up the laws of Spain, Portugal, England, Ireland, Scotland, Poland, Sweden and Denmark, and Bohemia. To all of them, he applied the same method he had used for the more familiar lands of Western Europe. In all of them, he mined the relevant local legal literature. Who would have supposed that an English lawyer in 1650 should have interested himself in the details of the laws of Poland or the Commune of Genoa? But Duck did, and he had a fair selection of works on the subject upon which to draw.[21]

The entry for Dr Duck in the *ODNB* rightly praises the *De usu iuris civilis* as Duck's 'great work'. The entry's coverage of the book's contents is quite brief, however, at least in comparison with its treatment of the various offices Duck held, and it ends rather blandly by describing the book as 'based on the best authorities'. That statement is true enough, but it does not convey either the magnitude of Duck's accomplishment or the amplitude of his learning.

---

[18]   Lib II, ch 5 §§ 1–43.
[19]   See Lib II, ch 5 § 35.
[20]   Ibid., 'Atque ita ius Romanum factum est ius Gallicum ex consuetudine Galliae, quae illud recepit, et ex consensu regum Galliae, qui ei iuris authoritatem tribuerunt'.
[21]   See Lipenius, *Bibliotheca realis iuridica*, vol II, pp 164–67.

14

William Somner (d. 1669)

With the notable exception of an article by Rosemary O'Day,[1] historians have paid little attention to the professional lives of the men who served as registrars in England's ecclesiastical courts. That they held a necessary place in diocesan administration has been widely recognized, but they themselves have long been overshadowed by the better-known advocates and judges active in the courts.[2] Perhaps their duty to act as scribes, faithfully recording and preserving the court *acta*, has made it appear that their work could not have counted for much intellectually. Even the few prominent men among them – of whom the subject of this chapter was certainly one – have been celebrated for accomplishments that had little connection with the law or their professional lives.[3] A closer look at the career of William Somner offers a chance to redress the balance. It also has a second advantage. In several ways he was typical of many of the registrars who served in England's spiritual forum.

Somner was a local man – born in Canterbury and a lifelong resident of the city. A wall plaque attached to the house where he lived, at 3 Castle Street, preserves his memory for local passers-by to see.[4] As White Kennett (d. 1728), his biographer and later bishop of Peterborough described his

---

[1]   R O'Day, 'The Role of the Registrar in Diocesan Administration', in R O'Day and F Heal (eds), *Continuity and Change: Personnel and Administration of the Church in England 1500–1642* (Leicester 1976), pp 77–94.

[2]   See, e.g., Tarver, *Church Court Records*, p 3; Ingram, *Church Courts, Sex and Marriage in England*, pp 62–63; Rodes, *Lay Authority and Reformation in the English Church*, p 176; Houlbrooke, *Church Courts and the People during the English Reformation*, pp 25–26.

[3]   See P Sherlock, 'William Somner', ODNB (Oxford 2004), online edn, www.oxforddnb.com/view/article 26030, accessed September 28, 2016; Churchill, *Canterbury Administration*, vol I, pp 452–56. This treatment is compatible with the presentation found in Ayliffe, *Parergon juris canonici Anglicani*, tit. 'Of a Notary or Register, and his Office'.

[4]   There is also a wall plaque in his honor in St. Margaret's Church in Canterbury, one the author has not been able to see.

subject's attachment to the cathedral city, 'neither his mind nor body could be mov'd any distance from it'.[5] His father, also named William, preceded him as registrar in the consistory court there, and if there is any truth to the story that the family's surname was derived from the term 'summoner', the men who served citations and process for the courts, both father and son came from a family long associated with the church's courts.

As was then normal, the office of registrar was granted for the life of the holder.[6] The father's name was found in the court records until the day he died. Then, if not in practice before that, the son began at once to act as *registrarius specialiter deputatus*. He had served as the clerk in the registry from the time he finished his own formal education at the free school in Canterbury, and after a short period he succeeded his father in the same office and with the same title. He held it until his own death more than thirty years later.[7] What intervened during his lifetime, of course, leaving him more leisure to undertake explorations of other fields of study, was the Interregnum. From that vantage point, he looked back at his office as having been both 'honest and worthy of praise'.[8] He lamented its demise. In hindsight, it now seems, the interval may actually have been fortunate. It allowed him to investigate and publish the scholarly works on the subjects upon which his reputation now rests.[9] At the time, however, he himself regarded the Civil War and Interregnum as an 'unhappy and destructive' period in the nation's history.[10]

OFFICE OF THE REGISTRAR

A respectable argument can be made that it was the registrar, rather than the chancellor, who occupied the most important place in the exercise of the ordinary jurisdiction of the English church's courts. The chancellors were the judges, of course, and as a rule they held academic qualifications that

---

[5] 'Life of William Somner', p 4, annexed to the beginning of W Somner, *Treatise of Gavelkind*, 2d edn (London 1726).

[6] A registrar's patent from the fifteenth century is printed in Woodcock, *Medieval Ecclesiastical Courts*, p 123.

[7] 'Life of William Somner', p 7.

[8] W Somner, 'Preface', *Dictionarium Saxonico-Latino-Anglicum* (Oxford 1659, reprint 1970), no 2.

[9] See 'Life of William Somner', p 39, remembering him as saying 'I was necessitated to betake myself to other thoughts' than the work of the ecclesiastical tribunals.

[10] Preface, *Dictionarium*, no 2. Little is known about his income during the Interregnum, but he was able to find at least occasional work as a notary; see J Houston, *Catalogue of Ecclesiastical Records of the Commonwealth 1643–1660 in the Lambeth Palace Library* (Farnborough 1968), p 10.

registrars lacked. Certainly they were in charge if they chose to be. However, it is remarkable how rare their appearances in many diocesan courts sometimes were. Of this feature of legal life in England the Canterbury act books from Somner's time provide a telling example. In the autumn of 1637, the chancellor was Sir Nathaniel Brent (1574–1652).[11] The registrar was William Somner. During the year that followed, the consistory court met twenty-one times, or a little more than once every three weeks. Between fifty and sixty causes were heard in most of these sittings.[12] However, in only two of the twenty-one sessions did Brent himself appear (December 20 and May 10). In nineteen the position of judge was taken by a deputy.[13] By contrast, in all but one of these sessions, the Act book records that the court met, 'in the presence of William Somner, notary public and registrar'.[14] He was always there, or at least almost always there. In other words, if anyone had reason to seek out the help of Canterbury's consistory court, it was to Somner or to his office, not to the chancellor, that they would have had recourse.

A letter from Archbishop Laud to Somner, preserved by chance, confirms the relevance of these attendance figures.[15] The Archbishop, prompted by what he described 'the common voice of the country' and being himself required to reside in London, desired to be more fully informed of the 'carriage of the clergy' in his diocese. Persistent rumors had reached him, giving reason to suspect that some incumbents had acted in 'disorderly or negligent' ways. To investigate further, he thought first of his chancellor, but concluded that Brent's 'living so much from Canterbury' made it impossible for him to provide the necessary information. The Archbishop turned instead to his principal registrar, saying that on this subject, 'You cannot but have better knowledge than other men'. We know no more about the results of this request, and we may question the propriety of seeking such information from the man who might have a say in the trial of any delinquents he named, but the incident is surely an indication of the central place Somner as registrar occupied in administration of the diocese. His biographer recorded that he

---

[11] The figures that follow were compiled from the manuscript Act book, Canterbury Cathedral Archives (CCA), Act book Z.2.1. For Brent's career, see Levack, *The Civil Lawyers in England*, pp 212–13.

[12] It is important to note, of course, that most causes required more than one sitting, so that the majority of causes heard in each session were continuations of those begun earlier.

[13] Generally styled a surrogate, who in the majority of sessions was the Revd Edward Aldey, rector of the church of St Andrew, Canterbury.

[14] The exception was the session of 24 May 1638, when Thomas Shindler acted 'in absentia registrarii'.

[15] It is found in *Works of the Most Reverend Father in God, William Laud, D D*, 7 vols (Oxford 1847–1857), vol VII, pp 268–69.

had 'prosecuted the duties of his office with prudence and integrity'.[16] This rings true. He was dependable.

SOMNER AND THE LAW

As was true of most registrars and proctors, Somner did not attend either of the two English universities. He was instead put to a clerkship in the office presided over by his father. We know so little about these offices (beyond their existence), that it would be idle to speculate about the education that took place within them. What we can legitimately ask is: How much law did young Somner learn there, and how much did he pick up in the course of his career as registrar? That is an answerable question, and we ask it first of the Roman and canon laws. The answer, manifest in his writings, is that he was familiar in fact with the texts of both laws and some of the learned commentaries written to explain and enlarge their contents. His first work, *Antiquities of Canterbury*, contains a series of 'Observations upon the Commissary of Canterbury'.[17] In it he made regular use of the resources of the *ius commune*. He was not, it seems, as full in his knowledge or as expert in its use as an advocate would have been, but he knew where to look and which texts to cite. In discussing the place of archpriests in the church's legal system, for example, he referred to the relevant title of the Gregorian Decretals and the specialized commentary relevant to the subject written by the French jurist Franciscus Duarenus (1509–59).[18] He also made the appropriate connection with the equivalent English office of rural dean by citing contents of William Lyndwood's *Provinciale*, adding a reference to material on the subject found in the *Summa Sylvestrina*.[19] He was capable also of using texts from the Roman law's Digest to explain current ecclesiastical practice in England, as in the manner of taking corporal possession of an ecclesiastical benefice. He noted two texts from the Digest to demonstrate what the requirement meant and what its derivation may have been.[20] More surprisingly, in discussing the extent of clerical immunities and the law of benefit of clergy, Somner invoked the authority not only of English

---

[16] 'Life of William Somner', pp 9–10.

[17] See W Somner, *Antiquities of Canterbury* (London 1640), pp 357–59

[18] Ibid., referring to X 1.24.1–4, and to F Duarenus, *De sacris ecclesiae ministeriis ac beneficiis* (Paris 1564), Lib. I, c. 8, but possibly taken from the edition also found in the *Tractatus universi iuris*.

[19] See Lyndwood, *Provinciale*, pp 14–15, v. *decanos rurales*; Sylvester Prierias (d. 1523), *Summa Sylvestrina*, (16th century), v. *archipresbyterii*.

[20] Somner, *Antiquities*, 177, describing the proper procedure as 'springing haply from these Laws in the Digest', citing Dig. 41.1.9 and Dig. 18.1.74.

sources like Lyndwood's glosses, but he also cited the work of the Spanish jurist, Diego de Covarrubias (1512–1577).[21] Somner and the Spaniard would not have seen eye to eye on many religious questions, but in the fashion that was accepted then but that is difficult to understand today, their differences did not prevent them from making use of reasoning and authorities found in the works of scholars across a religious divide.

A similar inquiry is possible to gauge the extent of Somner's knowledge of the English common law. Most of his professional work did not require use of common law sources, but few English civilians could ignore it entirely in a period when common lawyers were making aggressive use of writs of prohibition to limit the scope of ecclesiastical jurisdiction.[22] These attempts were much resented and resisted by the civilians, but they needed to know what they were up against. Very likely he did, but the primary reason for Somner's venture into the common law was not that. It was the preparation for his work on gavelkind, the system of land tenure and succession that prevailed in Kent.[23] It was published in 1660,[24] but he began years before that, and the enforced leisure he enjoyed following the abolition of the ecclesiastical courts in the 1640s provided him with the leisure necessary for the project's completion. The steps he took and the primary approach he adopted are evident in the Canterbury Cathedral Library, for the books with which he began are still there. They contain his marginal notations. He began with English statute books and with *Bracton, De Legibus*, using a 1660 edition of this thirteenth-century work. The annotations in it are those of a man learning the laws of England rather than an experienced common lawyer. His marginal notations drew attention to anything involving Kent and gavelkind.[25] They corrected the text of *Bracton* where Somner detected an error.[26] They provided additional references to works on the common law, as to those from Edward Coke, Ralph Hengham, Glanvill, and John Cowell.[27] And they drew conclusions from Bracton's text that were either mirrored or expanded in the practice of

---

[21] Ibid., 485, citing Covarrubias, *Liber practicarum quaestionum* (Venice 1566), Tom. II, c. 31.

[22] See Gray, *The Writ of Prohibition*; J H Baker, *Oxford History of the Laws of England: Volume VI 1483–1558* (Oxford 2003), pp 237–44.

[23] 'Life of William Somner', p 55, stating that it was this work that 'led him through a long course of Common Law and through the sense of very many Statutes'.

[24] W Somner, *Treatise of Gavelkind, both Name and Thing* (London 1660).

[25] E.g., Henricus de Bracton, *De Legibus* (London 1640), Canterbury Cathedral Library W/C-3–7, pp 92, 311.

[26] Ibid., p 373, correcting 'Henrici regis senis' to 'Henrici regis senioris'.

[27] Ibid., p 126 (Coke's *Institutes*); p 158 (Hengham's *Summa*); p 61 (Glanvill's *Tractatus de legibus*); p 26 (Cowell's *Interpreter*).

Somner's time.[28] What is missing is any attention to common law cases, either those from the Yearbooks or from contemporary practice. It seems, therefore, that Somner's interest in the secular law was limited by what he needed for his own work.

SOMNER AND THE COMMISSARY COURT

The years during which the ecclesiastical courts were in eclipse were not wasted years for Somner. It was then that he wrote not only the work on gavelkind, but also the other books upon which his reputation as a historian and antiquary rest. The Anglo-Saxon dictionary is the most celebrated of these, but he also published a *Treatise of the Roman Ports and Forts in Kent* (Oxford 1693) and several other minor works of the same character. He did not, however, forget his court, and he looked forward to its restoration. Among his unpublished works was a 'Defense of the right of the Commissary of Canterbury to prove prerogative wills and administrations'. Preserved in a manuscript at Lambeth Palace, its claims rested on what he described as 'such proofs and grants [as] have been made for 236 years' that were established 'by our bookes'.[29] It was, he alleged, a jurisdiction shared with the Prerogative Court of Canterbury in London.

He would have been comforted, then, by the fact that what he hoped for actually happened. He preserved the last act book from before the civil war. He kept it with him.[30] Its entries break off in 1643, and they had been confined to a few testamentary matters for the last few of these years. With the Restoration of the monarchy, however, the way for a return to the old ways opened up, and he did not miss the chance. Somner recorded *acta* for 15 July 1660 in the same act book and only a half folio away from the place where the last entry from 1643 is found. The new entry of this action records that it had been taken 'in the presence of William Somner, notary public and registrar'. These were the identical words found in the act books of the 1630s.

---

[28] Ibid., p 105, on the several royal courts where ordinary litigation took place.
[29] Lambeth Palace Library, London, MS 2014, no 10, f 150.
[30] It is now CCA, Z.2.4.

15

Richard Zouche (d. 1661)

Among seventeenth-century English civilians, none aimed higher than Richard Zouche. He was never reputed to be a man anxious for personal fame,[1] but he did not lack honorable ambition. He followed a path being laid out by the stellar European jurists of his time, men like Joachim Mynsinger (d. 1588), Hugo Grotius (d. 1645), and Antonius Faber (d. 1624). That path led to prominence in legal practice and appointment to a judgeship of one or more of the great European courts. It led to entry into political life, usually including prominent service in church or state. It led to appointment as professor in one or more of the law faculties in the principal European universities and to publication of multiple works of legal scholarship. And it led to an international reputation as a jurist, one not limited to a single land or to a single field of law. The career of Richard Zouche had all these. It was with good reason that Brian Levack described him as 'the most distinguished civilian that Oxford produced in the seventeenth century'.[2]

HIS LIFE AND CAREER

Zouche, scholar of New College from 1607, graduated BCL in 1614 and DCL in 1619; directly after which he was admitted as an advocate in the Court of Arches.[3] The very next year he also received appointment as Regius Professor of Civil Law at Oxford. A succession of upward steps followed, leading to several ecclesiastical offices and finally to his appointment as Judge of the High Court of Admiralty in 1641. During the years of the Interregnum, his role in

---

[1]   A Wood, *Athenae Oxonienses* (London 1813–20), vol 3, pp 511.
[2]   Levack, 'Law', p 563.
[3]   See T Holland, 'Introduction' to R Zouche, *Iuris et iudicii fecialis, sive, iuris inter gentes et quaestionum de eodem Explicatio* (Washington, DC 1911), pp i–ix.

government was limited by his own royalist sympathies, but he did not disappear from view. The parliamentary visitors permitted him to retain his academic posts in 1648, and he served as a member of the commission of lawyers appointed in the 1650s to deal with the internationally troublesome case of a murder said to have been committed by the Portuguese ambassador's brother. He held the Oxford Chair until his death, using it to write something like fifteen books on various aspects of the civil law.

It is the character of these law books, rather than the progression of his professional career, that deserves the special attention of modern English ecclesiastical lawyers. They mark out Zouche as a particularly notable civilian. They show the cosmopolitan road open to one of their predecessors in the hundred years after the accession of Queen Elizabeth. In some sense it was the high road. Whether it was the best road for a man like Zouche to have taken is a different question, one it is probably unfair to ask four hundred years later. At the time, however, it must have seemed a natural choice, perhaps also the wisest choice.

HIS WRITINGS

Zouche's writings on the law fall into one of four different categories, all of which were also staples of contemporary legal literature on the Continent.

Introductions to the Roman and Canon Laws

These works were meant primarily for law students, but they also proved useful beyond the earliest stages of a legal career. Zouche's entry in this field, *Elementa jurisprudentiae* (1st edn 1629), is like many similar introductory works written on the Continent; any comprehensive bibliography of the literature of the *ius commune* devotes many pages to them.[4] They were guides to the first steps in the study of the civil law, but depending on the predilections of their authors, they could also lead students further into the complexities of contemporary jurisprudence. Among them, Zouche's work is on the elementary side. It was addressed to 'the studious youth of Great Britain' and its stated purpose to encourage them to take the first steps towards mastery of the *ius commune*.[5] The book was not a failure; it was published again in Oxford in 1636, and in common with many of such works, Zouche's *Elementa* was

---

[4] E.g., Lipenius (1630–92), *Bibliotheca realis iuridica*, vol I, pp 723–54.
[5] See *Elementa*, pref. 'Iuventuti Magnae Britanniae iuris studiosae'.

several times reprinted on the Continent, both in Leiden and Amsterdam (1652, 1653, and 1681).

Collections of Interesting Legal Questions

Zouche's *Quaestionum iuris civilis centuria* (1st edn 1660) belongs to this class, as do a few others among the many he compiled.[6] The extent of the publication of similar works on the Continent during these years is quite astonishing. *Quaestiones, Singularia, Observationes, Resolutiones*, and others with some variant of these titles, poured forth from European presses during these centuries. Their popularity is particularly puzzling because most of them have no discernible order. Using them required either industry or an index. But it is apparent from the regularity with which at least the best among them were cited by other jurists that they served a purpose. Zouche would have known some of them very well. This was a natural field for a civilian to enter.

Investigations of Specialized Fields of Law

More than one of Zouche's books fit within this category. The best known of these is the *Iuris et iudicii fecialis sive iuris inter gentes … Explicatio* (1st edn 1650), best known today because it was reprinted and translated in 1911 as part of the Carnegie Institution's initiative to make available classic works of international law. The obvious Continental comparison is with Hugo Grotius' great work, *De iure belli ac pacis* (1st edn 1625), many times cited in Zouche's pages. It also made a connection with the work of Zouche's celebrated predecessor as Regius Professor, Alberico Gentili. Its success is shown by its publication on the Continent, including a translation into German.[7] Another work, devoted to maritime law, *Descriptio iuris et iudicii maritimi* (1st edn 1640) also fit within this tradition, as did his later topical treatment of crimes committed by ambassadors.[8]

Descriptions of Local Courts and Variants of the Ius Commune

The work titled *Descriptio iuris et iudicii ecclesiastici secundum canones et constitutiones anglicanas* (1st edn 1636) was Zouche's principal effort in this

---

[6] E.g., *Cases and Questions Resolved in the Civil Law* (Oxford 1652) (in English).

[7] Latin editions were published in Leiden in 1651, The Hague in 1659, and Mainz in 1661; The German edition, translated by Alfred Vogel, was published as *Algemeines Völkerrecht, wie auch algemeines Urtheil und Ansprüche aller Völker* in Frankfurt in 1666.

[8] *Solutio quaestionis veteris et novae, sive de legati delinquentis judice competente dissertatio* (1st edn, Oxford 1657).

field. Most European works like it are now forgotten, and it can be surprising
for a modern student of legal history to discover how many of them were
compiled. There were hundreds. In Italy, for example, works of *Praxis* were
compiled for virtually every important legal center.⁹ Like them, Zouche's
Descriptio provided straightforward exposition of ecclesiastical jurisdiction
in contemporary England. Also like most of them, its citations were more
often continental than they were local. In dealing with the law of benefices,
for instance, Zouche drew heavily upon the *Corpus iuris canonici*, together
with its glosses, and also substantive works on the subject by Panormitanus
(d. 1445), Petrus Rebuffus (d. 1557), Francis Duarenus (d. 1559), Marcus
Antonius Cucchus (d. 1565), Nicolaus Garcius (d. 1645), and Augustinus
Barbosa (d. 1649).

This last work probably retains the greatest interest for modern ecclesiastical lawyers. It was written by a civilian seemingly optimistic about the future.
It incorporated the additions to the law of the church made by Parliamentary
statutes and the 1603/04 canons, but it made no mention of the challenges
to the spiritual courts then being mounted by some common lawyers. It did
not deal with writs of prohibition or praemunire. It did not cite the opinions
of Sir Edward Coke. Instead, it proclaimed confidently that all 'violators of
ecclesiastical liberty' were ipso facto excommunicated.¹⁰ It treated the English
monarch's title of Supreme Governor not as a sign of surrender to lay power,
but as a guarantee that the English church would 'forever retain its liberty
and hold its rights and privileges fully and inviolate'.¹¹ Zouche was no crypto-
papist; he defended the clergy's right to marry and he regarded the power of
the popes as happily in the past.¹² But here he shied away from jurisdictional
dispute. Unlike the similar works of Cosin and Ridley,¹³ his *Descriptio* was
not a counter-attack against aggressive common lawyers. Zouche did know
something of the common law,¹⁴ and he was capable of entering the lists
of contemporary controversy.¹⁵ However, he did not confront opponents in

⁹ Lipenius, *Bibliotheca*, 646–63, lists works from Florence, Genoa, Lucca, Mantua, Milan,
   Pavia, Naples, Parma, Bologna, Rome, Ferrara, Perugia, Sicily, Venice, and Verona. In some
   cases, these included only statutes and *decisiones* drawn from the local courts.
¹⁰ *Descriptio*, Pt. IV § 8.
¹¹ *Descriptio*, Pt. I § 8: 'Et semper prospicere ut ecclesia sit libera et omnia iura et privilegia
   integra et inviolate retineat'.
¹² *Descriptio*, Pt. II § 4.
¹³ Cosin, *Apologie for Sundrie Proceedings by Iurisdiciton Ecclesiasticall*; Ridley, *View of the
   Civile and Ecclesiastical Law*.
¹⁴ See Levack, *The Civil Lawyers in England*, pp 1128, 1138, 1149.
¹⁵ Of this nature was R Zouche, *The Jurisdiction of the Admiralty of England Asserted Against
   Edward Coke's Articuli Admiralitatis* (London 1663). Note, however, that it was published after
   his death.

the *Descriptio*. It was an English example of a European-wide class of legal literature.

CONCLUSION

The character of this last work explains in some measure why Zouche has not attracted as much attention among modern historians as have some of the other civilians.[16] Historians are interested in conflict and in major events. Zouche's life was not filled with either. Of course, there are other reasons too. As a writer on the law, he was not the equivalent of a Grotius or a Covarrubias. And he was also unlucky. A large part of his professional career coincided with the Interregnum, when the spiritual courts had ceased to exist in England. Even in death, he may be thought unfortunate. He died in 1661 and so failed to share in the advantages which the Restoration brought to other English civilians. His life was far from tragic, however. He has not been altogether forgotten. His portrait – a handsome effort – is held by the National Portrait Gallery. One of his books was republished more than three hundred years after his death. But he deserves to be remembered today for more than this. His life and works should stand as a reminder of the international reputation to which an English civilian could legitimately aspire in the seventeenth century.

---

[16] E.g., Coquillette, *The Civilian Writers of Doctors' Commons, London*. John Cowell (d. 1611) is probably the best example of civilians whose fame rests on contemporary controversy; see, e.g., J Kenyon, *The Stuart Constitution* (Cambridge 1969), p 8.

16

Sir Leoline Jenkins (d. 1685)

Like many lawyers specializing in English ecclesiastical law, Leoline Jenkins came to his profession from Wales. Born to a Glamorgan family of quite modest means, he lived there until his matriculation at Oxford.[1] Unlike most other civilians of Welsh extraction, however, he became famous enough to be considered worthy of a biography. It was compiled in two volumes by his friend, William Wynne, and published almost forty years after Jenkins' death.[2] He also merited inclusion in *Aubrey's Brief Lives*. There he was described as possessing 'a strong body for study, indefatigable, temperate and virtuous',[3] and indeed his industry, piety, and integrity won him admirers throughout his professional career. They also won him a high place in government during his lifetime. The last of these admirable traits – virtue – was considered particularly noteworthy in his time; he refused requests for special favors even from men who could have done him material good.[4] In longer hindsight, Jenkins also has a special claim on the attention of modern ecclesiastical lawyers. He was one of the first English civilians whose contributions to the growth of English law marked him out as one of those who took a full part in shaping the realm's legal system.

JENKINS' LIFE AND CAREER

His early education was at Cowbridge Grammar School near to the place where he was born; it was a school he remembered with a gratitude sufficient

[1] A Marshall, 'Jenkins, Sir Leoline', *ODNB*; online edn, Jan 2008 www.oxforddnb.com/view/article/14732, accessed April 29, 2014.

[2] W Wynne, *The Life of Sir Leoline Jenkins* (London 1724).

[3] O Dick (ed), *Aubrey's Brief Lives* (London 1949), pp 174–76. See also Coote, *Sketches of the Lives and Characters of Eminent English Civilians*, pp 88–91.

[4] For his reputation, see, e.g., R Latham and W Matthews (eds), *The Diary of Samuel Pepys* (Berkeley and Los Angeles, CA 1974), vol VIII, p 133.

to move him to endow it liberally later in his life when his means allowed. In June 1641 he wènt up to Oxford, being admitted to Jesus College, an institution that was to figure largely in his career, but which he was obliged to quit in order to take up arms for the King's cause upon the outbreak of war. Already a royalist and episcopalian in conviction, Jenkins was among the men ousted from his College. Although he did return to live quietly in Oxford for a part of the Interregnum, he spent most of the years before the Restoration elsewhere, in a combination of private study and service as tutor to sons of the gentry. About the first of these, we know little. It certainly included the civil law; Aubrey recorded that he purchased a copy of the Commentary on the Institutes by Arnold Vinnius in 1653,[5] and in 1658 Sir William Whitmore invited him to live and study that law at Appleby in Shropshire, an invitation he accepted.[6] About the second – how he supported himself in those lean years – we know only a little more detail. We know, for example, that with his pupils he traveled into France, Holland, and Germany, residing for a time at several 'famous seats of learning' without, however, being overly impressed by the quality the education provided there. What is clear is that during these years he earned the praise of several admirers and future patrons. As a tutor Wynne also recorded that he was 'without the severity of a Master'. He became both friend and effective teacher to his students; his lessons were said to have been 'gentle and agreeable'.[7] These traits did not change. Some thought Jenkins a little dull,[8] but no one doubted his prudence, his conscientiousness, or his knowledge.

At the Restoration, Jenkins returned to Oxford, taking the DCL in 1661 and becoming Principal of Jesus College in succession to Francis Mansell in that same year. As Principal, he was energetic and successful.[9] He supervised the College's reorganization after the hard years of the Interregnum; he 'retrieved [its] credit and discipline'. He saw to the financing of a new library and the completion of a new quadrangle, in large part at his own expense. He continued in that office until 1673, but in 1662 he also became Deputy Professor of Civil Law, acting for Dr Sweit, who was both infirm in body and otherwise occupied as Dean of the Arches. Jenkins' lectures appear not to have survived, but contemporary sources tell us that they were marked by the special attention he paid to the civil law's titles on procedure, including evaluation of

5 *Brief Lives*, p 175.
6 Marshall, 'Jenkins, Sir Leoline'.
7 Wynne, *Life*, vol I, p vi.
8 See, e.g., G Burnet, *History of His Own Time* (London 1724–34), vol I, p 481: 'a man of exemplary life, and considerably learned; but he was dull and slow'.
9 E Hardy, *Jesus College* (London 1899), pp 136–40.

its application in the English tribunals where the civil law governed. His biographer recorded that Jenkins even 'occasionally shewed the agreement of the civil and common law of England' – surely a sign of his interest in the English legal system as a whole that would later serve him well.[10]

Oxford did not hold him for long. During the Interregnum he had gained the esteem and 'firm and happy friendship' of Gilbert Sheldon, who became Archbishop of Canterbury in succession to William Juxon, who died in 1663. The new archbishop encouraged him to move to the capital to take up the active practice of law. He did. Admitted at Doctors' Commons at the end of that year, almost as quickly he became deputy to the Dean of the Court of Arches. He then became assistant to Dr John Exton, judge of the Court of Admiralty, and succeeded him in that office upon the latter's death in 1668. He retained it until his death in 1685, winning praise for the sagacity and even-handedness of his maritime judgments.[11] In 1668 Archbishop Sheldon appointed him judge of the Prerogative Court of Canterbury, England's principal court in the exercise of ecclesiastical jurisdiction over last wills and testaments. He sat in Parliament for Oxford University in 1679–80 and 1680–81, and was named Secretary of State in 1680, although failing health compelled him to retire from that office a year before his death in 1685. All this time, he served frequently on diplomatic missions, most famously in helping to settle a dispute over the disposition of the estate of the Queen Mother, Henrietta Maria, who had died in Paris in 1669. It was a consequence of his achievement in these negotiations that he was knighted upon his return to England.

CONTRIBUTIONS TO MARITIME LAW

Outwardly spectacular as this career was, Jenkins' lasting reputation must rest today upon his substantive contributions to English law and his own profession. The affirmative case for his recognition is a strong one, first for his contributions to maritime law. The learning that stood behind his decisions in admiralty cases, his biographer tells us, 'rendered his name famous in most parts of Europe'.[12] His independence as a judge was itself much remarked upon at the time. It was one of the reasons for the high repute in which his opinions were held. This is worthy of note. The decision of Admiralty cases was then commonly thought to be subject to interference by the king's ministers.[13]

---

[10]   Wynne, *Life*, vol I, p x.
[11]   W Holdsworth, *History of English Law* (London 1922–66), vol XII, pp 659–61.
[12]   Wynne, *Life*, vol I, p xiii.
[13]   E Roscoe, *History of the Prize Court* (London 1924), pp 41–42.

It was tempting for a judge to decide them according to his nation's interest. Jenkins stood out against the practice. The Dutch War, declared in 1665, tested his resolve, but in 1672, he refused to accept the government's view on the status of Dutch ships taken before the War's declaration, tendering his resignation as judge rather than bend to political winds.[14] His definition of 'contraband goods' likewise excluded political manipulation of the category to the short-term benefit of his own country.[15]

Probably his best work as a judge – certainly the most celebrated – came in prize cases. He had a hand in the formulation of Rules for the Admiralty court in the adjudication of prizes issued in 1664,[16] and as a judge he made advances in dealing with difficult questions in the interpretation of accepted principles of prize law. Notable were cases involving ships and goods captured by the English. Maritime law held that neutral powers were entitled to trade with the enemy except where the goods they carried were used in the prosecution of war. It was not easy to know, however, whether goods and ships operating under neutral cover were enemy or neutral property. False papers and other subterfuges were used to give neutral cover to ships and goods actually under enemy control. One obstacle to a realistic decision in such cases was the doctrine that a ship's papers must be taken as conclusive. Jenkins, however, was not willing to yield to a rule so at variance with the facts. He allowed resort to the law of presumptions where fully satisfactory proof one way or the other was lacking. Students of the subject have shown that this approach to a difficult subject, one which the law later adopted, was first set forth in his early prize law decisions.[17]

CONTRIBUTIONS TO TESTAMENTARY LAW

As judge of the Prerogative Court of Canterbury, Jenkins was a natural 'resource person' to whom English common lawyers might turn for help in dealing with problems arising in the law of last wills and testaments. This remained a major part of the work of civilians, but there were problems.[18] Jenkins took a hand in solving them. One was the status of oral (nuncupative) wills. The ecclesiastical courts, which held primary jurisdiction over succession to chattels in

---

[14] Wynne, *Life*, vol I, p 702.
[15] D Llewelyn Davies, 'The Development of Prize Law under Sir Leoline Jenkins' (1935) 21 *Transactions of the Grotius Society* 149–60.
[16] R Marsen, *Documents Relating to Law and Custom of the Sea*, A.D. 1205–1767 (Publications of the Navy Records Society, 1915–16), vol II, pp 53–57.
[17] See Llewelyn Davies, 'Development', pp 158–60.
[18] Outhwaite, *The Rise and Fall of the English Ecclesiastical Courts*, pp 33–39.

England, had long allowed them, even to the point where an oral statement by a man on his deathbed could revoke or vary the terms of an earlier written testament.[19] Defended as the only way of securing the true last wishes of the deceased, this regime resulted in legal uncertainty and even unseemly squabbling at many a testator's deathbed, as friends and relatives sought to induce a dying man to vary the terms of an existing written testament in their own favor. Spoken words could do that. The Statute of Frauds (1677) dealt with this problem. It was widely said that Jenkins had assisted in its preparation,[20] and certainly the hand of a knowledgeable civilian is evident in several of the careful terms in the Act. Military wills were preserved, and ecclesiastical jurisdiction supported, but testaments made in writing were protected against casual oral change. Unless such declarations 'by word of mouth' by dying men were reduced to writing and read to the testator before his death, then confirmed to him and proved by the testimony of three witnesses, the prior written testament was to stand.[21] With a stroke, this troublesome problem was set right, or at least minimized. Evidence of practice before the Prerogative Court of Canterbury shows that the reform had its intended effect. The percentage of oral wills and revocations offered before the Court dropped from 31.8 percent of the total to 3.6 percent between 1661–76 and 1681–96.[22] No one can suppose that the Statute of Frauds 'solved' all the problems in any of the several areas of the law it touched, and of course it created new ones too. Even so, this provision was a step forward.

A second major contribution to testamentary law was equally sensible and equally needed: the Statute of Distributions (1670).[23] Jenkins himself prepared a memorandum outlining the case for statutory reform.[24] When a person died intestate, under English customary law going back at least to Magna Carta, the bishops were given control of the choice of the person appointed to administer the assets of the deceased. Their aim was to appoint someone who would know and implement the natural wishes of the intestate. In practice, the choice fell to the bishop's consistory courts, and ordinarily this process required at least

---

[19] L Bonfield, *Devising, Dying and Dispute: Probate Litigation in Early Modern England* (Farnham and Burlington, VT 2012), pp 109–29; for early confirmation, see the prologue to the Statute of Uses, 27 Hen VIII, c. 10 (1536), attributing the problem to 'greedy, covetous persons laying in wait upon them'.

[20] E.g., *Ash v Ardy* (1678), 3 Swans 664 (App), 36 Eng Rep 1015.

[21] 29 Car II, c 3 §21. See also C Withers, *Yorkshire Probate*, 5th edn (Chippenham 2006), pp 111–12.

[22] Bonfield, *Devising, Dying and Dispute*, p 73.

[23] 22 & 23 Car II, c 10.

[24] See Wynne, *Life*, vol II, pp 695–97.

the possibility of continued supervision by those courts. However, under what Jenkins regarded as a pretext that the continued process of supervision had led to abuses, early in the seventeenth century the common law courts had begun issuing writs of prohibition to prevent it.[25] The bishop's power was to end with appointment of the administrator.[26] Thus, if a man died intestate with five children, and administration were granted to the eldest among them, he (or she) would be free to take the whole estate after paying outstanding debts. The prohibition prevented correction by the courts – an obvious injustice to the other four. The statute restored the power of the bishops to require bonds of faithful administration and to require accounting from administrators, adding guidelines for the division of the assets of intestate estates. Jenkins claimed to regard the statute as simply 'an affirmance of the constant ancient practice',[27] but in fact it proved to be the model for the ubiquitous modern statutes of distribution that define with exactitude how the estates of intestates are to be divided among the next of kin. The statute itself later proved less effective in strengthening the powers of the ecclesiastical courts than Jenkins had envisioned, but in terms of its lasting effect on the future of the English (and American) common law it was a success.

CONCLUSION

Jenkins' biographer devoted by far the largest part of his *Life* to his subject's diplomatic career. It was dramatic in the events it included. It brought Jenkins renown among his contemporaries. It led him into participation in court circles. What he did as an emissary made a splash. From the perspective of the longer history of ecclesiastical law, however, the substantive contributions of Jenkins to testamentary and maritime law in England deserve pride of place. Earlier civilians had made a difference in the formulation of English statute law, but most of their efforts were to except the ecclesiastical courts from the scope of general legislation. 'Savings clauses' for spiritual jurisdiction were common. Statutes regulating usury,[28] perjury,[29] tithes,[30] marriage,[31] and drunkenness[32] all contained savings clause to preserve

---

[25] Gray, *The Writ of Prohibition*, vol IV, pp 1–40.
[26] E.g., *Tooker v Loane* (1618), Hob 191, 80 Eng Rep 338; *Hughes v Hughes* (1667), 1 Lev 233, 83 Eng Rep. 384. The statutory basis for this intervention was 21 Hen VIII, c 5 (1529–30).
[27] Wynne, *Life*, vol II, p 697.
[28] Usury Act 1571 (13 Eliz I, c 8).
[29] Perjury Act 1561 (5 Eliz I, c 9).
[30] Easter Offering and Tithes Act 1548 (2 & 3 Edw VI, c 13).
[31] Bigamy Act 1603 (1 Jas I, c 11).
[32] Drunkenness Act 1606 (4 Jas I, c 5).

ecclesiastical jurisdiction as it had long existed. The contributions of Leoline Jenkins, by contrast, were to the substance of English law. They amounted to a more direct kind of civilian participation in English legal life than had seemed suitable, perhaps even possible, for an ecclesiastical lawyer before his time. This was a choice on his part – a good one.

17

Hugh Davis (d. 1694)

Among post-Restoration civilians, Hugh Davis is a neglected but not insignificant representative of his profession. His life and work stand as testimony to the participation by civilians in the life of the nation and in larger legal currents of the times. Davis was the author of a treatise called *De jure uniformitatis ecclesiasticae* (London 1669). Begun in the heady years following the restoration of episcopacy, the treatise marshaled the traditional learning of the *ius commune*, combining it with the newer methods of the natural law school to defend and advance the cause of uniformity within the English Church. The text exhibits some of the scars of the Civil War and Interregnum without relying on them or even dealing with them directly. Davis looked beyond. Composed within the designedly irenic traditions exemplified by Richard Hooker, his treatise also belongs within that great movement of thought in which John Locke and Thomas Hobbes were the main English contributors.

LIFE AND CAREER

Davis was born in 1632 to a quite modest family. His father served as a cook at Winchester College.[1] The son, however, was a child of promise. He was chosen to be a scholar of the College in 1644 and he went up as a plebeian at Wadham College, Oxford, in 1651.[2] He soon transferred to the Wykehamist foundation, New College, where he was admitted as a Fellow in September

---

[1] See D Mateer, 'Hugh Davis's Commonplace Book: A New Source of Seventeenth-Century Song' (1999) 32 *Royal Musical Association Research Chronicle* 63–87. Except as noted the biographical information in this note comes from that article, whose author admirably explored the material in the archives in Winchester, Staffordshire, and Oxford for information about Davis. There is no entry for Davis in the *ODNB*.

[2] See R Barlow (ed), *The Registers of Wadham College, Oxford: Pt 1* (London 1889), p 193.

1654.[3] As is so often true, we know little of the nature and extent of his studies at New College, but they were certainly within the civil law faculty and they were certainly successful. When supplicating for admission to the BCL degree in 1657, he was described as a 'student of the Civill Law above six yeares standing of New College'. His later work, though not spent as a practicing lawyer at Doctors' Commons or any of the diocesan consistory courts, amply confirms his mastery of the traditions of the European *ius commune* as they were then taught in the civil law faculty.

Although there is little doubt that Davis sought and expected preferment, in the event he advanced no higher than the rectory of Dummer, a village about five miles southwest of Basingstoke within the diocese of Winchester. It was a middling living; in the 1870s the rectory had a value of £415.[4] He was first presented to the church in 1656. Then he was admitted again by the restored bishop of Winchester in 1661, seemingly by way of corroboration of his title. Despite the existence of a dispute between Davis and one segment of his parishioners and also a controversy over payment of first fruits of the benefice that was not settled until 1666, he held it up to the time of his death in 1694. The title page of his treatise, *De jure uniformitatis*, asserts that he was also chaplain to the Duke of Buckingham at the time of its publication, but that position led to no higher dignity in the church. Davis also left a commonplace book that contains texts of contemporary songs of interest to musicologists, but his claim to our attention must rest on the legal treatise upon which he labored over several years.

THE TREATISE

Despite its Latin title, *De jure uniformitatis ecclesiasticae* was written in English. Its subtitle gives an alternative and perhaps slightly more accurate description of what it contains: 'Three books of the rights belonging to an Uniformity in Churches'. Its arguments rest upon what Davis described as 'the chief things' that mattered in law. For him those things were the law of nature, the law of nations, and the divine law. The English common law did not come into it. In each of the three books Davis developed arguments from these basic sources of law in an effort to show that uniformity in religious practice was supported by the dictates of the law of nature and the needs of communal peace. The question, he wrote has been 'many times debated in the world

3   Foster, J (ed), *Alumni Oxonienses: The Members of the University of Oxford, 1500–1714* (London 1891, reprint Bristol 2000), vol I, p 380.
4   J Wilson, *The Imperial Gazetteer of England and Wales* (Edinburgh 1870–72), vol II, p 604.

with fire and sword'.[5] He hoped to enter the field peaceably. For him it was time for fire and sword to give way to a tranquility based upon conformity with the laws of nature. Davis concluded that this resting place meant consistency of religious practice in the nation. Uniformity was, he thought, essential in 'preserving and promoting the publick welfare'.[6]

The treatise is not well known today, and it must be admitted that it will not hold the attention of most readers for long. For understanding the contemporary status and utility of the *ius commune* within the Church of England, however, it furnishes an important vantage point on contemporary thought about the role of the law of nature in government of the church. In few other places is this perspective as easily accessible as it is in the treatise written by Davis. There are three pertinent points to be made about the work.

First, it continued to rely upon authorities drawn from the European *ius commune*. Davis cast a wide net in the authorities upon which his treatise was based, but almost all of them belonged within the traditions of European law. The text contains many references to the texts of the *Corpus iuris civilis*, and among the many civilians whose works he cited, Accursius (d. 1263), Bartolus de Saxoferrato (d. 1357), Baldus de Ubaldis (d. 1400), Paulus de Castro (d. 1441), Jason de Mayno (d. 1519), and Hugo Grotius (d. 1645) stand out as his announced favorites.[7] He relied upon the works of the canonists only slightly less often, reasoning that their authority 'in things just and regular, ought not to be the less regarded because it is papal'.[8] In confirmation of that attitude, one finds the works of Gratian (c.1140), Bartholomaeus Brixiensis (d. 1258), Panormitanus (d. 1445), and Didacus Covarrubias (d. 1577) cited as authorities in the treatise's pages. Davis even made use of St Thomas Aquinas to support his argument for the necessity of harmony between church and State.[9] What one does not find in the treatise is any regular reference to authorities from the English common law. There is no Sir Edward Coke (d. 1634); no Sir Anthony Fitzherbert (d. 1538); no William Sheppard (d. 1674). At least once, Davis did quote from *Bracton* and a treatise by Sir John Fortescue (d. c.1479),[10] but he went no further. In other words, his attitude was that of a traditionally minded English civilian. The treatise was as much concerned with political theory as it was with legal questions, and for that purpose the common lawyers may have seemed less relevant to Davis than did the works of Continental jurists.

---

[5] *De iure uniformitatis*, Dedication (to King Charles II).
[6] Ibid., Prolegomena.
[7] Ibid.
[8] Ibid.
[9] Ibid., Lib I, c 1 no 13.
[10] Ibid., Lib I, c 3 no 19.

Still, it is worthy of note that this kind of reliance upon the *ius commune* survived the Interregnum intact.

Second, it applied the law of nature as developed by continental jurists. Despite his traditional view of what counted as a relevant legal authority, Davis was 'up to date' on developments in the learned world. The sixteenth and seventeenth centuries witnessed sustained development of the law of nature as a guide and a tool for legal thought. It was the age of the Spanish scholastics – e.g. Francisco Suárez (d. 1617). It was the age of a German school of natural law – e.g. Samuel Pufendorf (d. 1694).[11] In particular the example set by Hugo Grotius seems to have been most influential with Davis. The law of nature has long been associated with reasoning by deduction from first principles. Grotius adopted this method, but he also took an additional tack. He frequently marshaled examples from history to establish and expand the understanding of the law of nature's tenets. The method has been called reasoning 'from the effect to the cause',[12] but it had this practical advantage. It employed examples from the past to put flesh on some of the quite abstract principles of the law of nature. Praiseworthy and blameworthy examples from the past helped Grotius, and others like him, come to grips with what the tenets of natural justice meant in practice.[13] The rules God had implanted in the hearts of men were knowable in part by the process of reasoning, but also in part by how they had been put into practice in the past. This is what Davis sought to do with ecclesiastical uniformity – to show its consistency with the law of nature through both abstract reasoning and historical precedent. So, for example, he used the example of the ancient Hebrews and that of the Assyrian and Persian monarchs to demonstrate the natural advantages of unity in religious practice.[14] And to prove that 'prelacy is from God', Davis called to mind testimonies from human history as well as 'the universally approved assertion of the [Schools]'.[15]

Third, it promoted ecclesiastical uniformity and the common good. Davis did not set out to prove that God had dictated the Thirty-nine Articles or even the Book of Common Prayer. He may have thought so, but he did not say so in the treatise. Nor did he draw any direct lessons from painful contemporary

---

[11] See O Robinson, T Fergus, and W Gordon, *European Legal History*, 3d edn (Oxford 2000) §§ 13.1.1–13.4.6.

[12] E.g., R Cumberland, *A Treatise of the Laws of Nature*, trans John Maxwell (London 1727), Introduction, § II.

[13] See the essays in M Barducci (ed), *Grozio ed il pensiero politico e religioso inglese 1632–1678* (Florence 2010).

[14] *De jure uniformitatis*, Lib II, c 9 §§ 10–13.

[15] Ibid., Lib I, c 3 § 3.

events in England. His argument went to the advantages of unity as the best source of concord in society as shown by reason and historical example. Without concord, 'the great fishes would swallow the small'.[16] In developing this theme, Davis did disagree with Grotius in one particular, even while adopting his method of analysis. Grotius had held that under some admittedly limited circumstances it was lawful to resist and even to wage war against one's sovereign.[17] Tyranny can reach a point where it need not be obeyed. Davis regarded this with suspicion. Though perhaps tenable in theory, in reality this approach leads to 'frequent risings' and to great harm to the commonweal.[18] That same applied in spiritual matters. Uniformity establishes 'a more facile and firm amity and peace among [the people]' than does competition between factions.[19] The great precept of the law of nature established that 'the Creator and Governor of the World is to be served and obeyed'.[20] That being so, wrote Davis, his own conclusion about resistance to authority was preferable to that of Grotius. It was in greater accord with the lessons that were taught by the law of nature and confirmed by history.

This view, expressed at length by Davis, sits quite uncomfortably with accepted principles in the twenty-first century. Who today does not think that it was right to resist Adolf Hitler or Pol Pot? And who does not endorse individual freedom of choice in religion? But we do not live in the seventeenth century. And we still admire the boldness of the thought of Thomas Hobbes. By a standard that recognizes the differences between now and then, Hugh Davis deserves at least a nod of recognition – perhaps even a salute – from those among today's ecclesiastical lawyers who take an interest in the history of their profession.

---

[16] Ibid., Lib II, c 3 § 9.
[17] P C Molhuysen (ed), Hugo Grotius, *De iure belli ac pacis libri tres* (Leiden 1919), Lib I, c 4 §§ 10–19. See D Baumgold, *Contract Theory in Historical Context: Essays on Grotius, Hobbes, and Locke* (Leiden and Boston, MA 2010), 27–49.
[18] *De jure uniformitatis*, Lib I, c 3 §§ 20–21.
[19] Ibid., Lib II, c 1§ 4.
[20] Ibid., Lib II, c 2 § 2.

18

George Lee (d. 1758)

The reputation of Sir George Lee in the history of ecclesiastical law stems from an achievement over which he had little control. He is recognized today principally as the earliest English civilian whose reports of decided cases appeared in print.[1] That publication did not, of course, take place until long after the common lawyers had paved the way in reporting cases from their own courts, and in a sense, Lee's own achievement seems almost accidental. When he died in 1758, his collection of cases and notes was still in manuscript,[2] and they remained in that state for almost three quarters of a century longer. Only in 1853 did Joseph Phillimore, then Regius Professor of Civil Law at Oxford, decide to publish two volumes from Lee's collection of cases.[3]

Lee was also not the earliest ecclesiastical lawyer to have made such a collection. What should count as a 'report' of ecclesiastical causes is a matter of opinion – some manuscript notebooks from the Middle Ages contained notations of actual causes together with miscellaneous notes from practice and summaries of the canon and civil laws. It is certain, however, that the collection of causes heard in the diocesan and provincial courts (and their later circulation in manuscript among English civilians) dates back at least to the reign of Elizabeth I.[4] The appearance in print of Lee's reports none-theless marks a moment in the history of the ecclesiastical law worthy of

---

[1]   J Wallace, *The Reporters*, 4th edn (Boston, MA 1882), pp 521–22.
[2]   This was also true, of course, for many contemporary reports from the royal courts; see Holdsworth, *Sources and Literature of English Law*, pp 100–03.
[3]   *Reports of Cases Argued and Determined in the Arches and Prerogative Courts of Canterbury and in the High Court of Delegates Containing the Judgments of the Right Hon. Sir George Lee* (2 vols, London 1832–33). Its principal coverage was for the years 1752–58, but a few cases from 1724 and 1733 were added.
[4]   The fullest example so far discovered is contained in Oxford, Bodleian Library, Tanner MS 427 (1597–1603) (from the London courts, chiefly the Court of Arches). The reporter is not known. See Baker, *English Legal Manuscripts*, vol II, p 150.

remembrance. It sought to put ecclesiastical causes on a level with cases from the royal courts.

LEE'S LIFE AND CAREER

The fifth son of Sir Thomas Lee, Bart, of Hartwell, Bucks, Lee entered Clare College, Cambridge, in 1716, but later moved to Oxford, where he matriculated at Christ Church. There he took degrees in law: the BCL in 1724 and the DCL five years later.[5] He was admitted as an advocate at Doctors' Commons in London in 1729, quickly establishing a reputation for legal ability. He later served as president of the Society and obtained the offices of Dean of Arches and Judge of the Prerogative Court of Canterbury in 1752. Beginning in 1742, he also served from time to time as one of the lords of the Admiralty. An intermittent member of Parliament from 1733 until his death in 1758, he was knighted in 1752. Lee died unexpectedly in London and was buried in the family vault in Hartwell church alongside his wife Judith, who had died before him in 1743.

Although Lee never abandoned (or slighted) his professional work as a civilian, he also took an active part in political life – so much so that almost the whole of his entry in the new *ODNB* deals with this aspect of his life. Not simply as an MP, Lee served as a trusted advisor to Frederick, Prince of Wales, whose conflicts with his father, King George II, came to an end only with the former's death in 1751.[6] It was said that he would have been named chancellor of the Exchequer had the Prince acceded to the throne, but the truth of the prediction has been disputed. What has not been disputed is his high reputation as a civilian.[7]

LEE'S REPORTS

For his volume of cases, Phillimore selected a sizable sample of the material in Lee's notebooks, but only a sample. Many other cases are to be found among those of Lee's manuscript notebooks that have survived. However, the selection

---

[5] This summary of his life was pieced together from M Kilburn, 'Lee, Sir George', *ODNB*; online edn, May 2009, www.oxforddnb.com/view/article/16283, accessed October 10, 2015; Squibb, *Doctors' Commons*, p 189; Coote, *Sketches of the Lives and Characters of Eminent English Civilians*, pp 113–15; and 'Memoir of Sir George Lee', in Phillimore, *Reports of Cases*, vol I, pp xi–xvii.

[6] A Foord, *His Majesty's Opposition, 1714–1830* (Oxford 1964), pp 273–79.

[7] E.g., in a manuscript letter of M Cottrell (1753), Lambeth Palace Library, MS 2873, fols 9–10; he is described as 'a man of great knowledge and understanding'.

that Phillimore did make provides a good indication of Lee's approach to law reporting. Almost all his cases came from the principal London tribunals: the Prerogative Court of Canterbury, the Court of Arches, and the Court of Delegates. In them, Lee's accounts followed a regular pattern.[8] Each entry began with a simple and brief statement of the nature of the case and the facts behind it, followed by a summary of the opening statements made by the advocate for each party. The proof offered in each came next, normally consisting of the testimony of each of the witnesses produced by the parties, but sometimes also including documents. Quite naturally, Lee paid much more attention to the evidentiary aspect of litigation than is found in most common law reports. In most circumstances, it was upon the probative force of the testimony of witnesses that judges were required to base their sentences, and the civil law of proof was not the free evaluation of evidence with which we are familiar today. Lee was careful to describe both with the qualifications and legal standing of witnesses and also the specific facts to which they had testified. To have done so fully in all of the cases would have been tedious in the extreme, however, and where many witnesses were produced, he sometimes recorded simply (after giving a fuller summary of a prior witness's testimony):

12. Thomas Chambers. – The same.
13. Ann Parks. – The same.[9]

After this record of the depositions, the next regular part of the entries in Lee's Reports was the arguments of counsel – sometimes only one for each side, sometimes more than one. Normally Lee's own brief judgment brought the entry to a close, although occasionally Lee also noted the case's outcome where it had been appealed to the Delegates.

The range of contentious matters being dealt with by eighteenth-century ecclesiastical courts shown in these reports remained wide, though not quite as wide as it had been 150 years before. Lord Hardwicke's Marriage Act 1753 (26 Geo II, c 33) ended the specific enforcement of private marriage contracts, but it did not end dissension about them in collateral litigation – chiefly in disputes about qualifications to administer estates,[10] and in suits brought for jactitation of marriage.[11] Tithe causes still appeared before the spiritual courts, although in much smaller numbers than had been true before 1640. Most likely this was

---

[8]   They are described by Holdsworth, *History of English Law*, vol XII, pp 666–69.

[9]   *Gardiner v Johnston* (1753), 1 Lee 358, 363, 161 ER 132, 134, Prerogative Court of Canterbury. Restraining the number of witnesses was an old problem, one that was never solved. See X 2.20.37 and DD ad id.

[10] E.g., *Plunkett v Sharp* (1754), 2 Lee 35, 161 ER 255, Court of Arches.

[11] E.g., *Butler v Dolben* (1756), 2 Lee 265, 312, 319, 161 ER 336, 352, 354, Court of Arches.

the result of the growth of a parallel jurisdiction in the temporal courts and the (by then) admitted principle that submitted questions regarding the proof and legality of tithing customs to the courts of the common law.[12] Disputes over pews or church seats and burial monuments, now fixed under the heading of faculty jurisdiction, are also to be found aplenty in Lee's Reports.[13] So (in lesser numbers) are defamation cases.[14] More than anything else, however, Lee's reports were dominated by testamentary causes. The Statute of Frauds 1677 (29 Car II, c 3) had not banished disputes about testamentary succession from the courts,[15] and the number of wills proved in the Prerogative Court had also risen from an average of 1,517 a year in the 1620s to more than double that by Lee's time.[16] Litigation ensued. In all, the evidence from Lee's reports vindicates the conclusion reached by the late Brian Outhwaite. He stressed the comparative and lasting imprint of the church's instance jurisdiction on English law and life. Nowhere did this make more of a difference than in the church's jurisdiction over last wills and testaments. He thought the common epithet 'bawdy courts' was a quite misleading way of describing the church's tribunals, and his conclusion is confirmed by Lee's reports.

THE HISTORICAL SIGNIFICANCE OF LEE'S REPORTS AND NOTEBOOKS

For legal historians, as for modern ecclesiastical lawyers, probably the most instructive lesson to be drawn from examination of Lee's reports, and also from the contents of his manuscript notebooks the author of this chapter was able to examine, comes down to a simple matter. They show that by the first half of the eighteenth century the shape of ecclesiastical jurisprudence in England had been integrated within the mainstream of English common law. Many historians have often quickly (and perhaps logically) assumed that this change must have taken place at the time of the Reformation. The evidence shows that it did not. The post-Reformation English civilians kept to their old ways.[17]

---

12 See Outhwaite, *The Rise and Fall of the English Ecclesiastical Courts*, pp 87–88; but see also *Harry v Littleton* (1753), 1 Lee 201, 161 ER 75, Court of Arches.

13 E.g., *Hopper v Davis et al.* (1754), 1 Lee 640, 161 ER 234, Court of Delegates.

14 E.g., *Ware v Johnson* (1756), 2 Lee 103, 161 ER 279, Court of Arches (on appeal from the commissary court of Buckinghamshire).

15 See Bonfield, *Devising, Dying and Dispute*, pp 133–223.

16 See Outhwaite, *Rise and Fall*, p 89; M Takahashi, 'The Number of Wills Proved in the Sixteenth and Seventeenth Centuries', in G Martin and P Spufford (eds), *The Records of the Nation* (Woodbridge 1990), pp 187–213, at p 196.

17 This is a principal theme of my *Roman Canon Law in Reformation England*; see also M Ingram, 'Church Courts in Tudor England (1485–1603): Continuities, Changes, Transformations', in V

Their methods and their sources of authority remained those of the European *ius commune*. By Lee's time, however, the balance had shifted towards what might be called the habits of mind characteristic of the common law. Not that the shift amounted to identity. The spiritual courts did not adopt the common law's trial by jury, and they retained a hold on most of the areas of subject matter jurisdiction that had long been theirs. The Doctors' Commons Library remained full of works on Roman and canon law,[18] and they were consulted. However, the century after the reconstitution of the courts in the 1660s had brought substantial changes in attitude and method to the English civilians. Lee's reports make this change evident in two particular ways.

The first lay in the acceptance of the authority of the common law courts in settling disputed matters of law. In the Middle Ages and the years before the Interregnum, the English civilians obeyed specific royal writs of prohibition when they received one, but they regarded many of these prohibitions as mere acts of power. Unlike the statutes enacted in Convocation and Parliament, prohibitions did not have the legitimate force of law. Long-established custom and specific statutes should determine the jurisdictional boundaries in England, the civilians believed, and these sources of law were more favorable to ecclesiastical jurisdiction than some of the aggressive uses of prohibitions in the hands of the common lawyers. Many of them amounted to unlawful innovation. Their use should therefore be curbed and things set right.[19] Perhaps the civilians were naïve in this assumption; certainly they were overly optimistic compared to what happened. But that is what they thought.

By Lee's time, however, this attitude had changed. So, for example, on the question of whether an ecclesiastical judge could require the giving of security for proper performance of an executor's duties, Lee cited only a case from Salkeld's Reports.[20] He did not turn to the abundant treatises on testamentary law from within the storehouses of the *ius commune* for support. Similarly, he accepted that when a question of interpreting the terms of a testamentary trust arose, it could only be done by the court of Chancery. Lee noted that in the relevant cause brought before him 'probably a prohibition would have been granted'.[21] In the same way, in his commonplace book his entry on the

---

Beaulande-Baraud and M Charageat (eds), *Les officialités dans l'Europe médiévale et moderne* (Turnhout 2014), pp 91–105.

[18] See *Catalogue of the Books in the Library of the College of Advocates in Doctors' Commons* (London 1818).

[19] Practical 'tips' for avoiding writs of prohibition were also circulated among the civilians; eg, Clement Colmore's Book (c 1610), Durham University Library, MS DDR/EJ/CCG/2/1, f 245v.

[20] Book of Cases of Sir George Lee, Lincoln's Inn Library, MS 158, f 80, citing as authority *R v Raynes* (1698), 1 Salk 299, 91 ER 265, KB.

[21] *Sutton v Smith* (1754), 1 Lee 275, 281, 161 ER 102, 104, Prerogative Court of Canterbury.

administration of estates stated that the correct interpretation of the Statute of Distributions 1670 (22 & 23 Car II, c 10) should be determined by the temporal courts.[22] He also accepted in principle the common law's decisions that the 1603/04 canons did not bind the laity.[23] His authority for this? The King's Bench had so held.[24]

The second change visible in Lee's reports and notebooks is a similar reliance on case law, both spiritual and temporal, for authority. In past times English civilians turned first to the texts of the Roman and canon laws. They took them as they had been interpreted by the great jurists of the *ius commune*. Bartolus, Panormitanus, and their successors were their habitual guides. Lee and the advocates who appeared in his reports still cited these treatises occasionally, but more often they argued on the basis of decided ecclesiastical causes. In a 1756 dispute over the scope of the appellate jurisdiction of the Court of Arches, for example, Lee based his decision on six prior cases decided in the Delegates and the Arches.[25] In a case from the next year, one that involved the use of affidavits in criminal cases, Lee looked for authority in five common law cases and one from the Prerogative court.[26] This reliance on cases was not Lee's alone; it was shared by the advocates who appeared before him. Many cases were argued and their outcome determined 'according to the constant determination of the Courts'.[27]

It would be a mistake to characterize this development as a full turn towards a regime of 'binding precedent' based on past cases. That regime is not evident in either Lee's reports or in his other manuscript notes. It was a shift in emphasis, not a sea change. Besides decided English cases, he also sometimes cited civil law texts and learned commentaries upon them, as in a defamation case involving a minor from 1740, where he made reference only to a text from the Codex and a seventeenth-century treatise on it.[28] He also referred to the commentaries by earlier English civilians – William Lyndwood's *Provinciale*, Henry Swinburne's treatise on wills, and Francis Clerke's *Praxis in curiis*

[22] Lincoln's Inn Library, MS 159, p 3, taking note of a case heard by the House of Lords and also one from the King's Bench, *Smith v Tracy* (1677), Vent 307, 86 ER 198, KB.

[23] *Lloyd v Owen and Williams* (1753), 1 Lee 434, 437, 161 ER 161, 162, Court of Arches. This was contrary to earlier practice, under which trusts were often established and regulated by the consistory courts, as in Estate of Bell (Bristol 1564), Bristol R O, Act book EP/J/1/6, p 47, where named trustees were to hold property 'ad usum et commodum' of the children of the testator.

[24] *Middleton v Thorpe* (recte Crofts) (1736), 2 Atk 650, 653 26 ER 788, 790, KB.

[25] *Hughes v Herbert* (1756), 2 Lee 287, 161 ER 343, Court of Arches.

[26] *Robins v Wolseley* (1757), 2 Lee 421, 443, 161 ER 391, 398, Court of Arches.

[27] *Keeling v M'Egan* (1754), 1 Lee 607, 612, 161 ER 222, 224, Prerogative Court of Canterbury.

[28] *Skinner v Wells* (1740), Lincoln's Inn MS. 158, f 59, London Consistory Court (reference to Cod. 5.34.11, and to Antonius Perez (d. 1673), *Praelectiones in duodecim libros Codicis* ad id).

ecclesiasticis, for example.[29] Moreover, as can be said of many common law reports, often no citations of any kind appeared in Lee's account of a case.

That fact is a reminder that these reports were not written for publication. If they were meant for anything beyond Lee's personal use, it was for circulation within a small community of professional lawyers. One sees this clearly enough in a suit for nullity of marriage from 1753, in which Lee concluded that, 'as there was no precedent, I must determine [the sentence] upon the general principles of law and reason'.[30] Here, he found, even Tómas Sanchez failed him. The important point, however, is that he had come within the common law world so convincingly described by Sir John Baker in *The Law's Two Bodies*.[31] Certainty about applicable principles of authority – even about the law itself – seems often to have eluded contemporaries, just as it sometimes does us.

CONCLUSION

Does George Lee deserve a special place among notable English civilians? If he does, it is not the place of a pioneer. He would not have claimed that for himself. He did only what others had done before him and he was then lucky enough to have one of his successors put his efforts into print. But it is (or was) an odd sort of lawyer who would stake his reputation on powers of invention. Particularly for a reporter of cases, accuracy in reporting, clarity in expression, and usefulness to his readers were what counted in those days. Even today, these straightforward virtues stand out in Lee's reports that Dr Phillimore chose to put into print. They merit some recognition.

---

[29] E.g., Lee's Commonplace Book, Lincoln's Inn MS. 159, p 1 (Lyndwood); *Andrews v Powis* (1728) 1 Lee 242, 260, 161 ER 90, 96, Serjeant's Inn (Swinburne).
[30] *Bird v Bird* (1753), 1 Lee 209, 212, 161 ER 78, 79, Court of Arches.
[31] J Baker, *The Law's Two Bodies: Some Evidential Problems in English Legal History* (Oxford 2001), pp 59–90.

19

Thomas Bever (d. 1791)

In past centuries, most of England's notable ecclesiastical lawyers prepared for their professional careers with the study of the civil law at Oxford or Cambridge. Both universities had established faculties where the *ius commune* was taught, and although attendance was by no means obligatory, these faculties provided the normal course of instruction for future civilians. What the students took away from their studies in those faculties is therefore a legitimate subject of inquiry in this book. It is not, however, an easy one. Historians have often repeated and amplified Edward Gibbon's woeful description of his encounters with the fellows of Oxford colleges during his fourteen-month stay as a student.[1] They have portrayed the dons as a class of men 'sunk in sloth and drunkenness' who roused themselves only occasionally to 'deliver rare and listless lectures'.[2] The revisionist scholarship of Dame Lucy Sutherland, among others, has provided a more balanced account of the subject than Gibbon's.[3] The life and writings of Dr Thomas Bever, fellow of All Souls College and colleague of Sir William Blackstone, add to it. They provide an instructive example of what can be learned about university education and the law during the eighteenth century, and it is far from all negative.

BEVER'S LIFE AND CAREER

Not a great deal is known about Bever's personal history. He was one of two sons of a Berkshire family who had owned land in Stratfield Mortimer at least

---

[1] E Gibbon, *Memoirs of my Life*, B Radice (ed) (London 1984), pp 75–91.
[2] H Bourguignon, *Sir William Scott, Lord Stowell, Judge of the High Court of Admiralty, 1798–1828* (Cambridge 1987), 34; see also J Barton, 'Legal Studies', in L Sutherland and L Mitchell (eds), *History of the University of Oxford V: The Eighteenth Century* (Oxford 1986), p 596, describing the law faculty as 'a comfortable refuge for the idle man'.
[3] Sutherland, *The University of Oxford in the Eighteenth Century*.

since the fifteenth century.⁴ Baptized in the parish church there in 1725, in due course Bever matriculated at Oriel College, Oxford, proceeding BA in 1748. He must quickly have been recognized for the 'good scholar and civilian' later described by Coote,⁵ for he was admitted as a jurist fellow of All Souls the following year. As such, Bever graduated BCL in 1753 and DCL in 1758. He was admitted to Doctors' Commons in London as an advocate in the latter year.⁶ He kept a house there as well as his rooms at All Souls. Bever was not without experience as a practicing lawyer, although Coote would later describe him as a 'better scholar' than he was an advocate. He served as a judge of the Cinque Ports and an advocate in the Court of Admiralty, and he also acted as chancellor and official principal in the dioceses of Lincoln and of Bangor.⁷ However, he devoted the great part of his intellectual life over the following thirty years to his work at Oxford, regularly delivering a course on the civil law to students he would later describe as 'many noble and accomplished youths, who have heretofore honored him with their constant and diligent attendance'.⁸

Bever died in London on November 8, 1791 and was buried in the parish church where he had been baptized. He had not married. He left behind two printed works and several collections of material that have remained in manuscript. Some of the latter are now preserved at All Souls College and others in the British Library and the Law Society in London.⁹ His will directed his executors not to permit publication of any of these papers and at their earliest opportunity to burn those not related to the law. These instructions were apparently carried out. Most of what can be said about Bever's place in and contribution to the history of English ecclesiastical law must be found, therefore, in the contents of his two printed works: the introductory *Discourse* just cited, which laid out and defended the principles on which his lectures were based, and the longer *History of the Legal Polity of the Roman State and*

---

⁴ The family's record and residence there was said to have been traceable to the Norman Conquest in 'Miscellaneous Remarks, Etc. – Account of Dr. Bever' (1798) 68 *Gentleman's Magazine* 753–54.

⁵ Coote, *Sketches of the Lives and Characters of Eminent English Civilians*, pp 125–26.

⁶ J Barton, 'Bever, Thomas', ODNB, Oxford University Press, 2004; online edn, Jan 2008 www.oxforddnb.com/view/article/2320, accessed March 24, 2016.

⁷ See 'Obituary of Considerable Persons; with Biographical Anecdotes' (1791) 61 *Gentleman's Magazine* 1068.

⁸ T Bever, *Discourse on the Study of Jurisprudence and the Civil Law; being an Introduction to a Course of Lectures* (Oxford 1766), p 39.

⁹ W Prest, *William Blackstone: Law and Letters in the Eighteenth Century* (Oxford 2008), p 115.

of the Rise, Progress and Extent of the Roman Laws, which was first published in Oxford in 1766.[10]

THE AIM AND SCOPE OF BEVER'S LECTURES

The traditional method of instruction in European faculties of civil law required lecturers first to read and then to comment upon the texts found in the *Corpus Iuris Civilis*, the great compilation of Roman law compiled in the sixth century at the instigation of the Emperor Justinian. This method of exposition had great strengths, strengths which help explain its continuation into the sixteenth century and beyond.[11] In skilled hands, it not only taught students the basic rules and principles of the civil law, it equipped them to employ the texts to deal with the new problems that arise constantly in legal practice.[12] However, it had weaknesses too, which had become particularly evident by the eighteenth century. Quite apart from the obsolete status of some of the material found in the Digest and Codex, the method was time consuming. Typical students spent something like six years or more mastering the craft, as Bever himself had done.[13] It was also repetitious in its method. The same juristic techniques were applied again and again – useful to some students, no doubt, but apt to become obvious or otiose in their long-continued repetition. Bever therefore adopted a different method for the lectures he began with the consent of Edward Jenner, Regius Professor of Civil Law from 1754 to 1767. His intent was to illustrate the great principles of reason and justice found in the Pandects and demonstrate their utility to his students. This method of course required attention to specific texts and to the meaning drawn from them by learned men of times past. However, it did not require entering all the nooks and crannies of Roman private law. Nor did it entail full exploration of each of the texts covered in traditional lectures.

This left him some freedom of choice. As Blackstone had done, so did Bever. He took his students as they were – most of them 'gentlemen of independent

---

[10] I have used the edition published in London in 1781. All subsequent references are to that edition. The work was translated into German and published as *Geschichte des römischen Staats und des römischen Rechts*, L Voelkel trans (Leipzig 1787).

[11] See 'Odofredus Announces his Law Lectures at Bologna', in L Thorndike, *University Records and Life in the Middle Ages* (New York 1944, reprinted 1971), pp 66–67; see also Brundage, *The Medieval Origins of the Legal Profession*, pp 249–62.

[12] My understanding of this subject is more fully explained in 'University Education and English Ecclesiastical Lawyers 1400–1650'.

[13] Rashdall, *The Universities of Europe in the Middle Ages*, vol III, pp 156–57.

estate and fortune'.[14] A few of them might become lawyers, but most would not. From the latter group, however, would be drawn many of the men who would be counted among the governors of English life and society. For this reason, they should form 'an accurate and comprehensive notion of those principles whereon the union and harmony of society in general depend',[15] and in Bever's view a study of some of the principal features of the civil law provided a proper vehicle for understanding those principles. The Pandects were, he thought, 'a rich magazine of good sense'.[16] In the law of last wills and testaments, for example, 'the civil law speaks with good effect, where the common law is silent or deficient'.[17] If students were to understand the law that regulated this part of human life, including limitations on the freedom of testation and instruction in what proper wills required, the approach Bever took offered them their best chance. Similarly, if they were to understand the dangers of giving way to luxury and extravagance in their own lives, the Roman law's provisions, meant to 'restrain the luxury and dissipation of the great and opulent', would provide salutary lessons.[18] In his view, the time spent in attaining an understanding of the civil law's basic rules against prodigality was not wasted.

This approach led Bever to deal at length with jurisprudential principles drawn from the law of nature. Some of what he wrote now seems overly abstract. It may even be right to conclude that 'today his lectures make dull and overly pious reading'.[19] However, this was not necessarily so at the time.[20] Legal positivism as found in the works of J L Austin (1790–1859) had not yet come to dominate the working assumptions of lawyers or magistrates. In the eighteenth century, the purpose of devoting attention to principles drawn from Roman and natural laws was, in the perceptive phrase of W H Bryson, 'to anchor the positive law and its study' in the wider world of ideas and justice.[21] The two worlds – the municipal law and the natural law – were connected.

---

[14] *Bl. Comm.* 15th edn (London 1809, reprint 1982), I *7.

[15] *Discourse*, p 2.

[16] Ibid., p 31.

[17] Ibid.

[18] *History*, p 149; see also A Manchester, *Modern Legal History of England and Wales 1750–1950* (London 1980), p 6.

[19] See Bourgignon, *Sir William Scott*, p 35; Holdsworth, *History of English Law*, vol XII, p 645.

[20] D Lieberman, *The Province of Legislation Determined. Legal Theory in Eighteenth-century Britain* (Cambridge 1989), p 39; M Lobban, *The Common Law and English Jurisprudence 1760–1850* (Oxford 1991), pp 19–26.

[21] See W Bryson, '"But I Know it When I See it" Natural Law and Formalism' (2016) 50 *University of Richmond Law Review Online*, 107.

BEVER'S VIEW OF THE ROMAN AND CANON LAWS

Bever was not an unqualified admirer of either the Roman or the canon law. Of the contents of the *Corpus iuris civilis*, he wrote that within its pages there was 'much to be seen to admire, much to emulate, and much to abhor'.[22] It was its intelligent study he sought to promote, making clear which was which. His estimate of the *Corpus iuris canonici* was similarly mixed. The parts of it that advanced the interests of 'the tyrannical politicians of the Romish communion' he rejected.[23] Yet he found within its contents 'a system of rules prescribed by the divine will of God to regulate our moral conduct'.[24] For him, study of both these laws did not carry with it a conclusion that the authority of the texts necessarily rested upon the status of the men in whose name they had been promulgated. For Bever, as for most other civilians of his time, the force of these learned laws was attributable 'merely to their own intrinsic worth'.[25]

Like most of his contemporaries, Bever also shared the view that principles of religion and morality were necessary parts of the law. He lived before legal positivism had secured its hold on the thought of most lawyers – a time when custom was still a legitimate source of law,[26] when desuetude could cause a statute to lose its force, and when generations of jurists had interpreted and shaped the ancient texts to conform with the needs of society and principles of right and wrong. He thus felt no incongruity in citing the opinions of Hugo Grotius (d. 1645), Samuel Pufendorf (d. 1694), Jacques Cujas (d. 1590), and Janus Gravina (d. 1718) as guides to the law to be applied in England.[27] Like Bever himself, these European jurists drew upon the *Corpus iuris civilis*, but they did not swallow it whole.[28] Bever cited their opinions to help promote understanding of the laws of Rome as having a 'title to universal law, above all others'.[29]

BEVER'S VIEW OF THE COMMON LAW

Bever's opinion of the English common law was similar to his view of the civil law – a mixture of praise and criticism. The municipal law of the realm

---

[22] *History*, p i.
[23] *Discourse*, p 5.
[24] Ibid., p 7.
[25] Ibid., p 16.
[26] See R Bursell, 'What is the Place of Custom in English Canon Law?' (1989) 1 *Ecc LJ* 12.
[27] *History*, pp 58, 69; *Discourse*, p 35.
[28] E.g., Stein, *Roman Law in European Legal History*, pp 64–67; Wolfgang Kunkel, 'The Reception of Roman Law in Germany: An Interpretation', in G Strauss (ed), *Pre-Reformation Germany* (New York 1972), pp 263–81.
[29] *Discourse*, p 24.

clearly did interest him, and he studied its contents more closely than had
been the norm among English civilians before the Interregnum. He chose,
for example, to explore the contents of Registers of Writs.[30] His judgment of
what he found was mixed. On the one hand, Bever praised the common law
as 'peculiarly adapted to the temper of the nation'.[31] He did not propose to
displace it with the Pandects. On the other hand, he also reacted as many
common lawyers long did at the start of their studies; what they found was a
'shapeless mass of juridical materials, which often staggers the resolution of
the most industrious student'.[32] To the tyro, *Coke on Littleton* offered more
discouragement than enlightenment.

For that enlightenment, he looked to the work of his colleague, William
Blackstone. Bever praised him and his *Commentaries* repeatedly. For him,
Blackstone was 'our modern oracle of English jurisprudence'.[33] The contents
of his *Commentaries* were 'a lasting and honorable monument' to the law of
England.[34] He saw no incongruity in this with his own high opinion of Roman
law; his settled opinion was that fairly considered, 'knowledge of the civil
law' would not 'lessen our veneration for the law of England'. He discovered
support for his opinion in Blackstone's own work.[35] Indeed, perusal of the text
of the first Vinerian Professor's Introduction to his *Commentaries* produces
so many shared opinions about the nature of law that it is easy and natural to
imagine the two men working together, comparing notes in harmony.

They were also in accord in believing that the common law had benefitted from ideas drawn from the European *ius commune*. This benefit was
not the major theme of either of their works, but that it had occurred from
time to time they agreed. Blackstone held that Roman laws had sometimes
'been introduced and allowed by our laws … their authority being wholly
founded upon that permission and adoption'.[36] Bever made the same point,
giving examples to prove the point. The dependence on the traditions of the
civil law, encouraged by the presence of so many ecclesiastics in the early
history of the Court of Chancery was the obvious and principal example, but
there were others. In one, he traced the probable origins of the English writ
De ventre inspiciendo to 'an ancient Praetorian edict, still preserved in the
Digest' (Dig. 25.4.1). It had been 'abridged and accommodated to the practice

---

[30] *History*, p 70.
[31] *Discourse*, pp 15–16.
[32] *History*, p 484.
[33] Ibid., pp 70–71.
[34] Ibid., p 484.
[35] *Bl. Comm.* I, *5.
[36] Ibid., p 14.

of an English court of justice' in the course of time, but it was 'evidently founded upon the same natural principle'.[37] Some of the examples may have been simple parallels; the similarity between the writ of habeas corpus and the *Lex Valeriana*, for instance.[38] But more often it had happened that the civil law had 'insensibly stolen into our own body' of laws.[39] For Bever, this silent entry provided another justification for the study of books of the civil law. Not the main reason of course. The lessons to be derived from familiarity with the 'collection of written reason' in the Pandects were the main reason. It was these lessons he sought to demonstrate to his students.

CONCLUSION

Study of the life and work of William Blackstone has enjoyed a revival of interest in our time.[40] Not so Thomas Bever. There is more than one good reason for the latter's neglect among historians of English law. It would be idle to suppose that the works of two men were equal in influence. However, for those of us who are interested in the history of ecclesiastical law in England, Bever does deserve our attention. He merits a place among the writers on the law of the English church. His general attitude towards law – both the civil and the common law – also connects us to a world from which we have wandered, but which we should not entirely forget.

---

[37] *History*, p 70. For a parallel, see *Bl. Comm.* I, *465 (citing D. 25.4.1–9 as the most likely source of the common law's rule for determining paternity).

[38] *History*, p 99.

[39] *Discourse*, p 14.

[40] See the essays in W Prest (ed), *Reinterpreting Blackstone's Commentaries: A Seminal Text in National and International Contexts* (Oxford and Portland, OR 2014) and W Prest (ed), *William Blackstone and his Commentaries: Biography, Law, History* (Oxford and Portland, OR 2009).

20

Francis Dickins (d. 1755)

A native of Hampshire and a student at Winchester College, Francis Dickins was admitted as a scholar at Trinity Hall, Cambridge, in August of 1699.[1] He proceeded LLB in 1705 and LLD in 1714, having also become a fellow of the college in January of 1704. It was a fellowship he held until his death in 1755, even though he ceased to reside in Cambridge during the last two or three years of his life because the 'noise, turbulence and ill manners' of another fellow of the college.[2] Most relevant for our appreciation of his place in the history of the ecclesiastical law in England, he became Regius Professor of Civil Law in 1714, and he occupied the chair for the remainder of his life. Apart from his tenure in that post, we do not know a great deal about his career. Perhaps there is not a lot to say about it. His name does not appear in the *ODNB* and no entry for him exists in either Charles Coote's *Sketches of Eminent English Civilians* (1804) or G. D. Squibb's survey of the profession of civilian lawyers in *Doctors' Commons* (1977).[3] No indication survives to show that he ever sought admission to Doctors' Commons in London. Indeed, Dickins seems to have been a true 'college man', rarely venturing outside Cambridge and not much interested in professional advancement.

---

[1]   The information in this paragraph comes from John and J A Venn, *Alumni Cantabrigienses* (Cambridge 1922–54), vol II, p 258. The records of Winchester College state that he was elected a scholar there in 1687 at the age of eleven (personal communications from Suzanne Foster, archivist of the College). The records of these two list him as coming from two different parishes; the records of Winchester College describe him as of Lyndhurst; those of Cambridge of East Meon.

[2]   Charles Crawley, *Trinity Hall, the History of a Cambridge College, 1350–1992* (Cambridge 1992), pp 124–25.

[3]   See also William Senior, *Doctors' Commons and the Old Court of Admiralty: A Short History of the Civilians in England* (London 1922), which deals almost exclusively with maritime law and makes no mention of Dickins.

His brother George, three years junior to Francis, followed a parallel track at Peterhouse, but as a Doctor of Medicine.

What we do know about Francis Dickins from Cambridge sources, however, stands to his credit. A contemporary described him as 'not only well esteemed for his learning, ... but [also] beloved by all who knew him for his sweetness of disposition and uncommon degree of humanity'.[4] A nice example comes from an account by one of his students, who recorded receiving 'a very angry letter from my father which disturbed me all the afternoon'. He found relief only when he 'went up to Doctor Dickins, who gave me some good advice and comforted me'.[5] Another Cambridge student recorded that although he had also 'attended the Law Lectures of that celebrated Professor Barbeyrac at Lausanne', he found that his pupils 'learned more from Dr Dickins in a week than they did from Barbeyrac's Lectures in a month'.[6]

What makes the elder Dickins' person and career of significance in the history of the profession of ecclesiastical law in England is the survival of what appear to have been his lecture notes as Regius Professor,[7] the same lectures praised by the disillusioned former Barbeyrac student. Those of Dickins' lectures that have been preserved dealt with matrimonial law, guardianship, property law, last wills and testaments, and the law of nature. They offer a valuable glimpse at eighteenth-century legal education in an English university, a subject about which not much reliable information has survived. Some of what does survive suggests that instruction at Cambridge and Oxford Universities scarcely existed. Life there was characterized only by academic torpor. It suggests that many of the college fellows and professors refused to provide students with any lectures at all. Dickins was not among that group.[8]

He himself must have wished to ensure that some notice be preserved of his lectures after his death. He directed that they be kept. The pastedown leaves of each of the manuscript volumes he left to the college contained a clear

---

4   *Memoirs of the Life and Writings of the Late Reverend Thomas Baker, D.D. of St. John's College in Cambridge* (Cambridge 1794), p 109.
5   Peter Pagnamenta (ed), *The Story Is Told in The Hidden Hall: Portrait of a Cambridge College* (London 2004), pp 18–19. The student's name was Spencer Penrice, admitted in Trinity Hall in 1736; he was the son of Sir Henry Penrice, judge of the Court of Admiralty until 1751.
6   Baker, *Memoirs*, pp 110–11.
7   They are Trinity Hall Library, MSS. 31, 44.1–4, 45.1–3, 46.1–4, 47, 48, 49, and 50. There is also a manuscript copy of one of them (which I have not been able to see) in the Wren Library, Trinity College, Cambridge, MS. B.16.45. Also, the Lincolnshire Archives Office, Lincoln, contains a manuscript that appears to be a student notebook based at least in part on Dickins' lectures, LAO.Form.20. Subsequent references to MSS. use TH to designate Trinity Hall as their location.
8   D A Winstanley, *Unreformed Cambridge* (Cambridge 1935), pp 122–23.

statement of his desire to have them preserved. They expressed his desire 'that the few manuscript books I shall leave behind me … may find a place in some remote part of the college library never to be taken out thence on any account whatsoever'.[9] Happily, the fellows of Trinity Hall have kept to his wishes, and the manuscript volumes, more than fifteen in number, are in the Library to be consulted. What of interest do they tell us?

COVERAGE OF THE LECTURES

They tell us several things. For the most part they were given in English. Latin appeared primarily when Dickins quoted from Latin texts or was otherwise necessary for legal precision. They also show that the lectures were organized by subject matter, not by the order found in the *Corpus iuris civilis*. At least to judge by the lectures Dickins chose to preserve, he took up the subjects most likely to have been of use and interest both to future lawyers and to English gentlemen. A comparison with the method found in the lectures of Dickins' slightly younger contemporary, Sir William Blackstone (1723–1780), is not farfetched. The traditional method of learning inherited from the Middle Ages had been for the lecturer to follow the order of the texts found in the Digest or the Institutes, as those texts were placed in the *Corpus Iuris Civilis*. The method took them one at a time, as they had been set forth in the 530s at the direction of the Emperor Justinian. This method was set out in the famous description given by the thirteenth-century jurist Odofredus.[10] It was textual, careful, and slow.[11] Perhaps it was even necessary for students who did not often own the books. In the era before the invention of the printing press, this would have been a normal state of affairs. Under the traditional system, the lecturer first described each of the texts; he then read them and went on to give summaries of their import; then he took up some of the questions they raised.

Dickins did not do this. He did take careful note of the important civilian texts; for example in his lecture on last wills and testaments he began by giving

---

9 Transcribed from TH, MS. 47a; there are slight differences in wording from one manuscript to another, but the sentiment and direction remain the same.

10 See his description in Thorndike, *University Records and Life in the Middle Ages*, p 67. This method was not easily or quickly abandoned; see, e.g., P Grendler, *The Universities of the Italian Renaissance* (Baltimore, MD 2002), pp 434–44.

11 The potential of this method can be appreciated by working through the text transcribed in A Lefebvre-Teillard, 'Un précieux témoin de l'École de droit canonique parisienne à l'aube du XIIIe siècle: le manuscrit 649 de la Bibliothèque municipal de Douai', (2017) 95 *Revue historique de droit français et étranger* 1–57.

what he described as 'the two most remarkable titles on this subject (Dig. 28.1 and Cod. 6.23), which were devoted to testamentary capacity and the basic requirements of their validity.[12] However, he then lectured more 'at large'. He tarried over questions of definition – something very much in the civilian tradition. He discussed the views of other jurists, some old, as for example the Roman jurists Ulpian and Modestinus, and also some more recent (Henning Goeden (d. 1521) and Arnold Vinnius (d. 1657), noting that the Roman law itself had developed over time. Dickins also asked whether the ability to make a will of one's property should be considered a natural right or simply one dependent upon municipal law, concluding that it had 'a mixt nature'.[13] He surveyed biblical teaching on the subject, concluding from passages in Isaiah, Genesis, Numbers, 2 Kings, Galatians, and Hebrews that it 'was not commanded in Holy Scripture ... yet it is authorized in several places'. He went on to discuss the current law of England relating to wills, including relevant statutes and even the views of Sir Edward Coke.[14] Thus, he took note that '[i]n England a will where lands are devised must be in writing and signed by three credible witnesses or the whole is void'.[15] He also discussed charitable bequests, surveying the texts of the Roman and canon laws on the subject, as well as saying something about current English practice in the area.[16] That English university law students would have learned nothing about the common law before William Blackstone became Vinerian Professor at Oxford is an exaggeration.

The Lectures also tell us something about what students in the civil law faculty would have learned of comparative law, including both the law of other lands and the principles that governed relations between civilians and common lawyers in England. As just noticed in the context of wills, the lectures given by Dr Dickins began with Roman law but also included coverage of the English common law. Blackstone was not the first man to mention the common law at one of England's universities. Dickins also included occasional comparisons of English law with the law that prevailed in other European lands. Some of the latter came from his reading in the works of Continental jurists, such as Hugo Grotius (d. 1645), for example, or Samuel

---

[12] He did the same for matrimonial law, see TH, MS. 44a, p 1: 'As to the civil law on the head of marriage consult [references to Dig. 23.2.1–68, Cod. 5.4.1–29, and Inst. 1.10.1–13]'.
[13] TH, MS. 47.1, p 6.
[14] TH, MS. 47.1, pp 183–84; he found fault with Coke's view of the age necessary for testamentary capacity.
[15] Ibid., p 18.
[16] Ibid., pp 62–64.

Pufendorf (d. 1694), or Cornelis van Bynkershoek (d. 1743).[17] He took the time to compare the burial practices prevalent in Holland with those that prevailed in England, for example.[18] He compared the realities of control of the sea in the Adriatic and the Baltic Seas with the ideal picture many drew out of *Mare liberum* by Grotius.[19] The lecture on the law of marriage is particularly full of comparative material, as for instance in comparing the place of parental consent in France with the then current situation in England.[20] To it, Dickins added his own comments about so-called Fleet marriages, which he considered 'a shame and reproach to the English nation'.[21] He even entered into a discussion of the merits and demerits of polygamy, comparing what he found in the biblical and historical record about its former place in human life; God tolerated polygamy in biblical times, Dickins concluded, which was not the same thing as actually approving it.[22] It is difficult to do more than guess at the reaction of students to the approach he took to the civil law. They did learn something of the basics of the ancient Roman law on the subject, including the relevant texts, but Dickins' lectures were very far from straightforward recitations of what those texts contained.

RELEVANCE OF THE LECTURES

Finally, although it would be far from the truth to describe the lectures preserved at Trinity Hall as platforms for law reform, Dickins did not hide his own opinions about current problems in discussing texts drawn from the civil law. His principal task was to explain what the law was and to interpret it for the students who attended his lectures, but he was not reluctant about sharing his opinions, just as Blackstone himself did, and in some instances he made concrete suggestions for improvement. For example, he took note of the uncertainties that arose from private and incomplete practices in making last wills and testaments, suggesting that 'it were to be wished that all testaments were of a public nature, made before a public notary and lodged in a publick

---

[17] TH, MS. 46.1, p 18. Further information about the extent of his own library can be found in Thomas Osborne, *Catalogue of the Libraries of the Following and Learned ... Persons* (London 1756–58), i, pp 190–92.
[18] TH, MS 46, pp 223–25.
[19] Ibid., pp 25–29.
[20] TH, MS. 44.1, pp 137–39.
[21] Ibid., p 139.
[22] TH, MS. 31, pp 16–24.

registry'.[23] He also expressed his view that most commercial monopolies served no purpose except 'to gratifie the avarice of a few'.[24] In his view, they should be curbed. Most of his critical comments about current practice, however, were tied to existing legal texts and aimed at preparing his students for avoiding problems by correctly interpreting the texts. Thus, for example, the canonical text *Malitia supplet aetatem* was the expression used in the classical canon law to validate marriage contracts of young girls below the age of twelve. If they had malice, it seemed to say, that was enough to make up for their lack of the age of consent (X 4.2.14). The texts themselves interpreted the phrase in a physical sense. Dickins did not. He suggested a more measured interpretation of the phrase. For him the term *malitia* should signify 'wisdom, prudence, discretion, and understanding of right and wrong'.[25] Similarly he stressed the importance of the definition of a last will and testament found in the texts as a *justa sententia* to argue that the law should not give blanket approval to the wishes of testators, but should instead pay attention to their reasonability. The example he gave was a testamentary direction ordering that a testator's 'funeral be solemnized by Morris dancers'.[26] Such an admonition should be ignored, he concluded, and it could be given due note by applying a correct understanding of the civil law's definition of what a testament was. In other words, the resources of the *ius commune* would supply the sensible answer to the question.

At the remove of three hundred years, it would be incautious to express a firm judgment on the merits of the lectures Francis Dickins delivered. How well they served the purposes of graduates who intended to serve as advocates and proctors in the ecclesiastical courts is not obvious. Dickins provided few examples of 'practice points' for aspiring civilians. Nor is it easy to assume, as many historians have done, that study of Roman law led Dickins and his students to embrace the theories of absolute monarchy. There is no hint of this in the lectures. It would not be incautious, however, to take note that his lectures were very far from purely doctrinal expositions of the civilian texts. They were introductory and interesting, ranging widely both in their subject matter and in the conclusions he drew about their contents. His friends in Cambridge described Dickins as 'agreeable company'.[27] Even after the passage of centuries, that quality shines through in his lectures.

---

23 TH, MS. 47.1, p 31.
24 TH, MS. 46.1, p 41.
25 TH, MS. 31, p 72: 'Malitia significat sapientiam, prudentiam, discretiionem, doli capacitatem'.
26 TH, MS. 47.1, p 17.
27 Baker, *Memoirs*, p 41.

21

Arthur Browne (d. 1805)

Born in Newport, Rhode Island, where his father served as rector of Trinity Church and took an active part in colonial American life, including the founding of the institution that would later come to be known as Brown University,[1] Arthur Browne's young life took an unfortunate and unexpected turn in 1771. His father died. The blow was even worse than such events usually are. His mother had herself died a few years before. This left Arthur a fifteen-year-old orphan. What to do? Luckily, he could count upon a small annuity secured for him through his father's foresight. Together with the help of funds contributed both by the Society for the Propagation of the Gospel (SPG) and his father's Newport congregation, he was able to finance the costs of a voyage back to Ireland, from which the family had come. There he matriculated in Trinity College, Dublin. The letter from the senior warden of Trinity Church in Newport to the SPG asserted that even as a boy, Arthur had shown 'marks of early genius'. It turned out that this was only a slight exaggeration.[2]

ACADEMIC AND PROFESSIONAL CAREER

Proceeding BA in 1776, MA in 1779, LLB in 1780, and LLD in 1784, Browne's merit as a scholar was soon obvious. He became a fellow of Trinity College by examination in 1777 and retained this fellowship to the end of his life. From an early date, the path of return to the American colonies was closed to him, even had he wished to pursue it, and he determined to make the best of

---

[1] Reuben Guild, *History of Brown University with Illustrative Documents* (Providence, RI 1867), p 146.

[2] The letter is quoted in Joseph C Sweeney, *The Life and Times of Arthur Browne in Ireland and America, 1756–1805* (Irish Legal History Society 26, 2017), p 32. Most of the biographical information in this essay comes from that volume, together with Paul O'Higgins, 'Arthur Browne (1756–1805): An Irish Civilian' (1969) 20 *NILQ* 255–73.

things as they stood. In 1777 he traveled to London to undertake study of the common law at Lincoln's Inn.[3] His experience there, like that of many others, was something of a disappointment. No mentor stepped forward to guide him, and he later recorded that he had 'sat down like most of my brethren to read at random', beginning with *Coke on Littleton* because of its 'great reputation'.[4] Discouraged, he had recourse to Blackstone's *Commentaries*, discovering then (as he himself ruefully recorded) that much of what he had learned from Coke's learned treatise had been the law of two hundred years in the past rather than the prevailing law of his own time. But he persevered, feeling obliged to 'read and read on, reports ancient and modern, cases, opinions, treatises, commentaries, all without order or method'.[5] Somehow, this random method of study was capable of producing able lawyers, at least if they were determined young men, as Browne certainly was. Although his own experience was later concentrated on the civil law, his experience at Lincoln's Inn brought him to an interest and knowledge of the common law, something he never lost. It later enabled him to serve clients in the temporal courts in Dublin, and, more surprisingly, it also made him into something like what we would now call a comparative lawyer.

Browne returned to Dublin and to the exposition of the civil law at Trinity College in 1779. He began his own course of lectures on the subject in 1785, consequent upon being named Regius Professor of Civil Law in that same year. In due course, he published two treatises that contained the substance of those lectures. It is upon their contents that any assessment of his contributions to the history of the profession of ecclesiastical law must depend. However, in several ways his career outside the academy was also a distinguished one. He regularly argued cases both in the common law courts and in the admiralty and ecclesiastical courts. He was named a KC in 1795 and a bencher of King's Inns in 1804. He was chosen as MP as a representative of the College in 1783–84, serving there for seventeen years until his change of mind and hesitant vote in favor of the Act of Union and the suppression of the Irish Parliament after the Irish rebellion of 1798 cost him a seat at Westminster by vote of the electors of the College.[6] Browne also served as the King's Prime Serjeant at Law in Ireland, indeed the last such Prime Serjeant. That office lapsed after

---

3   Sweeney, *Life and Times*, pp 57–73.
4   Arthur Browne, *Miscellaneous Sketches or, Hints for Essays* (London 1798), ii, p 373.
5   Ibid.
6   Long a matter of controversy, the subject of Browne's consistency and motive in coming to the opposite conclusion from the one he had earlier held is the subject of a long discussion, mostly favorable to Browne in Sweeney, *Life and Times*, pp 243–73.

his death from a sudden illness in 1805.[7] He was survived by his second wife, Bridget, and by five children.

COMPENDIOUS VIEW OF THE CIVIL LAW

Browne published two works based upon his lectures at Trinity College. They dealt with both the civil and the canon laws. The first and more celebrated of the two was *A Compendious View of the Civil Law and of the Law of the Admiralty* (1797).[8] The second was *A Compendious View of the Ecclesiastical Law of Ireland* (1799).[9] They both went into succeeding editions and the first of the two has even attracted modern reprints. In the Preface to this work, Browne recorded that the 'principal motive in publishing the following work' had been to 'prove his industry'. He must have been determined to demonstrate that the Regius Professorship he held was no sinecure.[10] The unstated but obvious comparison was with practice at Oxford and Cambridge, but this should not keep anyone from looking more closely at the insides of Browne's works. Doing so draws attention to the value of his lectures for understanding the place of the civil and the ecclesiastical laws in both Irish and English legal history.

The first point of interest is the approach Browne took to the Roman law. He divided his attention according to the traditional three-fold civilian division: first the law of persons, then the law of things, and finally the law of actions. However, his lectures did not take the methodical form, inherited from the Middle Ages, of moving slowly forward from one text in the Digest to the next,[11] reading and explaining each of them in turn. Many of the texts dealt with personal relations in force only in Rome, he explained. They were 'to the practicing lawyer now of little or no concern'.[12] Browne therefore moved quickly to subjects of current importance in his own day, beginning with the

---

[7]   See A R Hart, *History of the King's Serjeants at Law in Ireland* (Irish Legal History Society 9, 2000), pp 104–06.

[8]   Some appreciation for his place as an admiralty lawyer is also found in Kevin Costello, *The Court of Admiralty of Ireland 1575–1892* (Irish Legal History Society 20, 2011), pp 201–02, and Joseph Sweeney, 'The Admiralty Law of Arthur Browne' (1995) 26 *J. Maritime Law and Commerce* 59–132.

[9]   I have used what is described on the title pages as the second edition, published in Dublin in 1803.

[10] *Compendious View of the Civil Law*, p v.

[11] The classic contemporary statement of the traditional approach is that of Odofredus, 'Lectures at Bologna (13th century)', in Thorndike, *University Records*, pp 66–67. See also W Costello, *The Scholastic Curriculum at Early Seventeenth-Century Cambridge* (Cambridge, MA, 1958), pp 11–31 (with only a few references to lectures in the law faculty).

[12] *Compendious View of the Civil Law*, i, p 48 ('Prefatory Remark').

topic 'Husband and Wife' under the rubric of the law of persons. In it, he made careful reference to the basic civilian texts and institutions. In doing so, however, he was also careful to point out both those areas where the law of his own day matched Roman law and those areas where it did not. Thus, the principle that marriage was based upon free consent – '*consensus non concubitus facit nuptias*' – was one in which contemporary common law was identical to that stated in the Digest.[13] By contrast, the doctrine of *patria potestas* that had made consent of the father necessary to marital unions between unemancipated children had no formal place in contemporary English or Irish law. Statutes had confined the requirement of parental consent to a few specific situations.[14] Browne explained this simply, stating the law as it was. He did more, however. In the same lecture he added references to the history of the subject in French and Dutch laws, as well as several to apposite texts from the Bible. Texts taken from the formal canon law also filled in many of the blanks in his introduction to this aspect of the civil law. But so did English statutes and even some English cases. In other words, Browne's approach to the civil law left room both for the institutions drawn from the civil law and for contemporary changes and regional variations within the law.

A second point of interest lies in Browne's ambivalent attitude towards Roman law itself. He did not hesitate to say what he thought, and his thoughts contained both praise and blame. On the one hand, he repeatedly described it as 'the most perfect system of justice and equity between man and man, which has ever been produced by human invention'. He added that 'the principles of the civil law have been copiously borrowed by the English Jurists' and deservedly so.[15] On the other hand, Browne was also quick to criticize aspects of the civil law, as for instance its 'black code of personal slavery'.[16] Its introduction by English colonists into the West Indies was a blot on the reputation of their native land that otherwise excluded the institution.[17] Another of Browne's criticisms concerned the texts within it that could be read as supporting the unfettered power of rulers. The latter, buttressed by the famous text stating that the prince was not bound by the law (Dig. 1.3.31) 'breathes an arbitrary spirit'. Browne concluded it was a part of Roman law that 'cannot be explained away'.[18] Yet, he added, '[W]e should not shut our eyes to institutions

---

[13] Ibid., i, p 52; 'if then error, fear, or force intervened, the marriage was void, because consent, which is essential to it, was wanting'.
[14] Ibid., i, pp 58–59.
[15] Ibid., i, pp 21, 25.
[16] Ibid., i, pp 97–111.
[17] Ibid., i, pp 100–01.
[18] Ibid., i, pp 18–19.

containing much good, because they also contain some evil'.[19] Browne gave a
detailed treatment of many subjects, as for instance the laws regulating inheritance of land in Roman law, in which the rules of the civil law contrasted
favorably with those of the English common law on the subject.[20] Overall, he
thought, the balance stood in favor of the praiseworthy parts of the civil law.
There was good and bad in both.

A third subject of particular interest, already mentioned in passing, is
Browne's discussion of the influence of the Roman law on the common law
of England and Ireland. He had little doubt that it had occurred, although he
took it for granted that sometimes, 'by long use the debt is forgotten, and we
are apt to consider it as part of our original stock'.[21] His text provided examples
of clear influence, and they made a strong case. In the distribution of the
estates of men who had died intestate, he recorded 'our courts are chiefly
guided by the doctrine of one of Justinian's Novels.[22] So the Roman law's '*actio
quasi publica* was the parent of our qui tam action'.[23] And similarly the civil
law of the powers and capacities of corporations appeared to Browne to be so
like those of English law that a connection was all but certain.[24] Of course,
it may be said that this was part of a conscious effort to convince his students
of the merits of studying the civil law. Examples like these may have had that
purpose. Still, he did add that there were some plausible cases where no causa-
tive connection existed. That the Roman law of *fideicommissa* was the parent
of the English trust, as some contended, he regarded as quite unlikely. In that
case, he concluded, the 'resemblance is very remote'.[25]

COMPENDIOUS VIEW OF THE ECCLESIASTICAL LAW

This second work was also the product of lectures given by Browne at Trinity
College Dublin. The lectures followed the pattern just described in most
particulars, but there are three features worthy of note. First, it was a comparative work. Browne constantly drew upon what he knew of English ecclesiastical law to draw comparisons with the situation in Ireland. They had many
features in common – the scope of their subject matter jurisdiction being
the most obvious.[26] But they were not identical. The Act of Union raised the

---

[19] Ibid., i, p 20.
[20] Ibid., i, pp 222–33.
[21] Ibid., i, p 13.
[22] Ibid., i, p 7.
[23] Ibid., i, p 39.
[24] Ibid., i, p 144.
[25] Ibid., i, p 331.
[26] *Compendious View of the Ecclesiastical Law*, pp 364–71.

possibility that the Archbishop of Canterbury might exercise the powers of a metropolitan in Ireland, but Browne resisted the conclusion. The Archbishop of Armagh was the acknowledged primate, and the Act contained no change, express or implied, in this aspect of Irish church life.[27] He also contrasted the Irish canons on the age requisite for conferral of holy orders with those that prevailed in England,[28] and he took note that the practice of episcopal visitation of parishes required triennial exercise in England, but that visitation once a year was the more common practice in Ireland.[29] The lectures often took a comparative approach; wherever there was a Parliamentary statute on a subject, Browne provided both the English and the Irish examples.[30] He also regularly cited the works of English ecclesiastical lawyers – William Lyndwood, Henry Swinburne, and Thomas Oughton, for example – as often as not for comparative purposes. Indeed, Browne seems to have made a point of the existing differences between the two lands. He noted with apparent pride that although the English universities had been forbidden to offer degrees in the canon law during the reign of Henry VIII, the University of Dublin's law degrees had continued to be awarded 'in utroque jure tam civili quam canonico'.[31]

Second, Browne regularly made regular use of the resources of the European *ius commune* – both the canon and the Roman laws – in describing legal practice in Ireland. This usage had nothing to do with placating the large population of Catholics. It was his view that to understand the law and procedure used in ecclesiastical courts of the Church of Ireland, 'it is necessary to know the distinctions and orders of judges made by the canon law'.[32] On procedural matters, he made regular reference of the *Speculum iudiciale* of William Durantis (d. 1296). On the powers of archdeacons in Ireland, he looked to the title in the Gregorian Decretals (1234) for relevant authority.[33] To discuss the duties inherent in the office of a bishop, Browne turned to what he called 'a large volume on the duty of a bishop worthy of being consulted' by Augustinus Barbosa (d. 1649). It should be stressed that Browne was a convinced Protestant. He defended the established Church, expressing a strong desire that nothing he wrote would 'endanger this ancient and revered establishment'.[34] But like

---

[27] Ibid., pp 8–10

[28] Ibid., pp 35–37.

[29] Ibid., pp 67–68.

[30] Ibid., 327, giving both 21 Hen. VIII, c. 5 (England) and 28 Hen. VIII, c. 18 (Ireland) on the powers and duties of testamentary executors.

[31] Ibid., pp 122–23.

[32] Ibid., p 204.

[33] Ibid., pp 18–19.

[34] Ibid., pp 201–03.

the English civilians, he saw no incongruity in making use of the law of the medieval church and the many academic commentaries on it in the process of understanding and interpreting current ecclesiastical law.

Third, Browne was interested in current matters of debate and uncertainty among ecclesiastical lawyers and spoke about them in his lectures. He was, of course, a practicing lawyer as well as an academic. It should be no surprise that he added an appendix to his *Compendious View* which contained 'Ecclesiastical Cases Decided' since the time of Edward Bullingbrooke. Indeed, he made repeated references to matters of current interest or uncertainty in the courts in his lectures. For example, in speaking about the law of dilapidations, he apparently told students that recently his own views 'had been shaken by decisions of learned civilians'.[35] He used both the formal canon law and his own experiences to describe the laws of election relevant to the then current practice at Trinity College.[36] And he spoke of his own uncertainties when confronted by attempts to remove clergymen from their benefices. Was there, he asked, a real difference in result between being 'deposed, deprived, degraded, [or] suspended' from an office or benefice? Or were they just different words for the same thing?[37] In other words, Browne's lectures had an immediate and 'court-related' content.

CONCLUSION

English civilians, at least some of them, played important parts in the political and legal life of their nation. The names of Stephen Lushington (d. 1858) and William Scott, Lord Stowell (d. 1836), rough contemporaries of Browne, come immediately to mind as examples. Few of them, however, combined eminence in as many different arenas of public life as fully as did Arthur Browne. Perhaps Ireland has always been a smaller stage and offered more individual possibilities for advancement than existed across the Irish Sea. Fully considered, however, this difference is only one of degree. Both Browne's own career and his professional habits of mind matched those of many of the civilians whose careers are the subject of this volume. Although American by birth and Irish by residence, his life and his scholarship add to what we know about English ecclesiastical lawyers.

---

[35]   Ibid., 'Addenda'.
[36]   Ibid., pp 39–41.
[37]   Ibid., pp 58–59.

22

Henry Charles Coote (d. 1865)

Proctors were the workhorses of the ecclesiastical courts in England, as they were across most of Western Europe. They prepared the routine documents and made the required appearances on behalf of the parties in the civil causes that came before the tribunals.[1] Every English consistory court was served by a resident staff of proctors. For historians, however, it has not been the proctors, but instead the judges, advocates, and academics who have received the lion's share of attention.[2] That emphasis does seem appropriate. By contrast with the advocates, few proctors are found among the men admitted to fellowship in Doctors' Commons in London, and even fewer were authors of treatises that have claimed and retained a place in historical accounts of English ecclesiastical jurisdiction. As a rule, proctors were not university graduates; they were paid accordingly less for their services than advocates were, and they have left fewer marks on the historical record than the advocates.[3] The few among the English proctors who have attracted any modern interest (like the subject of this chapter) have done so because they did something else – something seemingly more worthy of note than the routine practice of ecclesiastical

---

[1] For what has been written about the proctors, see Churchill, *Canterbury Administration*, i, pp 450–52; Levack, 'The English Civilians, 1500–1750', pp 108–28; R H Helmholz, 'The Education of English Proctors, 1400–1640', in J Bush and A Wijffels (eds), *Learning the Law: Teaching and the Transmission of Law in England 1150–1900* (London and Rio Grande, OH, 1999), pp 191–210. Some of the duties of proctors are to be found in a treatise on procedure, printed in Logan, *The Medieval Court of Arches*, pp 90–97.

[2] Examples are Holdsworth, *History of English Law*, vol XII, pp 646–76; Storey, *Diocesan Administration in Fifteenth-Century England*; Brand, *The Origins of the English Legal Profession*, pp 148–57; Fournier, *Les officialités au moyen âge*, pp 32–41; C Donahue, Jr, 'The Ecclesiastical Courts: Introduction', in W Hartmann and K Pennington (eds), *History of Courts and Procedure in Medieval Canon Law* (Washington, DC 2016), pp 265–66.

[3] Coquillette, *The Civilian Writers of Doctors' Commons, London*, pp 44–94; Allmand, 'The Civil Lawyers'; Marchant, *The Church under the Law*, pp 52–56.

law. This neglect, natural though it has been, risks going too far in ignoring the contributions of the men who made up the great majority of ecclesiastical lawyers. Examination of the person and career of Henry Charles Coote demonstrates the worth of taking a closer look.

COOTE'S LIFE AND CAREER

Coote was the son of Charles Coote, the advocate who (among other accomplishments) compiled the work known as *Sketches of Eminent English Civilians*. It was the first published catalogue of the lives and careers of the men whose names were found in the subscription book of Doctors' Commons.[4] Wherever he could, the author added a description of their person and career that remains valuable to this day. The elder Coote was fifty-five years old at the time of his son's birth. By then it was certain that he would not be a financial success as an advocate. In the *Sketches*, he described himself as having 'rather patiently waited [for] employment than eagerly sought it'.[5] Too few clients came. Perhaps that points to one reason the son did not follow his father in the study of civil law at Oxford. The son nevertheless did follow the father in his choice of profession. He was admitted a proctor at Doctors' Commons in 1838.[6] Within the courts of the church, he subsequently made a specialty of practice before the Prerogative Court of Canterbury, the tribunal which exercised the archbishop of Canterbury's prerogative jurisdiction over wills and estates of persons who had died with property worth more than £5 in more than one diocese.[7] The PCC, as it was known, was the principal probate court in England, and of the church's hold on this segment of the English legal system, Coote was proud, even boastful. In his view, 'the nation has owed a deep debt of gratitude to the clergy and this court for the maintenance and defence of the freedom of testamentary disposition'.[8] As he wrote those words, the nation was about to renege on that 'deep debt'. Enactment of the Court of Probate Act in 1859 ended the church's hold on what remained of its jurisdiction over last wills and testaments. The PCC disappeared. The Act established a secular system of courts of probate in its place.[9]

---

[4] Coote, *Sketches of the Lives and Characters of Eminent English Civilians*.

[5] Ibid., p 133.

[6] Squibb, *Doctors' Commons*, p 195.

[7] See Ayliffe, *Parergon: Juris canonici Anglicani*, tit, 'Of Last Wills and Testaments, Codicils etc.', p 534; Kitching, 'The Prerogative Court of Canterbury'.

[8] H C Coote, *Practice of the Ecclesiastical Courts with Forms and Tables of Costs* (London 1847), p 31.

[9] Court of Probate Act, 20 & 21 Vict c 77 (1857).

Coote made the transition, however. Doctors' Commons was wound up, but its members were invited to continue as barristers and solicitors in England's other courts.[10] Even if it was a grudging choice, Coote accepted the invitation, extending and exercising his knowledge of the law of wills and trusts in its new setting. He became a solicitor and in 1858, he produced what would become the standard treatise on the subject – *Practice of the Court of Probate*. This work filled an obvious need. Coote's intent was to make 'the old learning of Doctors' Commons, in its new statutory context, available to the unspecialised legal profession'.[11] It was an immediate success. The first edition was followed by the second and third in 1859 and 1860. By the time of Coote's death on January 4, 1885 it had reached its 9th edition, and the treatise was not allowed to die with its author. Instead it was taken over and continued by T H Tristram (1825–1912). Long known as *Tristram and Coote's Probate Practice*, its most recent edition (the 31st) appeared in 2018[12]

By any measure, Coote's career was full of accomplishment. He also wrote a guide to the law and courts of admiralty.[13] He entered the field of historical controversy, first in journal articles and then in a small book called *A Neglected Fact in English History* (London 1864). Today, whatever reputation he enjoys among historians comes from the best known of his historical research efforts rather than for his work as a proctor or solicitor.[14] This book's theme, supported by numerous examples, was that many of the laws and institutions of Roman Britain did not disappear with the invasions of the Angles and the Saxons. They were taken into Anglo-Saxon practice and left a permanent mark on the later history of English law. Modern scholarship has returned to this subject,[15] although its students rarely mention Coote's *Neglected Fact*. Perhaps the work is 'extreme and over-simplified' in some of its treatment of the evidence.[16] It is nonetheless a book that can be read with profit.

---

[10] Squibb, *Doctors' Commons*, pp 102–09.

[11] Baker, *Monuments of Endlesse Labours*, p 169.

[12] A 'Second Supplement' to this edition was also published in 2018.

[13] *Admiralty Practice with the Practice of the Privy Council Relating Thereto* (London 1860).

[14] [Anon.], 'Coote, Henry Charles (1815–1885)', rev Nilanjana Banerji, ODNB, Oxford University Press, 2004, www.oxforddnb.com/view/article/6245, accessed November 17, 2016.

[15] See Hudson, *The Oxford History of the Laws of England, Volume II 871–1216*; P Wormald, *The Making of English Law: King Alfred to the Twelfth Century, Volume I: Legislation and its Limits* (Oxford 1999); H G Richardson and G O Sayles, *Law and Legislation from Æthelberht to Magna Carta* (Edinburgh 1966). None mentions Coote's work.

[16] It was so described in the *ODNB* entry noted above.

COOTE AS A PROCTOR

Whatever his other accomplishments, it is as a proctor that Henry Charles Coote deserves attention in a book devoted to the history of ecclesiastical lawyers. Most significant in this regard, he stands out as the compiler of a noteworthy formulary, a book of documents used in litigation, joined together with his own commentary on its contents. This work was published as *Practice of the Ecclesiastical Courts* (London 1847). It is a fine example of the contribution most characteristic of the work of English proctors. In fact, Coote's *Practice* followed and improved upon a tradition that stretches back to the thirteenth and fourteenth centuries, a tradition that was still alive in the nineteenth.[17] For centuries, proctors had collected the forms then used in the courts into what are now called either formularies or precedent books. Their compilers did so for their own use and for those who would come after them in the consistory courts. With the passage of time and the shrinkage of ecclesiastical jurisdiction in England, most of these collections have disappeared. But many also remain today – virtually all of them in manuscript.[18] They are to be found in some unexpected places, but most remain in diocesan and country record offices throughout England.[19] It is a large class with many variations; some of them are quite short, others are long and exhaustive. Probably their closest equivalent in the world of the common law would be the many books of entries that were compiled and used by generations of English common lawyers.[20]

Little attention has been paid to formularies in recent accounts of the work of the ecclesiastical courts. They seem both elementary and tedious to most modern students. Indeed, as a young man I myself described them as 'of little use in understanding actual practice' in the courts of the church.[21] This was a mistake on my part. It was true in a sense, but it ignored the function that formularies were meant to serve. They were designed to allow proctors both to understand and to make proper use of the procedures and formal documents needed in litigation. They were not intended to allow historians to draw conclusions about the frequency or the efficacy of particular features of the

---

[17] An informative predecessor, also compiled by a proctor, was Thomas Oughton, *Ordo Judiciorum; sive, methodus procedendi in negotiis et litibus in foro ecclesiastico* (London 1738).

[18] E.g., D M Owen, *Ely Records: A Handlist of the Records of the Bishop and Archdeacon of Ely* (Cambridge 1971), pp 29–34.

[19] Some have also been dispersed across the world. The University of Chicago, for example, has one copy. Joseph Regenstein Library, Special Collections, MS 1660.

[20] See Holdsworth, *History of English Law*, vol V, pp 383–86.

[21] R H Helmholz, *Marriage Litigation in Medieval England* (Cambridge 1974), p 22.

church's legal system. Without the forms and other aids found in formularies, proctors would have been at sea in serving their clients. With them, they could act effectively. That is what they were meant to accomplish and it is what they did accomplish. Coote's *Ecclesiastical Practice* thus belongs within a long and creditable tradition of his profession.

It is one of the best of its kind but of course necessarily also one of the last – 996 pages in an octavo edition, including 102 pages devoted to the author's scholarly introduction to the history and legal status of ecclesiastical jurisdiction in England. His treatment, the Introduction announced, would be 'confined to the more striking and curious features' of his subject.[22] This is true, at least in part. The volume contained controversial material, such as the forms taken from the disciplinary proceedings brought against Dr Edward Drax Free for gross sexual improprieties, a case that had scandalized Victorian society.[23] Coote also discussed the controversial subject of jactitation of marriage – false and malicious boasting of the existence of a marriage bond. Suits against such boasters were, he noted, 'of very unfrequent occurrence', but leading as they did to 'a judicial imposition of silence upon the offender', he held to the view that they were nonetheless 'of great practical utility'.[24]

Most of the Introduction, however, is taken up with a sober assessment of the origins of ecclesiastical jurisdiction and a description of its character. It is particularly full in explaining the slow steps that had led to the establishment of the archbishop of Canterbury's prerogative rights to administer the estates of those who had died with *bona notabilia* in more than one diocese.[25] His account takes full account of the canon law on the subject. It comes complete with citation of the texts and medieval commentary on texts found in the Gregorian Decretals and also an account of the force of custom in the *ius commune*. He also had at least some familiarity with English common law, citing authority found in the Yearbooks, Glanvill, the *Abbreviatio placitorum*, *Fleta*, and the works of John Selden.[26] Coote's Introduction demonstrates the extent of legal sophistication a proctor could achieve despite the lack of a university degree or association with the Inns of Court.

It is also balanced by the author's pride in the court system in which he had grown up and prospered. The convenience of the wide dispersal of spiritual courts among local communities, the 'precise and accurate method'

[22] *Ecclesiastical Practice*, p 102.
[23] Ibid., pp 158–76. A modern account of the case and its consequences is R B Outhwaite, *Scandal in the Church: Dr. Edward Drax Free, 1764–1843* (London and Rio Grande, OH 1997).
[24] *Ecclesiastical Practice*, pp 357–61.
[25] Ibid., pp 61–86.
[26] Ibid., pp 22, 90, 95–96.

of gathering evidence within them, and the base they long enjoyed in the 'refined and ancient' sources of Roman law, taken together, had produced what he called 'the most beneficial consequences for the English law and institutions'.[27] At the same time, Coote was frank in acknowledging the existence of a fault inherent in England's system of ecclesiastical courts. The weakness that afflicted spiritual jurisdiction, he wrote, 'always consisted in its inability to enforce its own decrees'.[28] The courts of the church depended upon the temporal sword to deal with contumacious defendants.[29] Even with this handicap, for him the lasting value of ecclesiastical jurisdiction over the centuries seemed evident. England's law had been enriched by its existence.

CONCLUSION

The greater part of Coote's *Ecclesiastical Practice* was not, of course, taken up by its author's discussion of the merits of the church's legal system. The book was mostly a collection of documents. It provided the forms, together with commentary, that were used by all proctors in the diocesan courts. They had been useful. Soon they would be useless. New forms would be needed. Despite Coote's passage to the status of solicitor, it is difficult not to believe he was anything but saddened when the greater part of the jurisdiction of the ecclesiastical courts was swept away by the Parliamentary statutes a few short years after this work's publication. There was no second edition. Coote had taken pride in his service as a proctor. A proctor's office, he wrote, had always been to assist 'the illiterate or inexperienced client', acting 'to guide him through the difficulties and niceties of his suit'.[30] Very soon thereafter, the disappearance of that office was to be a reality he had to accept.

[27] Ibid., pp 12–13.
[28] Ibid.
[29] The reference is to the process of Signification to the Chancery.
[30] *Ecclesiastical Practice*, p 12.

Bibliography

Treatises and Other Works on Law and Procedure Written Before 1800

Albericus de Rosate (d. 1354), *Dictionarium iuris tam civilis quam canonici* (Venice 1573, reprint 1971).

Ancharano, Petrus de (d. 1416), *Commentaria in libros decretalium* (Bologna 1580).

Andreae, Joannes (d. 1348), *In quinque decretalium libros novella commentaria* (Venice 1581, reprint 1963).

Proemium to Willelmus Durantis, *Speculum iudiciale* (Basel 1574).

Aretinus, Bonaguida (d. *c.*1263), 'Summa introductoria super officio advocationis in foro ecclesiae', Pt. II, tits. 5–25, in A Wunderlich (ed), *Anecdota quae processum civilem spectant* (Göttingen 1841), pp 183–218.

Atho, Johannis. See Ayton, John.

Ayliffe, John (d. 1732), *Parergon juris canonici Anglicani* (London 1726).

Ayton, John (d. 1350), *Constitutiones legatinae d. Othonis et d. Othoboni ... cum annotationibus Johannis de Athona* (Oxford 1679).

Azo (d. *c.*1230), *Summa codicis* (Basel 1563).

Baldus de Ubaldis (d. 1400), *In decretalium volumen commentaria* (Venice 1595, reprint 1971).

Bartolus de Saxoferrato (d. 1357), *Opera omnia* (Venice 1570–71).

Bertachinus, Johannes (d. *c.*1506), *Repertorium iuris utriusque* (Venice 1590).

Bever, T (d. 1791), *Discourse on the Study of Jurisprudence and the Civil Law; Being an Introduction to a Course of Lectures* (Oxford 1766).

History of the Legal Polity of the Roman State and of the Rise, Progress and Extent of the Roman Laws (Oxford 1766, reprint London 1781).

Blackstone, William (d. 1780), *Commentaries on the Laws of England* (Oxford 1765–69).

Bohic, Henricus (d. *c.*1350), *In quinque decretalium libros commentaria* (Venice 1576).

Browne, Arthur (d. 1805), *A Compendious View of the Civil Law and of the Law of the Admiralty* (Dublin 1797).

A Compendious View of the Ecclesiastical Law of Ireland, 2d edn (Dublin 1803).

Miscellaneous Sketches or, Hints for Essays (London 1798).

Bulgarus (*fl. c.*1130), *Summa de Iudiciis* in A Wunderlich (ed), *Anecdota quae processum civilem spectant* (Göttingen 1841).

Burn, Richard (d. 1785), *Ecclesiastical Law* (London 1762).

Burnet, G (d. 1715), *History of His Own Time* (London 1724–34).

Butrio, Antonius de (d. 1408), *Commentaria in libros decretalium* (Venice 1578, reprint 1967).

Cino da Pistoia (d. 1336), *In Codicem et aliquos titulos primi Pandectorum commentaria* (Frankfurt 1578, reprint 1964).

Clarus, Julius (d. 1575), *Liber sententiarum receptarum V § Practica criminalis* (Venice 1595).

Clerke, Francis (*fl.* 1596), *Praxis in curiis ecclesiasticis* (London 1684).

Coke, Edward (d. 1634), *First (Second etc.) Part of the Institutes of the Lawes of England* (1628–44).

Conset, Henry (*fl.* 1740), *The Practice of the Spiritual or Ecclesiastical Courts* (London 1685).

Corpus iuris canonici cum glossis (Venice 1615).

Corpus iuris civilis cum glossis (Venice 1606).

Cosin, Richard (d. 1597), *An Apologie of and for Sundrie Proceedings by Iurisdiction Ecclesiasticall* (London 1593).

  'Preface', *An Abstract of Certain Acts of Parliament, of Certain Canons, Constitutions and Synodells Provincial* (London 1584).

Covarrubias, Diego de (d. 1577), *Liber practicarum quaestionum* (Venice 1566).

Cowell, John (d. 1611), *Institutiones iuris Anglicani* (London 1630).

  The Interpreter or Booke Containing the Signification of Words (Cambridge 1607).

Cumberland, R (d. 1718), *A Treatise of the Laws of Nature*, trans John Maxwell (London 1727).

Damhouder, Jodocus (d. 1581), *Praxis rerum criminalium* (Antwerp 1601, reprint 1978).

Davis, Hugh (d. 1694), *De jure uniformitatis ecclesiasticae* (London 1669).

Decisiones Rotae Romanae. See Rota Romana.

Drogheda, William of (d. 1245), *Summa aurea*, published in L Wahrmund (ed), *Quellen zur Geschichte des römisch-kanonischen Prozesses im Mittelalter* (Innsbruck 1905–31).

Duarenus, F (d. 1559), *De sacris ecclesiae ministeriis ac beneficiis* (Paris 1564).

Duck, Arthur (d. 1648), *De usu et authoritate juris civilis romanorum* (Leiden 1654).

  Vita Henrici Chichele archiepiscopi Cantuariensis sub regibus Henrici V et VI (Oxford 1617).

Durantis, Willelmus (d. 1296), *Speculum iudiciale* (Basel 1574, reprint 1975).

Ellis, W (ed), *Summary of the Roman Law, taken from Dr. Taylor's Elements of the Civil Law* (London 1772, reprint 2005).

Ferrariis, Johannes Petrus de (*fl.* 1400), *Practica aurea* (Venice 1610).

Fliscus, Sinibaldus. See Innocent IV, Pope.

Fritsch, Ahasver (d. 1701), *Tractatus de peccatis advocatorum et procuratorum* (Frankfurt and Leipzig 1678).

Fulbecke, William (d. 1603), *A Parallele or Conference of the Civil, Canon, and the Common Law of England* (London 1602).

Geoffrey of Trani (d. 1245), *Summa super titulis decretalium* (Lyons 1519, reprint 1992).

Glanvill, Ranulf (d. 1190), *Treatise on the Laws and Customs of the Realm of England*, ed and trans G D G Hall (Oxford 1965).

Godolphin, John (d. 1678), *The Orphan's Legacy or a Testamentary Abridgment* (London 1701).

Guazzini, Petrus Paulus (*fl. c.*1700), *Opera omnia juridica et moralia* (Geneva 1738).

Harpprech, Ferdinand-Christopher (*fl.* 17th century), *Disputatio de procuratoribus* (Tübingen 1616).

Henricus de Segusio. See Hostiensis.

Hostiensis (d. 1271), *In decretalium libros lectura* (Venice 1581, reprint 1965).
   Summa aurea (Venice 1574, reprint 1963).

Huber, Ulric (d. 1694), *De ratione juris docendi et discendi diatribe,* ed M Hewett (Nijmegen 2010).

Innocent IV, Pope (d. 1254), *Apparatus in quinque libros decretalium* (Frankfurt 1570, reprint 1968).

Jacob, Giles (d. 1744), *New Law Dictionary* (London 1732).

Lancelottus, Joannes Paulus (d. 1590), *Institutiones iuris canonici* (Venice 1703).

Lanfrancus de Oriano (d. 1488), *Praxis iudiciaria aurea* (Lyon 1562).

Lipenius, Martin (d. 1692), *Bibliotheca realis iuridica* (Leipzig 1757, reprint Hildesheim 1970–71).

Lyndwood, William (d. 1446), *Provinciale (seu Constitutiones Angliae)* (Oxford 1679, reprint 1968).

Manz, Caspar (d. 1677), *Tractatus de advocatis, procuratoribus, defensoribus, syndicis et negotiorum gestoribus* (Ingolstadt 1659).

Maranta, Robertus (d. *c.*1530), *Tractatus de ordine iudiciorum ... intitulatus Speculum aureum* (Venice 1549).

Nicolaus de Tudeschis. See Panormitanus.

Odofredus (Bononiensis) (d. 1265), *Lectura super codice* (Bologna 1552, reprint 1968).

Oldradus da Ponte (d. 1335), *Consilia, seu responsa, et quaestiones aureae* (Venice 1570).

Osborne, Thomas (d. 1767), *Catalogue of the Libraries of the Following and Learned ... Persons* (London 1756–58).

Oughton, Thomas (d. *c.*1740), *Ordo Judiciorum; sive, methodus procedendi in negotiis et litibus in foro ecclesiastico* (London 1738).

Pacius, Julius (d. 1635), *Theses de procuratoribus et defensoribus* (Geneva 1597).

Panormitanus (d. 1445), *Commentaria super decretalium libros* (Venice 1615).

Pagula, William of (d. 1332), *Summa summarum* (MS. in Huntington Library, San Marino, CA).

Papa, Guido (d. 1487), *In augustissimo senatu Gratianopolitano decisiones* (Geneva 1667).

Paucapalea (*fl.* 1140s), *Die Summa des Paucapalea über das Decretum Gratiani,* ed J F von Schulte (Giessen 1890, reprint 1965).

Prierias, Sylvester (d. 1523), *Summa Sylvestrina* (16th century).

Pulton, Ferdinand (d. 1618), *De pace regis et regni* (London 1609).

Ridley, Thomas (d. 1629), *View of the Civile and Ecclesiastical Law* (Oxford 1662).

Rosate. See Albericus de Rosate.

Rota Romana. *Rotae Romanae auditorum decisiones novae, antiquae et antiquiores* (Venice 1570).

Ryves, Thomas (d. 1652), *The Poor Vicar's Plea for Tithes* (London 1620).

St German, Christopher (d. 1540), *Doctor and Student* (SS 91, 1974).

Sanchez, Thomas (d. 1610), *De sancto matrimonii sacramento tomi tres* (Lyons 1739).

Schneidewein, Joannes (d. 1568), *In Institutionum imperialium commentarii* (Venice 1701).

Scialoya, Angiolo *(fl.* 1645), *Tractatus de foro competenti* (Naples 1663).

Sinibaldus Fliscus. See Innocent IV, Pope.

Somner, W (d. 1669), *Antiquities of Canterbury* (London 1640).
'Preface', *Dictionarium Saxonico-Latino-Anglicum* (Oxford 1659, reprint 1970).
Treatise of Gavelkind, 2d edn (London 1726).

Speculator. See Durantis, William.

Stoughton, William *(fl.* 1584), *An Assertion for True and Christian Church-Policie* (Middelburg 1604).

Swinburne, Henry (d. 1624), *Brief Treatise of Testaments and Last Willes* (London 1590–91).
Treatise of Spousals or Matrimonial Contracts (London 1686).

Tancred (of Bologna) (d. 1236), 'Ordo iudiciarius', in F C Bergmann (ed), *Pillius, Tancredus, Gratia, Libri de iudiciorum ordine* (Göttingen 1842, reprint 1965), 111–23.
'Ordo judiciarius', C. 1 §§ 7–9, in L Rockinger (ed), *Briefsteller und Formelbücher des eilften bis vierzehnten Jahrhunderts* (Munich 1864, reprint 1961).

Tudeschis, Nicolaus de. See Panormitanus.

Tuschus, Dominicus (d. 1620), *Practicarum conclusionum iuris in omni foro frequentiorum* (Rome 1605–70).

Vantius, Sebastianus (16th century), *Tractatus de nullitatibus processuum ac sententiarum* (Venice 1567).

Wesenbecius, Matthaeus (d. 1586), *Commentarii in Pandectas juris civilis et Codicem Justinianeum olim dicta Paratitla* (Amsterdam 1665).

Wood, A (d. 1695), *History and Antiquities of the Colleges and Halls in the University of Oxford*, ed J Gutch (Oxford 1786).

Wood, Thomas (d. 1722), *Institute of the Law of England* (London 1772).

Wynne, W (d. 1745), *The Life of Sir Leoline Jenkins* (London 1724).

Zouche, Richard (d. 1662), *Algemeines Völkerrecht, wie auch algemeines Urtheil und Ansprüche aller Völker*, trans Alfred Vogel (Frankfurt 1666).
Cases and Questions Resolved in the Civil Law (Oxford 1652).
Descriptio iuris et iudicii ecclesiastici secundum canones et constitutiones anglicanas, 1st edn (Oxford 1636).
Descriptio juris et iudicii maritime, 1st edn (Oxford 1640).
Elementa jurisprudentiae (Oxford 1629).
The Jurisdiction of the Admiralty of England Asserted Against Edward Coke's Articuli Admiralitatis (London 1663).
Solutio quaestionis veteris et novae, sive de legati delinquentis judice competente dissertation, 1st edn (Oxford 1657).

Modern Works

Addy, J (ed), *The Diary of Henry Prescott, LL.B., Deputy Registrar of Chester Diocese, Volume I, 28 March 1704–24 March 1711* (Record Society of Lancashire and Cheshire, 127, 1987).

Allmand, C T, 'The Civil Lawyers', in C H Clough (ed), *Profession, Vocation and Culture in Later Medieval England* (Liverpool 1982), 155–80.

Andrich, G, *De natione Anglica et Scota iuristarum Universitatis Patvinae ab anno MCCXXII* (Padua 1892).

[Anon.], 'Coote, Henry Charles (1815–1885)', rev Nilanjana Banerji, *ODNB*, Oxford University Press, 2004, www.oxforddnb.com/view/article/6245, accessed November 17, 2016.

Armytage, G (ed), *Baptismal, Marriage, and Burial Registers of the Cathedral Church of Christ ... at Durham 1609–1896* (Harleian Society, vol XXIII, 1897).

Ascheri, M, *Laws of Late Medieval Italy (1000–1500)* (Leiden and Boston, MA 2013).

Aston, M, *Thomas Arundel: A Study in Church Life in the Reign of Richard II* (Oxford 1967).

Aylmer, G, *The King's Servants: The Civil Service of Charles I, 1625–1642* (New York 1961).

Aylmer, G and J Tiller (eds), *Hereford Cathedral: A History* (London and Rio Grande, OH 2000).

Baker, J H, *A Catalogue of English Legal Manuscripts in Cambridge University Library* (Woodbridge 1996).

English Legal Mansucripts, vol II (Zurich and London 1978).

Introduction to English Legal History, 4th edn (London 2002).

The Law's Two Bodies: Some Evidential Problems in English Legal History (Oxford 2001).

Monuments of Endlesse Labours: English Canonists and their Work 1300–1900 (London and Rio Grande, OH 1998).

Oxford History of the Laws of England: Volume VI 1483–1558 (Oxford 2003).

Baker, T, *Memoirs of the Life and Writings of the Late Reverend Thomas Baker, D.D. of St. John's College in Cambridge* (Cambridge 1794).

Bannister, A (ed), *Registrum Johannis Stanbury, episcopi Herefordensis, A.D. MCCCCLIII–MCCCCLXXIV* (C & Y Soc. 25, 1920).

Registrum Thome Myllyng, episcopi Herefordensis, A.D. MCCCCLXXIV–MCCCCLXCII (C & Y Soc. 26, 1920).

Registrum Thome Spofford, episcopi Herefordensis, A.D. MCCCCXXII–MCCCCXLVIII (C & Y Soc. 23, 1919).

Barducci, M (ed), *Grozio ed il pensiero politico e religioso inglese 1632–1678* (Florence 2010).

Barlow, R (ed), *The Registers of Wadham College, Oxford: Pt 1* (London 1889).

Barton, J L, 'The Faculty of Law', in J McConica (ed), *History of the University of Oxford III: The Collegiate University* (Oxford 1986), pp 257–93.

'Legal Studies', in L Sutherland and L Mitchell (eds), *History of the University of Oxford V: The Eighteenth Century* (Oxford 1986), pp 593–605.

Baumgärtner, I, 'Was muss ein Legist vom Kirchenrecht wissen? Roffredus Beneventanus und seine Libelli de iure canonico', in P Linehan (ed), *Proceedings of the Seventh International Congress of Medieval Canon Law* (Vatican City 1988), pp 223–45.

Baumgold, D, *Contract Theory in Historical Context: Essays on Grotius, Hobbes, and Locke* (Leiden and Boston, MA 2010).

Beilby, M, 'The Profits of Expertise: The Rise of the Civil Lawyers and Chancery Equity', in M Hicks (ed), *Profit, Piety and the Professions in Later Medieval England* (Gloucester 1990), pp 72–90.

Bellomo, M, *The Common Legal Past of Europe 1000–1800*, trans L Cochrane (Washington, DC 1995).

Bennett, M, *Richard II and the Revolution of* 1399 (Stroud 1999).

Berman, H, *Law and Revolution: The Formation of the Western Legal Tradition* (Cambridge, MA 1983).

Bethmann-Hollweg, M A, *Der Civilprozeß des gemeinen Rechts in geschichtlicher Entwicklung* (Bonn 1864–74).

Black, A, *Monarchy and Community: Political Ideas in the Later Conciliar Controversy* 1430–1450 (Cambridge 1970).

Bonfield, L, *Devising, Dying and Dispute: Probate Litigation in Early Modern England* (Farnham and Burlington, VT 2012).

Bourguignon, H, *Sir William Scott, Lord Stowell, Judge of the High Court of Admiralty,* 1798–1828 (Cambridge 1987).

Bowker, M (ed), *An Episcopal Court Book for the Diocese of Lincoln,* 1514–1520 (Lincoln Record Society 61, 1967).

Boyle, L, 'The Curriculum of the Faculty of Canon Law at Oxford in the First Half of the Fourteenth Century', in *Oxford Studies Presented to Daniel Callus* (Oxford Historical Society, n.s. 16, 1964).

Pastoral Care, Clerical Education and Canon Law, 1200–1400 (London 1981).

Bradford, P and A McHardy (eds), *Proctors for Parliament: Clergy, Community and Politics, c.*1248–1539 (C & Y Soc. 107, 2017).

Brand, P A, *The Origins of the English Legal Profession* (Oxford and Cambridge, MA 1992).

Brasington, B, *Order in the Court: Medieval Procedural Treatises in Translation* (Leiden and Boston, MA 2016).

Bray, G (ed), *The Anglican Canons* 1529–1947 (London 1998).

Tudor Church Reform: The Henrician Canons of 1535 *and the Reformatio legum ecclesiasticarum* (London 2000).

Brooke, C N L, 'Gilbert Foliot', in *ODNB*, www.oxforddnb.com/, accessed October 17, 2017.

Brooke, Z N, *The English Church and the Papacy* (Cambridge 1952).

Brooks, C, *Law, Politics and Society in Early Modern England* (Cambridge 2008).

Lawyers, Litigation and English Society since 1450 (London and Rio Grande, OH 1998).

Brundage, J A, 'From Classroom to Courtroom: Parisian Canonists and their Careers' (1997) 83 ZRG *(Kan. Abt.)* 352–53.

'Legal Learning and Professionalization of Canon Law', in H Vogt and M Münsteer-Swendsen (eds), *Law and Learning in the Middle Ages: Proceedings of the Second Carlsberg Academy Conference on Medieval Legal History* 2005 (Copenhagen 2006), pp 5–28.

'My Learned Friend: Professional Etiquette in Medieval Courtrooms', in M Brett and K Cushing (eds), *Readers, Texts and Compilers in the Earlier Middle Ages* (Farnham and Burlington, VT 2009).

Medieval Canon Law (London 1995).

Medieval Origins of the Legal Profession: Canonists, Civilians, and Courts (Chicago, IL 2008).

'The Teaching and Study of Canon Law in the Law Schools', in W Hartmann and K Pennington (eds), *History of Medieval Canon Law in the Classical Period,* 1140–1234 (Washington, DC 2008), pp 98–120.

Bryson, W, '"But I Know it When I See it" Natural Law and Formalism' (2016) 50 *University of Richmond Law Review Online* 107.

Burger, M, *Bishops, Clerks, and Diocesan Government in Thirteenth-Century England* (Cambridge 2012).

Bursell, R, 'What is the Place of Custom in English Canon Law?' (1989) 1 *Ecc LJ* 12.

Cairns, J W and P J du Plessis (eds), *The Creation of the Ius Commune: From Casus to Regula* (Edinburgh 2010).

Calendar of Entries in the Papal Registers Relating to Great Britain and Ireland, Papal Letters (London 1893–1960).

Cambrensis, Giraldus, 'Vita St Remigii' c 28, in *Opera*, Rolls Series 21:7 (1877).

Carlton, C, *Archbishop William Laud* (London 1987).

Carpenter, D, *Magna Carta* (London 2015).

Carruthers, M, *The Book of Memory: A Study of Memory in Medieval Culture*, 2d edn (Cambridge 2008).

Caspary, G, 'The Deposition of Richard II and the Canon Law', in S Kuttner and J Ryan (eds), *Proceedings of the Second International Congress of Medieval Canon Law* (Vatican City 1965), pp 189–201.

Cencius, L, *Tractatus de procuratoribus* (Florence 1857).

Chapman, C, *Ecclesiastical Courts: Their Officials and their Records* (Dursley 1992).

Cheney, C R, *From Becket to Langton: English Church Government 1170–1213* (Manchester 1956).

'The Church and Magna Carta' (1965) 65 *Theology* 265–72.

Cheney, M G, 'Pope Alexander III and Roger, Bishop of Worcester, 1164–1179: The Exchange of Ideas', in S Kuttner (ed), *Proceedings of the Fourth International Congress of Medieval Canon Law* (Vatican City 1976), pp 207–27.

Roger, Bishop of Worcester 1164–1179 (Oxford 1980).

'Roger (c.1134–1179), Bishop of Worcester', in *ODNB* (2004–12).

Cheney, M, D Smith, C Brooke, and P Hoskin (eds), *English Episcopal Acta 33: Worcester 1062–1185* (Oxford 2007).

Churchill, I, *Canterbury Administration: The Administrative Machinery of the Archbishopric of Canterbury Illustrated from Original Records* (London 1933).

Cobban, A, *The King's Hall within the University of Cambridge in the Later Middle Ages* (Cambridge 1969).

'Theology and Law in the Medieval Colleges of Oxford and Cambridge' (1982) 65 *Bulletin of the John Rylands Library* 57–77.

Coing, H, 'Das Schrifttum der englischen Civilians und die kontinentale Rechtsliteratur in der Zeit zwischen 1550 und 1800' (1975) 5 *Ius Commune* 1–55.

Coote, C, *Sketches of the Lives and Characters of Eminent English Civilians* (London 1804).

Coote, H C, *Admiralty Practice with the Practice of the Privy Council Relating Thereto* (London 1860).

A Neglected Fact in English History (London 1864).

Practice of the Court of Probate (1858).

Practice of the Ecclesiastical Courts with Forms and Tables of Costs (London 1847).

Coquillette, D R, *The Civilian Writers of Doctors' Commons, London: Three Centuries of Juristic Innovation in Comparative, Commercial and International Law* (Berlin 1988).

Corbett, P E, *The Roman Law of Marriage* (Oxford 1930, reprint 1969).

Cortese, E, *Il Rinascimento giuridico medievale*, 2d edn (Rome 1996).

Costello, K, *The Court of Admiralty of Ireland 1575–1892* (Irish Legal History Society 20, 2011).

Costello, W, *The Scholastic Curriculum at Early Seventeenth-Century Cambridge* (Cambridge, MA 1958).

Courtenay, W, *Schools and Scholars in Fourteenth-Century England* (Princeton, NJ 1987).

Cox, J C, *Bench-Ends in English Churches* (Oxford 1916).

Crawley, C, *Trinity Hall, the History of a Cambridge College, 1350–1992* (Cambridge 1992).

Cressy, D, *Travesties and Transgressions in Tudor and Stuart England* (Oxford 2000).

Crook, J A, *Legal Advocacy in the Roman World* (Ithaca, NY 1995).

Davies, J, *The Caroline Captivity of the Church: Charles I and the Remoulding of Anglicanism 1625–1641* (Oxford 1992).

Davies, R, 'The Episcopate', in C Clough (ed), *Profession, Vocation, and Culture in Later Medieval England* (Liverpool 1982), pp 51–89.

Davis, H, 'The Canon Law in England' (1914) 34 ZRG (Kan. Abt.) 349–50.

Derrett, J D M, *Henry Swinburne (?1551–1624) Civil Lawyer of York* (York 1973).

'The Works of Francis Clerke, Proctor (A Chapter in English Romano-Canonical Law)' (1974) 40 *Studia et documenta historiae et iuris* 52–66.

Dick, O (ed) *Aubrey's Brief Lives* (London 1949).

Doe, N (ed), *Christianity and Natural Law* (Cambridge 2017).

Fundamental Authority in Late Medieval English Law (Cambridge 1990).

Domingo, R, *Roman Law: An Introduction* (London and New York 2018).

Donahue, C, Jr, 'The Ecclesiastical Courts: Introduction', in W Hartmann and K Pennington (eds), *History of Courts and Procedure in Medieval Canon Law* (Washington, DC 2016), pp 265–66.

'Introduction', *Select Cases from the Ecclesiastical Courts of the Province of Canterbury, c.1200–1310* (SS 95, 1981).

'Procedure in the Courts of the Ius commune', in W Hartmann and K Pennington (eds), *History of Courts and Procedure in Medieval Canon Law* (Washington, DC 2016), pp 74–124.

Douglas, D (ed), *English Historical Documents: Volume II 1042–1189* (London 1968).

Druwé, W, *Scandalum in the Early Bolognese Decretistic and in Papal Decretals (c.1140–1234)* (Leuven 2018).

Duggan, A (ed), *Correspondence of Thomas Becket* (Oxford 2000).

Duggan, C, *Twelfth-Century Decretals Collections and their Importance in English History* (London 1963).

Duncan, G I O, *The High Court of Delegates* (Cambridge 1971).

Dunning, R W, 'The Wells Consistory Court in the Fifteenth Century' (1962) 106 *Proceedings of the Somersetshire Archaeological and Natural History Society* 46–61.

Edwards, K, *English Secular Cathedrals in the Middle Ages*, 2d revised edn (Manchester 1967).

Emanuel, H, 'Notaries Public and their Marks Recorded in the Archives of the Dean and Chapter of Hereford' (1953) 8 *National Library of Wales Journal* 147–62.

Emden, A, *Biographical Register of the University of Cambridge to 1500* (Cambridge 1963).

Biographical Register of the University of Oxford to A.D. 1500 (Oxford 1959).

Feenstra, R, 'Grotius' Doctrine of Liability for Negligence: Its Origin and its Influence in Civil Law Countries until Modern Codifications', in E J H Schrage (ed), *Negligence: The Comparative Legal History of the Law of Torts* (Berlin 2001).

Ferme, B E, *Canon Law in Medieval England: a Study of William Lyndwood's Provinciale with particular reference to Testamentary Law* (Rome 1996).

Fielding, J, 'Arminianism in the Localities: Peterborough Diocese, 1603–1643', in K Fincham (ed), *The Early Stuart Church 1603–1642* (Stanford, CA 1993), pp 93–113.

Fincham, K, *Prelate as Pastor: The Episcopate of James I* (Oxford 1990).

(ed), *The Early Stuart Church 1603–1642* (Stanford, CA 1993).

Flahiff, G, 'The Writ of Prohibition to Court Christian in the Thirteenth Century (parts 1 & 2)' (1944 & 1945) 6 & 7 *Medieval Studies* 261–313 and 229–90.

Flather, A, *The Politics of Place: A Study of Church Seating in Essex, c.1580–1640* (Leicester 1999).

Foord, A, *His Majesty's Opposition, 1714–1830* (Oxford 1964).

Foster, J (ed), *Alumni Oxonienses: The Members of the University of Oxford, 1500–1714* (London 1891, reprint Bristol 2000).

Fournier, P, *Les officialités au moyen âge* (Paris 1880, reprint 1984).

Fowler-Magerl, L, *Ordines Iudiciarii and Libelli de Ordine Iudiciorum* (Turnhout 1994).

Ordo iudiciorum vel ordo iudiciarius. Begriff und Literaturgattung (Frankfurt 1984), in *Ius commune*, Sonderheft 19.

Fraher, R, 'The Theoretical Justification for the New Criminal Law of the High Middle Ages: *Rei publice interest, ne crimina remaneant impunita*' (1984) *University of Illinois Law Rev.* 577–95.

Franklin, R, 'Sir Richard Steward and the Crisis of the Caroline Regime', in S Green and P Horden (eds), *All Souls under the Ancien Régime* (Oxford 2007), pp 38–54.

Fried, J, *Die Entstehung des Juristenstandes im 12. Jahrhundert* (Cologne and Vienna 1974).

Fuller, T, *History of the University of Cambridge*, ed M Prickett and T Wright (Cambridge 1840).

Gardiner, S R (ed), *Constitutional Documents of the Puritan Revolution, 1625–1660*, 3d edn revised (Oxford 1906, reprint 1962).

Gardner, J F, *Women in Roman Law and Society* (Bloomington, IN 1986).

Gasquet, Cardinal, *Old English Bible and Other Essays* (London 1897).

Gibbon, E, *Memoirs of My Life*, ed B Radice (London 1984).

Gilmore, M, *Argument from Roman Life in Political Thought 1200–1600* (Cambridge, MA 1941, reprint 1967).

Given-Wilson, C (ed and trans), *The Chronicle of Adam Usk 1377–1421* (Oxford 1997).

Goering, J, 'Burgh John (fl. 1370–1398)', in *ODNB*, Oxford University Press, 2004, www.oxforddnb.com/view/article/2912, accessed July 14, 2015.

'The Changing Face of the Village Parish: The Thirteenth Century', in J Raftis (ed), *Pathways to Medieval Peasants* (Toronto 1981), pp 323–33.

'Leonard E. Boyle and the Invention of Pastoralia', in R Stansbury (ed), *Companion to Pastoral Care in the Late Middle Ages (1200–1500)* (Leiden and Boston, MA 2010), pp 7–20.

Gottschalk, G, *Über den Einfluss des römischen Rechts auf das kanonische Recht* (Mannheim 1866, reprint 1997).

Gouron, A, 'Le rôle de l'avocat selon la doctrine romaniste du douzième siècle', in A Gouron, *Pionniers du droit occidental au Môyen Âge* (Aldershot 2006).

'Some Aspects of the Medieval Teaching of Roman Law', in J Van Engen (ed), *Learning Institutionalized: Teaching in the Medieval University* (Notre Dame, IN 2000), pp 161–76.

Gray, C M, *The Writ of Prohibition: Jurisdiction in Early Modern English Law* (New York 1994).

Greenberg, D (ed), *Stroud's Judicial Dictionary of Words and Phrases*, 7th edn (London 2006).

Greenidge, A H J, *The Legal Procedure of Cicero's Time* (London 1901, reprint 1971).

Grendler, P, *The Universities of the Italian Renaissance* (Baltimore, MD 2002).

Guild, R, *History of Brown University with Illustrative Documents* (Providence, RI 1867).

Güterbock, K, *Bracton and his Relation to the Roman Law* (Philadelphia, PA 1894).

Haigh, C, *The Plain Man's Pathways to Heaven: Kinds of Christianity in Post-Reformation England, 1570–1640* (Oxford 2007).

'Slander and the Church Courts in the Sixteenth Century' (1975) 78 *Transactions of the Lancashire and Cheshire Antiquarian Society* 1–13.

Hardy, E, *Jesus College* (London 1899).

Harries, J, 'Cicero and the Law', in J Powell and J Paterson (eds), *Cicero the Advocate* (Oxford 2004), pp 147–63.

Harris, K, 'The Patronage and Dating of Longleat House MS 24, a Prestige Copy of the Pupilla Oculi illuminated by the Master of the Troilus Frontispiece', in F Riddy (ed), *Prestige, Authority and Power in Late-Medieval Manuscripts and Texts* (York 2000), pp 35–54.

Harriss, G, *Shaping the Nation: England 1360–1461* (Oxford 2005).

Hart, A R, *History of the King's Serjeants at Law in Ireland* (Irish Legal History Society 9, 2000).

Hartmann, M, 'The Letter Collection of Abbot Wibald of Stablo and Corvey and the Decretum Gratiani" (2011–12) 29 *Bulletin of Medieval Canon Law*, n.s. 37–40.

Haselmayer, L A, 'The Apparitor and Chaucer's Summoner' (1937) 12 *Speculum* 43–57.

Heales, A, *History and Law of Church Seats or Pews* (London 1872, reprint 1998).

Helmholz, R H, 'Assumpsit and fidei laesio' (1975) 91 *LQR* 406–32.

'The Education of English Proctors, 1400–1640', in J Bush and A Wijffels (eds), *Learning the Law: Teaching and the Transmission of Law in England 1150–1900* (London and Rio Grande, OH 1999), pp 191–210.

'Ethical Standards for Advocates and Proctors in Theory and Practice', in S Kuttner (ed), *Proceedings of the Fourth International Congress of Medieval Canon Law* (Vatican City 1976), pp 283–99.

'Introduction' in *Select Cases on Defamation to 1600* (SS 101, 1985), pp xliii–xlv.

Marriage Litigation in Medieval England (Cambridge 1974).

Roman Canon Law in Reformation England (Cambridge 1990).

Three Civilian Notebooks 1580–1640 (SS 127, 2010).

'University Education and English Ecclesiastical Lawyers 1400–1650' (2011) 13 *Ecclesiastical L J* 132–45.

Heseltine, P and H Stuchfield, *Monumental Brasses of Hereford Cathedral* (London 2005).

Heward, E, *Masters in Ordinary* (Chichester 1990).

Hill C, *Economic Problems of the Church: From Archbishop Whitgift to the Long Parliament* (Oxford 1956, reprint 1963).

Society and Puritanism in Pre-Revolutionary England (New York 1964).

Hill, M, *Ecclesiastical Law*, 2d edn (Oxford 2001).

Hill, M and R H Helmholz (eds), *Great Christian Jurists in English History* (Cambridge 2017).

Hoeflich, M H, and J M Grabher, 'The Establishment of Normative Legal Texts: The Beginnings of the Ius commune', in *History of Medieval Canon Law in the Classical Period* (Washington, DC 2008), pp 1–21.

Hogan, J, *Judicial Advocates and Procurators* (Washington, DC 1941).

Holdsworth, W, *History of English Law* (London 1922–66).

Sources and Literature of English Law (Oxford 1925, reprint 1952).

Holland, T, 'Introduction' to R Zouche, *Iuris et iudicii fecialis, sive, iuris inter gentes et quaestionum de eodem Explicatio* (Washington, DC 1911), pp i–ix.

Hope, A, 'Bishops' Deputies and Episcopal Power in Medieval Law, c.1150 to c.1350', in P Coss et al. (eds), *Episcopal Power and Local Society in Medieval Europe, 900–1400* (Turnhout 2017), pp 195–217.

Horn, J (ed), *Le Neve, Fasti Ecclesiae Anglicanae 1300–1541, VII Chichester Diocese* (London 1964).

Le Neve, Fasti Ecclesiae Anglicanae, 1300–1541, II Hereford Diocese (London 1962).

Le Neve, Fasti Ecclesiae Anglicanae 1300–1541, III Salisbury Diocese (London 1962).

Le Neve, Fasti Ecclesiae Anglicanae 1541–1857 III Canterbury, Rochester and Winchester Dioceses (London 1974).

Houlbrooke, R, *Church Courts and the People during the English Reformation, 1520–1570* (Oxford 1979).

Houlbrooke, R, 'Dun [Donne], Sir Daniel (1544/5–1617)', *ODNB*; online edn 2008, www.oxforddnb.com/, accessed December 20, 2013.

Houlbrooke, R A (ed), *The Letter Book of John Parkhurst, Bishop of Norwich, Compiled During the Years 1571–5* (Norfolk Record Society 43, 1974–75).

Houston, J, *Catalogue of Ecclesiastical Records of the Commonwealth 1643–1660 in the Lambeth Palace Library* (Farnborough 1968).

Houston, R A, 'The Composition and Distribution of the Legal Profession and the Use of Law in Britain and Ireland c.1500–c.1850' (2018) 86 *Tijdschrift voor Rechtsgeschiedenis* 123–56.

Hudson, J, *Oxford History of the Laws of England, Volume II 871–1216* (Oxford 2012).

Hughes, J, *Pastors and Visionaries: Religion and Secular Life in Late Medieval Yorkshire* (Woodbridge 1998).

Hughes, P L and J F Larkin (eds), *Tudor Royal Proclamations, Volume I: the Early Tudors (1485–1553)* (New Haven, CT 1964).

Hurter, H, *Nomenclator literarius theologiae catholicae theologos* (Innsbrook 1903–13).

Ingram, M, *Church Courts, Sex and Marriage in England, 1570–1640* (Cambridge 1987).

'Church Courts in Tudor England (1485–1603): Continuities, Changes, Transformations', in V Beaulande-Baraud and M Charageat (eds), *Les officialités dans l'Europe médiévale et moderne* (Turnhout 2014), pp 91–105.

'Reformation of Manners in Early Modern England', in P Grittiths et al. (eds), *The Experience of Authority in Early Modern England* (New York 1996), pp 47–88.

Jacob, E, *Essays in the Conciliar Epoch* (Manchester 1963).

James, M R, C N L Brooke, and R A B Mynors (eds), *Walter Map De Nugis Curialium* (Oxford 1994).

Johnson, C (ed), *Registrum Hamonis Hethe* (C & Y Soc. 49, 1948).

Jolowicz, H F, 'The Assessment of Penalties in Primitive Law', in P Winfield and A McNair (eds), *Cambridge Legal Essays* (Cambridge 1926).

Jones, B (ed), *Le Neve, Fasti Ecclesiae Anglicanae 1300–1541: Coventry and Lichfield Diocese* (London 1964).

Jones, T (ed), *The Becket Controversy* (New York 1970).

Jones, W R, 'Relations of the Two Jurisdictions: Conflict and Cooperation in England during the Thirteenth and Fourteenth Centuries', in W Bowsky (ed), *Studies in Medieval and Renaissance History*, vol VII (Lincoln, NE 1970), pp 79–210.

Kantorowicz, H, *Bractonian Problems* (Glasgow 1941).

Kelly, H, 'Penitential Theology and Law at the Turn of the Fifteenth Century', in A Firey (ed), *A New History of Penance* (Leiden and Boston, MA 2008), pp 239–317.

Kenyon, J, *The Stuart Constitution* (Cambridge 1969).

Ker, N R and W Pantin, 'Letters of a Scottish Student at Paris and Oxford c.1250', in *Formularies which Bear on the History of Oxford c.1204–1420*, vol II (Oxford Historical Society n.s. 5, 1942).

Kilburn, M, 'Lee, Sir George', ODNB; online edn, May 2009, www.oxforddnb.com/view/article/16283, accessed October 10, 2015.

Kitching, C, 'The Prerogative Court of Canterbury from Warham to Whitgift', in R O'Day and F Heal (eds), *Continuity and Change: Personnel and Administration of the Church in England 1500–1642* (Leicester 1976), pp 191–214.

Knowles, D, *The Episcopal Colleagues of Archbishop Thomas Becket* (Cambridge 1951).

Kunkel, W, 'The Reception of Roman Law in Germany: An Interpretation', in G Strauss (ed) *Pre-Reformation Germany* (New York 1972), pp 263–81.

Ladeur, K-H, *Der Anfang des westlichen Rechts* (Tübingen 2018).

Landau, P, 'Gratian and the *Decretum* Gratiani', in W Hartmann and K Pennington (eds), *History of Medieval Canon Law in the Classical Period, 1140–1234* (Washington, DC 2008), pp 48–49.

Jus Patronatus: Studien zur Entwicklung des Patronats im Dekretalenrecht und der Kanonistik des 12. und 13. Jahrhunderts (Cologne 1975).

'The Origin of Civil Procedure', in U Blumenthal, A Winroth, and P Landau (eds), *Canon Law, Religion and Politics: Liber Amicorum Robert Somerville* (Washington, DC 2012), pp 136–43.

Lander, S, 'Church Courts and the Reformation in the Diocese of Chichester, 1500–58', in R O'Day and F Heal (eds), *Continuity and Change: Personnel and Administration of the Church in England 1500–1642* (Leicester 1976), pp 215–37.

Lange, T, *Excommunication for Debt in Late Medieval France: The Business of Salvation* (Cambridge 2016).

Lapsley, G, *Crown Community and Parliament in the Later Middle Ages*, ed H Cam and G Barraclough (Oxford 1951).

Latham, R and W Matthews (eds), *The Diary of Samuel Pepys* (Berkeley and Los Angeles, CA 1974).

Laud, W, *Works of the Most Reverend Father in God, William Laud, D D*, 7 vols (Oxford 1847–57).

Leader, D, *History of the University of Cambridge, vol I: The University to 1546* (Cambridge 1988).

Le Bras, G, *L'Evolution générale du procurateur en droit privé romain des origines au IIIe siècle* (Paris 1922).

Lefebvre-Teillard, A, *Les officialités à la veille du Concile de Trente* (Paris 1973).

'Un précieux témoin de l'École de droit canonique parisienne à l'aube du XIIIe siècle: le manuscrit 649 de la Bibliothèque municipal de Douai' (2017) 95 *Revue historique de droit français et étranger* 1–57.

Lepine, D, *Brotherhood of Canons Serving God: English Secular Cathedrals in the Later Middle Ages* (Woodbridge 1995).

'"A Long Way from University": Cathedral Canons and Learning at Hereford in the Fifteenth Century', in C Barron and J Stratford (eds), *The Church and Learning in Later Medieval Society: Essays in Honour of R. B. Dobson* (Donington 2002), pp 178–209.

Lepsius, S and T Wetzstein (eds), *Als die Welt in die Akten kam: Prozeßschriftgut im europäischen Mittelalter* (Frankfurt 2008).

Levack, B, *The Civil Lawyers in England 1603–1641* (Oxford 1973).

'The English Civilians, 1500–1750', in W Prest (ed), *Lawyers in Early Modern Europe and America* (London 1981), pp 110–11.

'Law', in N Tyacke (ed), *History of the University of Oxford*, vol IV (Oxford 1997), pp 559–68.

Lévy, J P, *Le problème de la preuve dans les droits savants du Moyen Age* (Recueils de la Société Jean Bodin 17, 1965).

Lieberman, D, *The Province of Legislation Determined. Legal Theory in Eighteenth-Century Britain* (Cambridge 1989).

Llewelyn Davies, D, 'The Development of Prize Law under Sir Leoline Jenkins' (1935) 21 *Transactions of the Grotius Society* 149–60.

Lobban, M, *The Common Law and English Jurisprudence 1760–1850* (Oxford 1991).

Logan, F D, 'The Cambridge Canon Law Faculty: Sermons and Addresses', in M J Franklin and C Harper-Bill (eds), *Medieval Ecclesiastical Studies in Honour of Dorothy M. Owen* (Woodbridge 1995), pp 151–64.

Excommunication and the Secular Arm in Medieval England (Toronto 1968).

The Medieval Court of Arches (C & Y Soc. 95, 2005).

MacCulloch, D, 'Bondmen under the Tudors', in C Cross, D Loades, and J J Scarisbrick (eds), *Law and Government under the Tudors* (Cambridge 1988), pp 91–110.

The Boy King: Edward VI and the Protestant Reformation (Berkeley and Los Angeles, CA 1999).

Maitland, F W, 'English Law and the Renaissance', in H Cam (ed), *Selected Historical Essays of F. W. Maitland* (Boston 1957), pp 122–51.

Introduction, *Select Passages from the Works of Bracton and Azo*, SS 8 (London 1895).

'Magistri Vacarii Summa de Matrimonio' (1897) 12 *LQR* 133–43, 270–87.

Roman Canon Law in the Church of England (London 1898).

Malden, H E, *Trinity Hall* (London 1902).

Manchester, A, *Modern Legal History of England and Wales 1750–1950* (London 1980).

Manning, R B, *Religion and Society in Elizabethan Sussex* (Leicester 1969).

Marchant, R A, *The Church under the Law: Justice, Administration and Discipline in the Diocese of York* (Cambridge 1969).

Marsen, R, *Documents Relating to Law and Custom of the Sea, A.D. 1205–1767* (Publications of the Navy Records Society, 1915–16).

Marshall, A, 'Jenkins, Sir Leoline', *ODNB*; online edn, Jan 2008 www.oxforddnb.com/view/article/14732, accessed April 29, 2014.

Mateer, D, 'Hugh Davis's Commonplace Book: A New Source of Seventeenth-Century Song' (1999) 32 *Royal Musical Association Research Chronicle* 63–87.

Mausen, Y, 'Arthur Duck et le droit romain: Ius commune ou peregrinae leges?' (2009) 20 *Rivista Internazionale di Diritto Comune* 179–207.

Veritatis adiutor: la procédure du témoignage dans le droit savant et la pratique française (XIIe–XIVe siècles) (Milan 2006).

Mayali, L, 'Procureurs et representation en droit canonique médiéval' (2002) 114 *Mélanges de l'Ecole française de Rome. Moyen-Age* 44–57.

Mayr-Harting, H, 'Master Silvester and the Compilation of Early English Decretal Collections' (1965) 2 *Studies in Church History* 186–96.

Merryman, J H and R Pérez-Perdomo, *The Civil Law Tradition*, 3d edn (Stanford, CA 2007).

Merzbacher, F, 'Die Parömie "Legista sine canonibus parum valet, canonista sine legibus nihil"' (1967) 13 *Studia Gratiana* 273–82.

Milsom, S F C, *Historical Foundations of the Common Law* (London 1969).

Mitchell, R, 'English Students at Padua, 1460–75' (1936) 8 *Transactions of the Royal Historical Society*, 4th series, 101–17.

Molhuysen, P C (ed), *Hugo Grotius, De iure belli ac pacis libri tres* (Leiden 1919).

Morey A and C N L Brooke (eds), *Gilbert Foliot and his Letters* (Cambridge 1965).

Morrill, J, 'The Attack on the Church of England in the Long Parliament, 1640–1642', in D Beales and G Best (eds), *History, Society and the Churches: Essays in Honour of Owen Chadwick* (Cambridge 1985), 105–24.

Morris, C, 'From Synod to Consistory: The Bishops' Courts in England, 1150–1250' (1991) 22 *Journal of Ecclesiastical History* 115–23.

Morris-Jones, J, 'Adam Usk's Epitaph' (1921) 31 Y *Cymmrodor* 112–34.

Muldoon, J, 'Hugo Grotius, Medieval Canon Law and the Creation of Modern International Law', in P Landau and J Mueller (eds), *Proceedings of the Ninth International Congress of Medieval Canon Law* (Vatican City 1997), pp 1155–65.

Muller, J A (ed), *The Letters of Stephen Gardiner* (Westport, CT 1933, reprint 1970).

Mullinger, J, *The University of Cambridge from the Earliest Times to the Royal Injunctions of 1535* (Cambridge 1911, reprint 1969).

Musson, A, 'Men of Law and Professional Identity in Late Medieval England', in T Baker (ed), *Law and Society in Later Medieval England and Ireland: Essays in Honour of Paul Brand* (London and New York 2018), pp 225–53.

Musson, A and N Ramsay, *Courts of Chivalry and Admiralty in Late Medieval Europe* (Woodbridge 2018).

Mynors, R and R Thomson, *Catalogue of the Manuscripts of Hereford Cathedral Library* (Woodbridge 1993).

Nörr, K W, *Romanisch-kanonisches Prozessrecht* (Heidelberg 2012).

O'Day, R, *The English Clergy: The Emergence and Consolidation of a Profession 1558–1642* (Leicester 1979).

The Professions in Early Modern England, 1450–1800: Servants of the Commonweal (Harlow 2000).

'The Role of the Registrar in Diocesan Administration', in R O'Day and F Heal (eds), *Continuity and Change: Personnel and Administration of the Church in England 1500–1642* (Leicester 1976), pp 77–94.

O'Day, R and A Hughes, 'Augmentation and Amalgamation: Was There a Systematic Approach to the Reform of Parochial Finance, 1640–60?' in R O'Day and F Heal (eds), *Princes and Paupers in the English Church 1500–1800* (Leicester 1981), pp 167–93.

Ogle, A, *The Tragedy of Lollards' Tower* (Oxford 1949).

O'Higgins, P, 'Arthur Browne (1756–1805): An Irish Civilian' (1969) 20 *NILQ* 255–73.

Ornsby, G (ed), *Correspondence of John Cosin* (Surtees Society 52, 1869).

Outhwaite, R B, *The Rise and Fall of the English Ecclesiastical Courts, 1500–1860* (Cambridge 2006).

Scandal in the Church: Dr. Edward Drax Free, 1764–1843 (London and Rio Grande, OH 1997).

Owen, D M, *Ely Records: A Handlist of the Records of the Bishop and Archdeacon of Ely* (Cambridge 1971).

The Medieval Canon Law: Teaching, Literature, and Transmission (Cambridge 1990).

Owen, D M (ed), Introduction, *John Lydford's Book* (London 1974), pp 5–11.

Owen, E, 'The Will of Adam of Usk' (1903) 18 *EHR* 316–17.

Pagnamenta, P (ed), *The Story Is Told in The Hidden Hall: Portrait of a Cambridge College* (London 2004).

Pantin, W, *The English Church in the Fourteenth Century* (Notre Dame, IN 1962).

Parks, E P, *The Roman Rhetorical Schools as a Preparation for the Courts under the Early Empire* (Baltimore, MD 1945).

Pedersen, O, *The First Universities*, trans R North (Cambridge 1997).

Pennington, K, 'Due Process, Community and the Prince in the Evolution of the Ordo iudiciarius' (1998) 9 *Rivista internazionale di diritto commune* 9–47.

Pope and Bishops: The Papal Monarchy in the Twelfth and Thirteenth Centuries (Philadelphia, PA 1984).

'Representation in Medieval Canon Law' (2004) 64 *The Jurist* 361–83.

'Roman Law at the Papal Curia in the Early Twelfth Century', in U-R Blumenthal, A Winroth, and P Landau (eds), *Canon Law, Religion and Politics: Liber Amicorum Robert Somerville* (Washington, DC 2012), pp 233–52.

Peters, E, 'The Sacred Muses and the Twelve Tables: Legal Education and Practice', in K Pennington and M Eichbauer (eds), *Law as Profession and Practice in Medieval Europe: Essays in Honor of James A Brundage* (Farnham 2011), pp 137–51.

The Shadow King: Rex Inutilis in Medieval Law and Literature, 751–1327 (New Haven, CT 1970).

Peters, R, *Oculus Episcopi: Administration in the Archdeaconry of St. Albans 1580–1625* (Manchester 1963).

Phillimore, J, *Reports of Cases Argued and Determined in the Arches and Prerogative Courts of Canterbury and in the High Court of Delegates Containing the Judgments of the Right Hon. Sir George Lee* (2 vols, London 1832–33).

Polden, P, 'The Civilian Courts and the Probate, Divorce, and Admiralty Division', in W Cornish et al. (eds), *Oxford History of the Laws of England*, vol XI (Oxford 2010), pp 692–714.

Pollock, F and F W Maitland, *History of English Law before the Time of Edward I*, 2d ed. (Cambridge 1898, revised 1968).

Poos, L R (ed), *Lower Ecclesiastical Jurisdiction in Late-Medieval England* (Oxford 2001).

Post, G, *Studies in Medieval Legal Thought: Public Law and the State, 1100–1322* (Princeton, NJ 1964).

Prest, W (ed), *Lawyers in Early Modern Europe and America* (London 1981).

    The Professions in Early Modern England (London and New York 1987).

    Reinterpreting Blackstone's Commentaries: A Seminal Text in National and International Contexts (Oxford and Portland, OR 2014).

    William Blackstone and his Commentaries: Biography, Law, History (Oxford and Portland, OR 2009).

    William Blackstone: Law and Letters in the Eighteenth Century (Oxford 2008).

Radding, C M, *Origins of Medieval Jurisprudence: Pavia and Bologna, 850–1150* (New Haven, CT 1988).

Rashdall, H, *The Universities of Europe in the Middle Ages* (Oxford 1936).

Rathbone, E and S Kuttner, 'Anglo-Norman Canonists' (1949/51) 7 *Traditio* 279–358.

Reynolds, S, 'The Emergence of Professional Law in the Long Twelfth Century' (2003) 21 *Law & History Review* 347–66.

Richardson, H G, 'Azo, Drogheda, and Bracton' (1944) 59 *EHR* 22–47.

Richardson, H G (ed), *Formularies which Bear on the History of Oxford c.1204–1420*, vol II (Oxford Historical Society n.s. 5, 1942).

Richardson, H G and G O Sayles, *Law and Legislation from Æthelberht to Magna Carta* (Edinburgh 1966).

Richardson, W C, *History of the Court of Augmentations 1536–1554* (Baton Rouge, LA 1961).

Ritchie C A, *The Ecclesiastical Courts of York* (Arbroath 1956).

Robinson, O, T Fergus, and W Gordon, *European Legal History*, 3d edn (Oxford 2000).

Rodes, R E, *Lay Authority and Reformation in the English Church* (Notre Dame, IN 1982).

Roscoe, E, *History of the Prize Court* (London 1924).

Salonon, K, *Papal Justice in the Late Middle Ages* (Oxford and New York 2016).

Saul, N, *Richard II* (New Haven, CT and London 1997).

Sayers, J E, 'An Evesham Manuscript Containing the Treatise Known as *Actor et Reus* (British Library, Harley MS. 3763)', in *Law and Records in Medieval England* (London 1988).

    Papal Judges Delegate in the Province of Canterbury, 1198–1254 (Oxford 1971).

    'William of Drogheda and the English Canonists', in P Linehan (ed), *Proceedings of the Seventh International Congress of Medieval Canon Law* (Vatican City 1988), pp 205–22.

Scarisbrick, J J, *The Reformation and the English People* (Oxford 1984).

Schmoeckel, M, 'Procedure, Proof, and Evidence', in J Witte Jr. and F S. Alexander (eds), *Christianity and Law: An Introduction* (Cambridge 2008), pp 143–62.

Schulte, J F von, *Die Geschichte der Quellen und Literatur des canonischen Rechts* (Stuttgart 1875).

Schulz, F, *History of Roman Legal Science* (Oxford 1946, reprint 1963).

Scrutton, T, 'Roman Law Influence in Chancery, Church Courts, Admiralty, and Law Merchant', in *Select Essays in Anglo-American Legal History* (Boston, MA 1907), vol I, pp 208–47.

Senior, W, *Doctors' Commons and the Old Court of Admiralty: A Short History of the Civilians in England* (London 1922).

Sharpe, J A, *Defamation and Sexual Slander in Early Modern England: The Church Courts at York* (York 1980).

Sheils, W J, 'The Right of the Church: The Clergy, Tithe and the Courts at York, 1540–1640', in W J Sheils and D Wood (eds), *The Church and Wealth* (Oxford 1987), pp 231–55.

Shepard, A, 'Trinity Hall Civil Lawyers and the Cambridge University Courts, c.1560–1640', *Trinity Hall 2000: Legal Education and Learning* (n.d.).

Sherlock, P, 'William Somner', *ODNB* (Oxford 2004), online edn, www.oxforddnb .com/view/article 26030, accessed September 28, 2016.

Shinners J and W Dohar (eds), *Pastors and the Care of Souls in Medieval England* (Notre Dame, IN 1998).

Smith, D M, *Guide to the Archive Collections in the Borthwick Institute of Historical Research* (York 1973).

Smith, J A C, *Medieval Law Teachers and Writers: Civilian and Canonist* (Ottawa 1975).

Smith, L B, *Tudor Prelates and Politics 1536–1558* (Princeton, NJ 1953).

Smith, M G, *The Church Courts, 1680–1840: From Canon to Ecclesiastical Law* (Lampeter 2006).

Spurr, J, *The Restoration Church of England, 1646–1689* (New Haven, CT and London 1991).

Squibb, G D, *Doctors' Commons: A History of the College of Advocates and Doctors of Law* (Oxford 1977).

Steig, M, *Laud's Laboratory: The Diocese of Bath and Wells in the Early Seventeenth Century* (London 1982).

Stein, P, 'Duck, Arthur (1580–1648)', in *ODNB*, http://oxforddnb.com, accessed August 27, 2014.

'English Civil Law Literature', in *Ins Wasser geworfen und Ozeane durchquert: Festschrift für Knut Wolfgang Nörr* (Cologne 2003), pp 979–92.

Roman Law in European History (Cambridge 1999).

'A Seventeenth-Century English View of the European jus commune', in *Excerptiones iuris: B Durand and L Mayali (eds), Studies in Honor of André Gouron*, (Berkeley, CA 2000), pp 717–27.

Storey, R, *Diocesan Administration in Fifteenth-Century England*, 2d edn (York 1972).

Strier, R, 'From Diagnosis to Operation', in D L Smith, R Strier, and D Bevington (eds), *The Theatrical City: Culture, Theatre and Politics in London, 1576–1649* (Cambridge 1995), pp 224–59.

Sutherland, L, *The University of Oxford in the Eighteenth Century: A Reconsideration* (Oxford 1973).

Swanson, R N, *Church and Society in Late Medieval England* (Oxford 1989).

Swanson R and D Lepine, 'The Later Middle Ages, 1268–1535', in G Aylmer and J Tiller (eds), *Hereford Cathedral: A History* (London and Rio Grande, OH 2000), pp 48–86.

Sweeney, J, 'The Admiralty Law of Arthur Browne' (1995) 26 *J. Maritime Law and Commerce* 59–132.

The Life and Times of Arthur Browne in Ireland and America, 1756–1805 (Irish Legal History Society 26, 2017).

Takahashi, M, 'The Number of Wills Proved in the Sixteenth and Seventeenth Centuries', in G Martin and P Spufford (eds), *The Records of the Nation* (Woodbridge 1990), pp 187–213.

Taliadoros, J, 'Law and Theology in Gilbert of Foliot's (c.1105/10–1187/88) Correspondence' (2005) 16 *Haskins Society Journal: Studies in Medieval History* 77–94.

Taliadoros, J, *Law and Theology in Twelfth-Century England: The Works of Master Vacarius (c.1115/20–c.1200)* (Turnhout 2006).

Tanner, N P, *The Church in Late Medieval Norwich, 1370–1532* (Toronto 1984).

Tardif, A, *La procédure civile et criminelle aux XIIIe et XIVe siècles* (Paris 1885).

Tarver, A, *Church Court Records* (Chichester 1995).

Tate, J, 'Glanvill and the Development of the English Advowson Writs', in J Witte, S McDougall, and A di Robilant (eds), *Texts and Contexts in Legal History: Essays in Honor of Charles Donahue* (Berkeley, CA 2016), pp 129–44.

Taylor, N (ed), *Guide to the Professional Conduct of Solicitors*, 7th edn (London 1996).

Thieme, H, 'Le rôle des *Doctores legum* dans la Société allemande du XVIe siècle', in *Individu et sociétè à la Renaissance* (Brussels 1967), pp 159–69.

Thorndike, L, *University Records and Life in the Middle Ages* (New York 1944, reprinted 1971).

Torquebiau, P, 'Contumace', in R Naz (ed), *Dictionnaire de droit canonique* 4 (Paris 1935–65), pp 506–21.

Trevor-Roper, H, *Archbishop Laud 1573–1645* (London 1963).

Trusen, W, 'Advocatus – zu den Anfängen der gelehrten Anwaltschaft in Deutschland und ihren rechtlichen Grundlagen', in H Kipp et al. (eds), *Um Recht und Freiheit: Festschrift für August Freiherr von der Heydte zur Vollendung des 70. Lebensjahres* (Berlin 1977), vol II, pp 1235–48.

Gelehrtes Recht im Mittelalter und in der frühen Neuzeit (Goldbach 1997).

'Die gelehrte Gerichtsbarkeit der Kirche', in H Coing (ed), *Handbuch der Quellen und Literatur der neueren Europäischen Privatrechtsgeschichte* (Munich 1973), vol I, pp 467–83.

Tucker, P, *Law Courts and Lawyers in the City of London, 1300–1550* (Cambridge 2007).

Ullmann, W, *Law and Politics in the Middle Ages: An Introduction to the Sources of Medieval Political Ideas* (Ithaca, NY 1975).

Underwood, M, 'The Structure and Operation of the Oxford Chancellor's Court, from the Sixteenth to the Early Eighteenth Century' (1978) 6 *Journal of the Society of Archivists* 18–27.

Usher, R, *Rise and Fall of the High Commission* (Oxford 1913, reprint 1968).

Uzelac, A and C H van Rhee (eds), *Landscape of the Legal Professions in Europe and the USA: Continuity and Change* (Cambridge and Antwerp 2011).

Vage, J, 'Records of the Bishop of Exeter's Consistory Court c.1500–c.1660' (1982) 114 *Reports and Transactions of the Devonshire Association* 79–98.

Van Hove, A, *Prolegomena ad Codicem iuris canonici* (Mechelen and Rome 1945).

Venn, J and J A Venn, *Alumni Cantabrigienses* (Cambridge 1922–54).

Waddams, S M, *Law, Politics, and the Church of England: The Career of Stephen Lushington, 1782–1873* (Cambridge 1992).

Waelkens, L J M, 'Medieval Family and Marriage Law: From Actions of Status to Legal Doctrine', in J W Cairns and P J du Plessis (eds), *The Creation of the Ius Commune: From Casus to Regula* (Edinburgh 2010), pp 103–25.

Wahrmund, L, *Quellen zur Geschichte des Römisch-kanonischen Prozesses im Mittelalter*, 5 vols (Innsbruck 1905, reprint 1962).

'Die Summa aurea des Wilhelmus de Drokeda', in *Quellen zur Geschichte des römisch-kanonischen Prozesses im Mittelalter* (Innsbruck 1905–31), vol 2:2, pp 1–432.

Walther, H G, 'Learned Jurists and their Profit for Society – Some Aspects of the Development of Legal Studies at Italian and German Universities in the Late Middle Ages', in W J Courtenay and J Miethke (eds), *Universities and Schooling in Medieval Society* (Boston, MA 2000), pp 100–26.

Wallace, J, *The Reporters*, 4th edn (Boston, MA 1882).

Wauters B and M de Benito, *History of Law in Europe: An Introduction* (Cheltenham and Northampton, MA 2017).

Webster, T, *Godly Clergy in Early Stuart England* (Cambridge 1997).

Weijers, O, *A Scholar's Paradise: Teaching and Debating in Medieval Paris* (Turnhout 2015).

Weimar, P, 'Die legistische Literatur und die Methode des Rechtsunterrichts der Glossatorenzeit', in P Weimar, *Zur Renaissance der Rechtswissenschaft im Mittelalter* (Goldbach 1997).

Wenzel, S (ed and trans), *Fasciculus Morum: A Fourteenth-Century Preacher's Handbook* (University Park, PA 1989).

Wetzstein, T, 'Prozeßschriftgut im Mittelalter – einfürende Überlegungen', in S Lepsius and T Wetzstein (eds), *Als die Welt in die Akten kam: Prozeßschriftgut im europäischen Mittelalter* (Frankfurt 2008), pp 1–27.

Wieacker, F, *History of Private Law in Europe*, trans T Weir (Oxford 1995).

Wijffels, A, 'A Seventeenth Century English Commentary "De regulis iuris" (D.50.17)', in O Condorelli (ed), *Panta rei. Studi dedicati a Manlio Bellomo*, vol V (Rome 2004), pp 473–96.

Williams, C H (ed), *English Historical Documents, 1485–1558* (London 1967).

Wilson, J, *The Imperial Gazetteer of England and Wales* (Edinburgh 1870–72).

Winnington-Ingram, A, *Monumental Brasses in Hereford Cathedral*, 3d edn (Hereford 1972).

Winroth, A, *The Making of Gratian's Decretum* (Cambridge 2000).

Winstanley, D A, *Unreformed Cambridge* (Cambridge 1935).

Withers, C, *Yorkshire Probate*, 5th edn (Chippenham 2006).

Wood, A, *Athenae Oxonienses* (London 1813–20).

Woodcock, B, *Medieval Ecclesiastical Courts in the Diocese of Canterbury* (Oxford 1952).

Woolfson, J, *Padua and the Tudors: English Students in Italy, 1485–1603* (Toronto 1998).

Wormald, P, *The Making of English Law: King Alfred to the Twelfth Century, Volume I: Legislation and its Limits* (Oxford 1999).

Wouw, H van de, 'Brocardia Dunelmensia' (1991) 108 ZRG *(Rom. Abt.)* 241–42.

Wright, T (ed), *The Anglo-Latin Satirical Poets and Epigrammatists of the Twelfth Century*, Rolls Series 59:1 (1872).

The Political Songs of England (Camden Society 6, 1839).

Wrigley, E A and R S Schofield, *Population History of England, 1541–1871* (Cambridge, MA 1981).

Zimmermann, R, *Contemporary Law, European Law: The Civilian Traditions Today* (Oxford 2001).

'Europa und das römisches Recht' (2002) 2 *Archiv für die civilistische Praxis* 243–316.

Zonto, G and J Brotto (eds), *Acta graduum academicorum Gymnasii Patavini* (Padua 1969–2008).

Zulueta, F De, 'William of Drogheda', in J van Kan and F de Zulueta (eds), *Mélanges de droit romain dédiés à Georges Cornil* (Paris 1926), vol II, pp 641–57.

Zulueta, F De and P Stein, *The Teaching of Roman Law in England around 1200* (SS, Supplementary Series 8, 1990).

Zutshi, P N R, 'Notaries Public in England in the Fourteenth and Fifteenth Centuries' (1996) 23 *Historia instituciones documentos* 421–33.

Index